December '72

DRESSAGE

The Art of Classical Riding

DRESSAGE

THE ART OF
CLASSICAL RIDING

SYLVIA LOCH

Foreword by
Brigadier General Kurt Albrecht
Formerly Director of the
Spanish Riding School, Vienna

Trafalgar Square Publishing

NORTH POMFRET, VERMONT

First published in the United States of America in 1990 by
Trafalgar Square Publishing, North Pomfret, Vermont 05053

First published in Great Britain 1990 by The Sportsman's Press

To my mother, Barbara,
and my late father Alexander Beauchamp Cameron
from whom I learned my fundamental appreciation of Art and Nature and
a sense of History

ISBN 0-943955-32-7

Library of Congress Catalog Card Number: 90-70211

Printed in Great Britain

CONTENTS

Acknowledgements and Gratitude

T hat feeling of elation which suffuses the writer when the precious completed manuscript is handed to the publisher can only be compared to the first apprehensive sight of the finished *oeuvre*; but before that precious moment there lies one more important and pleasurable task. Mine is to acknowledge and express heartfelt thanks to all those who bore both my singlemindedness and inaccessibility during the last two years; they so often helped with or took over my other duties. These particularly include Liz McCurley, Samantha Hullah and Nuala Garnsey. As for Richard, my deeply understanding and highly imaginative lawyer husband, my generous mother and very forgiving daughter, I once again thank them from the bottom of my loving heart.

To research, write and rewrite, illustrate and collate a book worthy of the subject of Classical Dressage is both enlightening and humbling. The more I explored the writings of the equestrian masters, old and new, well-recognised and little-known, the more the feeling of humility and wonder at their achievements increased. It is above all their story and not mine that I have unfolded in these pages. To share the reiteration of their thoughts and to place them in a coherent modern context before the reader has been a great privilege.

To all those equestrian authors, living or dead, whose books are recorded in my bibliography, I am therefore deeply grateful. I owe also a particular debt of gratitude to the following: General Kurt Albrecht for his kind patience in translating and reading through my text before writing such a generous Foreword, Dr Oulehla, present Director of the Spanish Riding School and of the Piber Stud in Austria for the greatest practical assistance, Anthony J. Fox for editorial advice and painstaking translations from the old and modern French and Arsenio Raposo Cordeiro in Lisbon for the use of so many beautiful photographs from his own 1989 publication. Equally important support and generosity has come from many quarters including Austrian Airways in London, the Austrian Tourist Office in London and Vienna, and especially Marion Telsnig and Traudl Lisey. Much kindness has been received from Dr Zundritsch, the Austrian Cultural Attaché, and Dr Walter Foster at the Anglo Austrian Society in London; particular encouragement came from Madame Eva Podhajsky. In France, I received assistance from M. Michel Henriquet at Versailles as well as support from the École Nationale d'Equitation at Saumur. In London, David Fuller of Arthur Ackermann's in Bond Street, has contributed so much to my picture research, and from America there has been similar help from the Paul Mellon Foundation. In the Iberian Peninsula the historical researches and translations of Dr Fernando d'Andrade and Alfredo Baptista Coelho have proved invaluable.

Innumerable other people have also made their various contributions including Bente Branderup in Denmark, Ivan Bezugloff in the United States, Jimmy Carvalho e Silva and Janet Fragoso in Portugal, Eleanor Duval in Belgium, Joy Howley in Australia, Dr Reiner Klimke in West Germany, Arthur Kottas and Johann Riegler in Vienna, Els Wyler in Holland, as well as so many friends and colleagues at home including Colonel Jamie Crawford, Colonel Richard Felton and his wife, Marga, Joan Gold, Pat Grover, Elwyn Hartley-Edwards, Jane Kidd, Daphne Machin-Goodall, Julia Wynmalen, Lady John Fitzgerald, antiquarian bookseller

Gregory Way at Borrough Green, Newmarket, Irene Benjamin, Veronica Quarm at Wilton, Bruce Irving at the National Portrait Gallery, and bibliophile John Woods. Finally I thank Bob Rowland for his beautiful drawings and Alan O'Neill at Charles Hodge Photography for his painstaking contribution to my artwork.

From the administrative and editorial world, the British Horse Society Dressage Office, English Heritage, together with publishers, J. A. Allen of London and Howley & Russell of Australia, and magazines *Horse and Hound, Horse and Rider, Dressage, Riding, Equestrian World, Dressage and CT* (United States) and *The Horse* (Australia) have all been extremely helpful with information and permission to reproduce material.

Finally, my grateful thanks to Madeleine McCurley for photographing myself and my horses for the jacket on one of that year's coldest days, and once again, most especially to my indefatigable Editor, Sue Coley for giving her support one hundred and ten per cent and having the sensitive intelligence to understand my subject even although she is not yet a rider herself . . .!

List of Colour Plates

1 A painting by Meytens of the *Damenkarussell*, celebrated on 2 January 1743 in the Winter Riding School, Vienna.

2 Two fine portrayals of Spanish Baroque horses by George Hamilton (1672–1737).

3 The equestrian portrait of Emperor Charles VI by George Hamilton, which dominates the interior of the Winter Riding School.

4 Queen Marie-Antoinette in hunting costume, painted by Louis-August Brun in 1783.

5 Monsieur de Nestier (1684–1754), royal *écuyer*, mounted on Le Florido.
   A study of the head of an early Lipizzaner by George Hamilton.

6 Morier's painting of Henry Herbert, 10th Earl of Pembroke, who taught the classical airs of the High School.
   A portrait of an unknown Englishman in an indoor manège, painted by Thomas Parkinson in 1766.

7 *Groom schooling a bay horse*, by Alfred de Dreux (1810–1860).
   A study in oils of Waloddi Fischerstrom, equerry at the Swedish Court in 1868, on a powerful Swedish cavalry horse.

8 A rider of the *Cadre Noir* at Saumur demonstrating the courbette.

9 The piaffe, executed by a rider of the Portuguese School of Equestrian Art, on a Lusitano stallion from the royal Alter stud.
   Gentleman riders from the Portuguese School of Equestrian Art.

10 Nuno Oliveira, known worldwide as the Master.
   Author and master of equitation, Don Diogo Bragança (Lafoes).

11 Riders of the Spanish Riding School of Vienna entering the Winter Riding School.
   Bereiter Johann Riegler greets his Lipizzaner at Wembley Arena in 1989.

12 Granat, ridden by Christine Stückelberger, in an extended trot at Goodwood, 1978.
   The half-pass of world champion Christine Stückelberger's Granat.

13 Jennie Loriston-Clarke working-in prior to competing with Masterlock Recruitment's Dutch Bid.
   Ahlerich, ridden by Reiner Klimke at the 1984 Los Angeles Olympics.

14 Dutch Courage and Jennie Loriston-Clarke, enjoying an outing in the New Forest.
   Nicole Uphoff on Rembrandt, during the Seoul Olympics.

15 Monica Theodorescu on Ganimedes, 1988 Olympics.
Dusan Mavec of Yugoslavia on Pluto Canissa IV at the 1989 European Championships.

16 Cynthia Ishoy of Canada on Dynasty, Seoul Olympics.
Margit Otto-Crepin on Corlandus, preparing to ride for France at Goodwood House.

FOREWORD
By Brigadier General Kurt Albrecht

Any writer who creates a work about the Classical Art of Riding which throughout its twenty chapters explores this Art to its innermost depths not only has to be deeply familiar with the subject but must be truly inspired by it. This can be said with an absolutely clear conscience about this author.

Sylvia Loch has already shown this same closeness of relationship in her previous publications. Her searching desire always to seek out and make available to the reader the true values of this Art is clearly recognisable. Now, in this book, all that researched knowledge and truth, practically acquired over many years, has been concentrated into twenty chapters.

She begins with the original sources of which the work of Xenophon certainly ranks amongst the most important, since his writing embraces, with unsurpassed clarity, the heart of the matter. Then follows the great period of Portuguese, Italian, French, Spanish and English influences as well as the important classical period within the German-speaking world. Finally we arrive at the present day, when the classical teachings, now clothed in the form of competitive dressage, have leapt across the Atlantic, there to find an unexpectedly strong response.

Sylvia Loch's work is of real and special significance since it highlights the fundamental values which have survived over thousands of years. This is particularly important at a time when the present enthusiasm for dressage has pushed that most vital aspect, namely the Art, somewhat into the background so that it is not always accorded its true place of value.

Not one single period has been omitted. Thus the lifework of many important equestrian personalities has been recalled from the past. Now, works which did not receive the necessary recognition even in their own time, have found a deserved place in this book, thus emphasising even more the true objectivity of this author.

By laying bare the basic elements of classical teaching and reminding us of our own creativity so that, instead of turning the horse into an oppressed servant, we may allow him to be a friend working with us in collaboration, Sylvia Loch's book demonstrates that this, beyond all else, is the most important concern for us all. I therefore most sincerely hope and believe that this book will achieve the true and real recognition it deserves throughout contemporary equestrian circles.

Brigadier General Kurt Albrecht,
(Director of the Spanish Riding School from 1974–1985)
Vienna

'All human beings love horses. I think everyone is thankful for the many ways a horse will make himself useful, giving willingly of the work we expect from him, and also the pleasure he gives us in so many other ways. A rider who loves not his horse will only bring danger upon himself. When I speak of strength and courage, I do not mean brutal and daring riders, but I mean the relaxed strength of the rider who allows the horse to move in a more natural, balanced and elegant way. These characteristics of the good rider lead him on the road to perfection.

'Difficulties have to be overcome by allowing sufficient time to strengthen the horse's muscles. It is this which makes many think that dressage is pointless. Thus many riders neglect those gymnastic exercises so necessary to achieve suppleness, balance, obedience and collection. Without these exercises, no horse will show good free movements and allow the rider to sit comfortably, regardless of the use to which the horse is put by the rider – fox hunting, jumping, the riding of intricate figures, or all of these pursuits. Therefore, it does not make any sense to debate these unwarranted opinions. Art speaks for itself.'

La Guérinière, Paris, 1733

François Robichon de la Guérinère (*c*1688–1751).
(*Courtesy Museé de Versailles*)

Frontispiece of Richard Berenger's translation of Bourgelat (1754) and of his own book, *A History and Art of Horsemanship* (1771).

Introduction

This book recounts the development of Classical Equitation over a period of more than two thousand years. What is conceived today as the execution of good dressage by competitors, trainers and judges alike is the result of that vital and practical evolution. Too often however this historical aspect is unappreciated, to the general disadvantage of the Art.

The present objectives and standards of national and international dressage competitors will at times widely differ from those of people who simply enjoy schooling their horses for quiet self-fulfilling pleasure, yet, recognising it or not, both are influenced to a very great extent by that long and complex history of horsemanship.

Indeed, for the English speaking world, many, even of the cognoscenti, fail to realise that up until only two hundred and fifty years ago, England was as important a centre as any European country for the development of classical riding. A number of her masters enjoyed and still enjoy the most illustrious reputation abroad. As we shall see, England regrettably surrendered her principles and the practice of academic riding at a time of religious and political upheaval, so that today dressage riders from the English-speaking world generally believe they follow the teachings of one of the great Romanic or Germanic Schools, both here also to be fully recounted and reviewed. Their tenets have played an important and formative role in the definitions and standards of modern competition dressage but the whole spectrum of classical riding is much older and wider than this; the necessary awareness will only improve if all concerned are able to accept this and review past received truths.

It is possible that these were well understood when the first recorded dressage competition took place in 1873 in Pressburg (then part of the Austrian Empire, and now Bratislava in Czechoslovakia). It may also have coloured riding and judging in 1902 when the first truly international horse show to include a dressage event, took place in Turin, Italy. (This was won by the Austrians, followed by the French and the Germans.) Thereafter however, as dressage competitions increased in popularity, culminating in the first equestrian events at the 1902 Stockholm Olympic Games, it became increasingly necessary to lay down some firm guidelines. How in fact were these implemented?

In order to establish international standards for the future of competitive dressage, the FEI (Federation Equestrienne International) was officially convened in May 1921 in Paris. This body, drawn from top international equestrians immediately began work on a complete set of rules and codes of practice, in order to regulate international competitions and 'unify the basic principles of drawing up programmes for all international tests.'[1] In 1930 a code was published which reads:

> 'The FEI instituted an International Dressage Event in 1929 in order to protect the Equestrian Art from the abuses to which it can be exposed and to preserve it in purity of its principles,

[1] From *The History of the F.E.I.* by E.A. Saracin.

so that it could be handed on intact to generations of riders to come.'

The standard laid down for Dressage (the Object and General Principles) which is incorporated into the Rules for each national federation (eg. the British Horse Society) reads:

The object of Dressage is the harmonious development of the physique and ability of the horse. As a result, it makes the horse calm, supple, loose and flexible, but also confident, attentive and keen, thus achieving perfect understanding with his rider.

These qualities are revealed by:

The freedom and regularity of the paces;

The harmony, lightness and ease of the movements;

The lightness of the forehand and the engagement of the hindquarters, originating in a lively impulsion;

The acceptance of the bridle, with submissiveness thoughout and without any tenseness or resistance.

The horse thus gives the impression of doing of his own accord what is required of him. Confident and attentive he submits generously to the control of his rider, remaining absolutely straight in any movement on a straight line and bending accordingly when moving on curved lines.

His walk is regular, free and unconstrained. His trot is free, supple, regular, sustained and active. His canter is united, light and cadenced. His quarters are never inactive or sluggish. They respond to the slightest indication of the rider and thereby give life and spirit to all the rest of his body.

By virtue of a lively impulsion and the suppleness of his joints, free from the paralysing effects of resistance, the horse obeys willingly and without hesitiation and responds to the various aids calmly and with precision, displaying a natural and harmonious balance both physically and mentally.

In all his work, even at the halt, the horse must be 'on the bit'. A horse is said to be 'on the bit' when the hocks are correctly placed, the neck is more or less raised and arched according to the stage of training and the extension or collection of the pace, and he accepts the bridle with a light and soft contact and submissiveness throughout.

The head should remain in a steady position, as a rule slightly in front of the vertical, with a supple poll as the highest point of the neck and no resistance should be offered to the rider.

The horse shows cadence when its movements are well marked, rhythmic and harmonious.

In the following pages, all the important historical events, personalities and rationale which resulted in this FEI statement are recounted.

The FEI definitions themselves are fundamentally true to the spirit of the great equestrian philosophers. Indeed, there is a remarkable commonalty between the FEI Rules and the ideals of every master from Xenophon to Oliveira. Yet, all of us who practise dressage and watch its judging at national and international events are aware of increasing disparate interpretations and this gives concern to many people.

Let us therefore now retrace the history of equitation and try to find true perspective through the words of the great authors. We owe this to the horse, for in loving him, there has to be a common path ahead – a path which is inviting, sure, smooth, and clear – not necessarily for ourselves, but for him.

ONE

What is the Classical Art of Riding?

Over many centuries, long before the inception of the FEI and its widely accepted code to protect the Equestrian Art, there has been a continuous debate on the art of horsemanship. The ancient Greeks were the first to explore this art mainly in relation to the preparation of the horse for war; likewise the Romans in relation to their cavalry campaigns in Africa and in Spain. After the Renaissance[1] in Italy, all the civilised countries of the world embraced the concept so that whole Schools and Academies sprang up to teach and perpetuate this Art, universally regarded as truly noble.

Today, the equestrian term Classical Art has become fashionable again, particularly in countries which not so long ago cared little for the aesthetic in relation to riding, and where the objective with horses was to ride hard and fast and to hell with any fanciful ideas of what many still consider as foppish finery. In those isolated areas where the artistic concept of riding had remained however, little changed. Today, the term Equestrian Art may not be fully understood, but nevertheless it appeals to the average rider since it instantly raises equitation into a higher sphere than other forms of riding which are firmly regarded as a sport.

Achieving the Definition

Aesthetic ideas are too often clothed in mystery. There is no lacuna however of the objectives of the Classical Art of riding; nor less about the means by which we may achieve it.

> 'The object of the Classical Art of Riding is to train the horse not only to be brilliant in the movements and exercises of the High School, but also to be quiet, supple, and obedient, and by his smooth movements to make riding a true pleasure.' (Alois Podhajsky, 1967)
>
> 'Riding is pleasant and can be made an Art. And who would not be an artist? Only those, however, who try with their whole soul to understand the horse's psychic disposition and who endeavour to establish perfect harmony by sensitive feel instead of crude force, are entitled to be called artists. . .' (W. Müseler, 1937).
>
> 'The ideal is to train the horse and so obtain harmony and perfection in all movements between rider and horse so that they appear to be as one.' (R. Wätjen, 1958).

The quotations above are all of this century; they come from the Austro-German School which since dressage competition began has tended to dominate the competitive world. The following thoughts, equally appealing are from the English-speaking world a century or more earlier.

> 'Equitation is confessedly a science; every science is founded upon principles and theory must indispensably be necessary, because what is truly just and beautiful cannot depend upon chance.' (Earl of Pembroke, London, 1778)
>
> 'When is a horse considered to be in his proper equilibrium? When he goes well, light in hand. . .without seeking support from, or on, the rider's hand – when even the reins

---

[1] The great revival of learning and art based on classical realism which started in Italy and lasted throughout fifteenth and sixteenth century Europe. It took for its inspiration much of that accomplished under the Greeks and the Romans.

are let loose, and he still continues for some time to retain himself in that upright, airy position of the head, and action of the fore-hand; and by the slightest touch of the hand, he is halted.' (J. G. Peters, London, 1835)

'The best saddlehorse is of course the one which will absolutely follow his master's mood; upon whose neck the reins can be flung if one wishes . . . but who, at request, can show his paces to the best advantage.' (Colonel T.A. Dodge, New York, 1894).

It is really an inescapable conclusion that if more people had listened to the voice of their own experts, however unfashionable, there would be less disparity between the different schools of teaching today, and a higher common standard of dressage worldwide.

The ancient Greeks taught us that nothing can be achieved correctly or harmoniously without a strict adherence to the laws of the universe which made the distinction between the classical and the non-classical.

Taking all this into consideration, we may now define the Art of Classical Riding as the ability to teach the horse through the use of kindness, logic and exercises based on nature's laws of balance and harmony, to submit himself happily and proudly to the will of the rider without in any way upsetting his natural way of moving.

In the Name of Art

Before we examine the meaning of the word dressage, let us look a little more closely at the idea of art. Where for example does art end and sport begin, or vice versa?

In the days when art could never in the public's wildest imagination comprise of a canvas daubed with huge bold brush strokes of raw colour accompanied by an apparently random use of squiggles and blobs, blurs and bobs, definitions were undoubtedly easier. A heap of bricks thrown apparently at random on the floor in the name of art three hundred years ago might have ensured the perpetrator's burning at the stake, but not his celebrity as an artist.

To our forefathers, art represented the definite and *classical*. This meant that it pertained to reality, reflected the beauty and order of nature and was determined always by the laws of balance and light. Logic and symmetry prevailed at all times. The opposite of classicism

Lightness upon the hand and roundness under saddle . . . This *Ecuyer en chef* at Saumur (turn of the century), on his Thoroughbred horse, demonstrates all the classical ideals. (*Photo courtesy of the Ecole National d'Equitation de Saumur*)

was chaos, disorder, darkness, a breaking of the rules – something quite unacceptable.

Nowadays, tastes have changed. Revolutionary ideas hold the arts in their thrall and the adherents of modernism reject the work of the classicists for being predictable. Yet modernism, far from introducing freedom is often rigidly oppressive. The classicists argue that where modernism prevails, there is an avoidance of Nature's laws. There is the feeling that modernistic paintings, furniture and architecture in particular will deteriorate with age whereas classic work improves, mellows and never looks out of place. Fair comment? probably so.

Where therefore does this fit into our conception of Dressage, to which the FEI refers to as the Classical Art, the subject of this book?

Describing *Dressage*

The word dressage, because it means different things to different people, has become a somewhat emotive word in the English language; yet in other languages the meaning is precise. Several derivations are advanced. The important equestrian one comes from the French, *dresser*. Whilst the English verb 'to dress' has been used historically in relation to horses, the noun 'dressage' only became popular at the turn of the present century. Nevertheless, many today are still bemused by the word. If the more accurate description 'schooling' was introduced for the lower levels of equitation, many more riders might find the discipline of dressage attractive.

The Oxford English Dictionary of Historical Terms informs us in a more accurate light that in the sixteenth century 'to dress' meant to place or set in position, to put into alignment, or to prepare according to certain principles. Later on, the term also indicated to clothe (as most people use it today) but by the end of that century, it implied rather more than that, namely to array, equip or adorn. One of the first references to the dressing of horses is made in Shakespeare's *Richard II*,[2] and contemporaneously, England's Gervase Markham was using it with reference to horses which he had trained or 'dressed'.

The Dressed Horse

The French translation is even more exacting. By the end of the seventeenth century *dresser* meant not merely the putting in place, but also conveyed the raising of the head and neck of the horse, both of which cannot naturally take place until the horse is trained to collection. In England, it was also understood that the horse was not 'dressed' unless able to carry out full collection, with his hocks under him, the poll raised, and the head carried in the vertical. Since no European king, prince, captain or gentleman prior to the 1800s would consider taking exercise on a horse which could not be fully collected in this way, all good horses, or horses of the blood were dressed. Thus throughout the civilised world, there grew up not only horsebreeders, but a vast population of horse *dresseurs*, expert horsemen or horsemasters, whose living depended on the Classical Art of riding.

Modern Use

Returning to the present, the word dressage in English is loosely used for virtually any form of ring or school riding. Yet in France, with typical precision, the word is used in its simplest sense and then qualified. Thus there is the world of difference between *Dressage d'obstacles* (schooling over fences), *Dressage de Manège* (general schooling in the manège) and *Dressage*

---

[2] Published in 1597–8.

Sculpture from the Place de la Concorde, Paris, by G. Coustou (1677–1746). Powerful and free! An image of the horse which has inspired sculptors, artists and riders since the civilised world began.

Academique which denotes fairly advanced manège work, possibly leading to the *haute école* or High School.

One of the most sensible passages on the philosophy of dressage or schooling the horse comes from the pen of the late Franz Mairinger (1915–1978) a former *Bereiter* of the Spanish Riding School. The following words reflect the idealism of the ancient Greeks.[3]

'If you want to know how a horse should be ridden, see how he moves by himself when free. How he walks, trots and canters . . . Have a close look and see the beauty, the rhythm and harmony of his movements. Then sit down, close your eyes and try to burn this picture of effortless grace, beauty and harmony deep into your mind, your heart. Never forget it. Because that is the way you should ride your horse. There in a few words is all the knowlege of the world, and your training goal!

'Preserve his natural gaits. Preserve his personality. Preserve his instinct to go forward. Do this and you must be successful because you are respecting nature's wisdom.

'Give him back his natural balance, with your additional weight on his back. That is the essence of schooling, training or *dressage*. . .'

It was this vision of a beautiful, free-moving horse, man's gift from the Creation, that inspired the ancient Greeks to define a philosphy of horsemanship. Today, whatever we conceive of God or the Creation, that thought should always be with us, lest the spirit of the art of riding be extinguished.

In this book, the word dressage will be used where relevant. For most of us however, this must traditionally denote manège work *above* elementary level, i.e., when the horse is collected and able to execute those free, natural movements despite our weight on his back. 'Dressage should mean the advanced special education of some horses with particular aptitudes, after completion of the elementary education that all horses should receive. . .' wrote General Albrecht.[4]

Ironically, in the days when dressage was rarely talked about, and certainly there were no competitions, the general standard of the average riding horse worldwide was very much higher. Schooling was undertaken as a matter of course and there were sufficient grooms, nagsmen[5] or professional horse copers about who made it their business to ensure that every

[3] From *Horses are Made to be Horses*.
[4] From *A Dressage Judge's Handbook*.
[5] See Glossary.

horse which passed through their hands received a basic education. Without this, the horse would not be considered suitable for a gentleman or lady to ride. Almost all of that breed of horseman has long since disappeared with predictable consequences.

Not very English

Another reason that dressage has become an emotive word, is that once the term was accepted into the English language to denote a separate discipline from general horsemanship, it invited derision amongst the jumping, hunting and polo fraternity. Whilst some regarded it as a threat to sporting riding, there were others who disdained it for being precious, and worse, oh so very much worse in British eyes, something rather *foreign*.

With the disappearance of the training groom, it was soon conveniently forgotten that elementary dressage improved all horses and riders. Thus in this century, between the wars, the remark, 'he does dressage', did not so much indicate a person who was seriously engaged in the schooling of the horse for purposes of suppling and achieving a more obedient mount, it often implied a rider who did not possess the nerve for the other disciplines.

Court Riding

As we will discover, in Italy, Portugal, France, Prussia, Austria, Bohemia, Hungary, Denmark, Sweden, Spain, Holland and so on, indoor or manège riding played an important and integral role in the life at court until the break-up of old Europe in the Napoleonic Wars. Those great

This English engraving, no 1, by John Vanderbank (1694–1739) from a series of drawings engraved by John Sympson and published as *Twenty-Five Actions of the Manège Horse* is entitled 'The Scholar placed in the Saddle without stirrups'.

écuyers or riding masters who were attached to the King or Emperor were regarded as artists in their own right; they were as vital to the prestige of the monarch as the court painter or court musician, and often held the highest rank amongst all the courtiers.

In England the demise of High School riding came earlier, but under the Catholic Tudor and Stuart kings and queens of England, equitation flourished as brilliantly as at any European court. Italian and French was the tongue of the English and Scottish nobles, and there was a rich interchange of European cultures. Today, Italian is still the language of music and opera, whereas French has given us the terms of the riding school, i.e. manège, haute école, renvers, travers, piaffe, levade and so on.

The Influence of the Horse

Jane Kidd, the equestrian travel writer and dressage correspondent for *Horse and Hound* has said 'I have come to the conclusion after travelling all over Europe that people ride to suit the horse of their country.'[6] This perceptive remark may be extended to include the whole world from the dawn of civilisation to the present day, and in particular explains why Britain broke away from the Classical Art. With the creation of the English Thoroughbred, a wonderful amalgam of genes resulting in a new race which bred true, the thrills of sporting riding gripped the nation. To suit the extended gaits of the long-necked, horizontally balanced Thoroughbred, a complete change in riding style and attitude took place. With the Restoration, the sport of chasing and racing swiftly superceded the collected riding of the manège, whilst hunting – once the sport of kings – became available to all horsemen.

A Competitive Spirit

The English-speaking nations in general, have never been able to resist a wager. It was natural therefore that with racing, came betting, and even on the hunting field, dares and bets were made as to which horse could gallop the faster between one point or steeple and another; hence the amateur sports of steeplechasing, or point-to-pointing. As these competitive pursuits developed and spread worldwide together with polo, another dashing sport, the riding fraternity not only resisted the idea of collected riding but some actually saw it as counter-productive to the freedom of crosscountry riding.

It is very likely that dressage would have remained unaccepted by the British, North Americans, Canadians and Australians, now so deeply steeped in the traditions of outdoor riding had it not been for the introduction of competitive riding in the Olympic Games of 1912.[7] Dressage, so long concealed from public view in the private manèges of the titled and wealthy, and behind the closed doors of those illustrious academic and military establishments of Europe, was now displayed for all to see. With its new competitive face, and despite the intervention of two world wars, it was found appealing enough dramatically to change the English-speaking world's attitude to this once spurned discipline. Through competition, dressage had suddenly become respectable.

Whilst a very few still practise dressage for its own sake, the great preoccupation therefore, which has mushroomed in the last decade, is to train the horse to compete in memorised dressage tests to compare the standard of one's horse against those of others.

Only at the highest levels does financial reward count sufficiently to make the time, effort

---

[6] Personal conversation during interview with author, November 1987.

[7] The first Olympiad is generally accepted to have taken place in 776 BC in Ancient Greece, when chariot races but no mounted events took place.

and expense materially worthwhile, but the majority of modern dressage riders love a challenge and accept this. Their object is to go out week after week, from competition to competition throughout the spring, summer and autumn, determined to score better places for which the achievement is to have their horses improved and upgraded to the next level.

Enthusiasts of the early English hunting field were not only bold, but often extremely competitive across country. Engraving by Henry Alken (1785–1851).

Asking a Question of Ourselves

With its changing face from virtuosity to competition, let us return to the question of art. Is today's competitive dressage really the Classical Art as indicated by the FEI in 1921, or has it, with its brave new face – so different from the days of courtly equitation – been unwittingly transformed into yet another equestrian sport? This is a question which lingers on the lips of those who have travelled the world and seen dressage in all its moods . . . stately versus energetic, private versus public, light versus robust. Should one add classical versus competitive?

Perhaps it is only by withdrawing from our own involvement, disregarding simultaneously our own country's method and breed of horse, that we can truly achieve an objective view.

This book presents a history of the Classical Art of riding. Through these chapters, the reader may familiarise himself with the influence of different cultures, different ideals, and different objectives, all set against a backcloth of different periods and personalities. Even more important to our story will be the influence of different horses. The horse of the Bourbon kings for example was not the horse of today's Olympic stars. That one facet alone, can alter the whole interpretation.

Many today feel dressage has developed into two forms – one arising out of the classical or traditional school, the other closer to what the French might term *dressage sportif*. Now it is up to the reader to decide for himself. Do we adhere to the letter of the FEI guidelines, or are we in danger of losing its spirit?

Perhaps the time has come to reconsider the true meaning of the words 'Classical Art'. Not only does classical imply the use of proven laid-down rules which are derived from nature's own laws and therefore create an end result which is not out of harmony with that of our universe. In riding, it implies rather more than that; it must include the kind and discreet handling of the horse so that despite responding to our requests, he remains happy in himself.

The Spanish Riding School of Vienna, the only academy of dressage which has remained virtually intact and unchanged in its approach over an illustrious history of four hundred years serves the modern world as a firm custodian of the art of classical dressage. Riders see their foremost task as bringing the horse to the heights of his physical ability, without losing his essential joie de vivre.

Reward

For this reason, the message of Xenophon of Athens, written over two thousand years ago is strictly followed at Vienna: 'The art of riding is based on rewards and punishments.' The rules therefore are clearcut for the classical school. Reward is constantly given, and punishment is applied not so much in the application of a harsh heel or spur, but in the cessation of praise or reward. In less knowledgeable hands however, this is not always understood. When force prevails, dressage ceases to be classical. A horse may be trained through discomfort or pain, but he will never be dressed in the classical sense of the word.

Punishment

Certainly there was nothing of art in the early revival of dressage under the sixteenth century Italian masters. Whilst Grisone (see Chapter 4), known by his contemporaries as the 'Father of the art of equitation', repeated almost word for word the teachings of Xenophon, we know from excerpts and illustrations that he interpreted punishment all too literally and had little understanding of the mind of the horse. Due to ignorance, so-called art in this case became a travesty.

Yet cruel practices are not merely confined to history. In today's world of materialist values and the constant quest for fame and success, it is inevitable that methods of schooling horses can stray from these ideals of Xenophon and twentieth century Vienna. Unwittingly, trainers concentrate on the punishment side of schooling and quite forget the important aspect of reward. Punishment may take many forms such as the endless trotting in circles which we see today, the horse bent like a bow on a fixed rein contact, driven unremittingly forward by relentlessly active legs. With never a break or a pat to relieve the physical and mental pressure and show him he has done well, this is unacceptable discipline.

The French Count Montigny,[8] who trained and later taught at the Spanish Riding School, wrote in his *L'Equitatation des Dames* '. . . the abusive use of immoderate and constant force

---

[8] Inspector General of all the French Cavalry Schools in the nineteenth century. He was also a chief rider at the Spanish Riding School of Vienna from 1842–1845 and served in a Hungarian cavalry regiment.

is without effect; it extinguishes and paralyses all efforts; in other words, this force leads to insensitivity and to complete indifference to the aids.'

The same enlightened French thinking led the great eighteenth century La Guérinière (1688-1751) to insist that that the asking action of the legs must be followed by the giving of the legs, and that in each stride, each movement, there must be a moment of reward with hand and leg – i.e. cessation of the aid: '. . . *Descente de main, et de jambes* . . .' These terms will become the clearer through each chapter of this book. Discipline must exist, but because of the innate sensitivity of the horse, classical equestrian art can only be achieved through delicacy and tact.

Modern Pressures

Today, the task for competitors and judges alike in international dressage competition is not an easy one. Tests are written, so that judgements can be made more easily. Unfortunately, because of layout and the allocation of marks, accuracy often takes precedence over flow and style. Riding to markers leaves little room for choice, no allowance for the horse to be asked at the right time for him. Since timing is all-important in the execution of a difficult movement, this can cause abruptness, thus accuracy is often obtained to the discomfort of the horse. Artistry is therefore lost.

The true artist however will continue to train with the ultimate suppleness, happiness and beauty of the horse in mind, and the discerning judge will observe the merit of soft, flowing movement against accurate but overtly mechanical steps. Whether this combination will win medals is however, open to doubt. The judge's task is not an enviable one.

Ephemeral opinions can also detract from the original classical values. It is tempting to judge a dressage horse by its sheer presence, size and strength, when inside may lie hidden deep stress and resistance brought about by fear of retribution. Again, the discerning judge will be in a position to note these signs, apparent in the tension of a horse's jaw, or the sad resigned equine face, particularly the look in the eye. Mankind has always been prey to outward appearances; it takes a true horseman or woman, in every sense of the word, to distinguish between genuine gaiety in the horse's work as opposed to the artificial sparkle often produced by anxiety. The greatest criteria, irrespective of breed, size or type, of what constitutes the Classical Art, must be the horse's physical and psychological state at the end of training. We can therefore do no better than to quote Colonel Handler, who wrote in his beautiful *oeuvre, The Spanish Riding School in Vienna* the following passage:

> If training has not made a horse more beautiful, nobler in his carriage, more attentive in his behaviour, revealing pleasure in his own accomplishment with a twitching of his ears and a lively expression in his eyes, he may have been dressed, but he has not been truly schooled, in the classical sense of dressage.'

TWO

Xenophon and the Birth of Classical Equitation

Lightness! Agility! Balance! Those essentials of the classically trained horse were as relevant two and a half thousand years ago as they are today. From contemporary equestrian art and pottery, we can remark that not every ancient cavalryman had the benefit of proper training. Since there was little if any literature on the subject, cavalry commanders passed on the techniques of hand to hand combat, and how to train the horse to be obedient and manoeuvrable in battle by word of mouth.

Schooling for a Purpose

The Greek commander Xenophon, born about 430 BC was a man of active service during the last of the Pelopennesian Wars as well as many other recorded campaigns. He has left us the first surviving treatise of horsemanship with a number of schooling principles still recognised today. In his work, he mentions an earlier writer of the time, Simon of Athens, but sadly, scarcely a fragment of that work has been preserved.[1] Xenophon's valuable *Hippike*, translated as The Art of Horsemanship,[2] as well as other works[3] by this talented and prolific writer, provide the basic classical ideals for all future horsemen.

Some form of school or ring riding had probably begun as long ago as 1500 BC. That is plain from Xenophon's accounts of preparing the horse for the skirmish of battle through suppling and collecting exercises on the circle and the volte as well as the the change of rein through the demi-volte to enable the horse to be equally responsive on either rein. One of the traditional battle movements which had to be practised in those days was a very fast impulsive gallop down the career (see Glossary) where the horse had to be brought back sharply on his hocks and turned immediately in either direction. For this collection and flexion was required and the best horses according to Xenophon, must be supple through the jaw and utterly permeable in the rider's hands.

Difficulties existed however, since, although the curb bit then existed in Persia, historians are convinced the Greeks only used a jointed snaffle. Greek cavalrymen did not have the support of stirrups or a proper saddle (hence the popularity of comfortable 'double-backed' horses).[4] Without these artificial aids of control, teaching the horse collection until it became second nature to him was a *sine qua non*.

Battle!

Try to imagine the scene! Once a battleground was chosen, able officers led the field carefully forward, their horses collected and 'well in hand', as prescribed by Xenophon,[5] to maintain

---

[1] Only a discourse on conformation remains.

[2] Xenophon, *The Art of Horsemastership*, translated by M.H. Morgan PhD, J.A. Allen 1979 edition.

[3] The *Anabasis* (379–371 BC); the *Cyropaedia*; the *Hellenica* (after 362 BC); the *Memorabilia*; the *Oeconomics*; the *Cynegetica* (an essay on hunting); the *Hippiarchicus* (on a good cavalry commander); the *Hiero*; the *Agesilaus*; the *Symposium*; *The Revenues of Athens* (355 BC) and possibly *The Apology*.

[4] See *The Art of Horsemanship*, Chapter 1, page 17. Xenophon meant by this expression horses with well developed dorsal muscles which were comfortable to ride compared to those with a protruding backbone.

[5] *ibid*, Chapter 8, page 47.

ordered formation. Soon each horse and rider would be enclosed on three sides by his own compatriots. Ahead lay death or victory. Think of the noise of these bloody confrontations! The Bible describes them very well, the clash of steel and of cymbals, the neighing and screaming of horses and men. Only a confident horse of fire would prove an enthusiastic partner to a cavalryman dependent on an equal sharing of courage and dexterity.

In the mêlée that ensued, the more gymnastic and responsive the horse, the better chance for the rider of emerging from the fray, unscathed. Unlike the nomadic tribes of Asia who rode mares or geldings, Xenophon and his men rode stallions since they were the more brave, showing greater aptitude for the exercises of pirouetting, leaping, turning, moving sideways and curvetting away or into the enemy lines.

The first priority therefore was total manoeuvrability. The rider's hands were occupied with shield and sword, so the desired result was an easily balanced warhorse, trusting and obedient.

In Chapter 1, we remarked that no gentleman or officer prior to 1800 would consider riding an animal other than a dressed horse (i.e., one schooled to collection). In Xenophon's time, the relevance of collection was even more important since there were only crude weapons to assist the attack over the most harsh and unforgiving ground.

A Deep Balanced Seat

For all this life or death struggle on horseback, Xenophon insisted on what has come to be known as the classical seat, the seat from which the rider can gather his horse. The efficacy of this classical seat is still applicable today, wherever and whenever riders have the need of precision.

'I do not approve of a seat which is as though the man were on a chair,' wrote Xenophon, referring to the hunting seat of the nomads (whom we shall discuss shortly). Xenophon required the rider to be as balanced on horseback as if we were on the ground, '. . . rather as though he were standing upright with his legs apart.' Only in this balance, explained Xenophon, could the horse be kept 'collected for the turns'.

Subsequent writers through history have attempted to explain the effect of the weight aids of the seat on the horse's balance. As the French writer Colonel Jousseaume wrote, 'It is enough for the rider to feel the state of balance of the horse and know how to modify it if necessary . . .' Xenophon's seat made allowances for these minute modifications and conclusively passed the test of time.[6]

Xenophon, the founder of classical equitation, from a French engraving by Charles Aubrey, Paris, 1833 (*Histoire Pittoresque de L'Equitation Ancienne et Moderne*). From early pictorial evidence, we have every reason to believe that this artist's impression of Xenophon's style of riding, his armour, clothing and skins in place of a saddle, is reasonably accurate. (Stirrups were not used until after the time of the Romans.)

[6] From *Progressive Equitation* by André Jousseaume.

The Forward Seat

From contemporary pictorial evidence we know the forward or hunting seat existed alongside that of Xenophon. Even certain Greek riders are depicted in a far from classical position. Casually seated, sometimes too far back, sometimes crouched over the withers, warriors have their knees drawn up, the thigh bone almost horizontal instead of stretched down, and the horses themselves running free and uncollected on a loose rein.

This form of riding was obviously well-known to Xenophon. It came from the fierce Mongul warriors, the Etruscans and the Scythian peoples[7] who occupied the great grassy plains of the Kuban and the Ukraine far to the north and east of Greece. Nomadic, travelling people, their horses were of the handy pony type, long backed and short limbed which travelled best in a flat easy canter on the forehand. In the manner of latter-day hunters, the nomadic tribes gripped with their knees and leant forward with the body. We know from their magnificent coloured pottery that their great delight on horseback was, above all, the chase.

This was the logical start of the forward seat, and in war the Scythians made formidable adversaries. Not for them however, the brilliant manoeuvres in battle on the hotblood warhorse favoured by Xenophon. Their style was to make daring raids on their fast little ponies, gallop in, loot and burn, then out again. It was their numbers, surprise and shock tactics which won them the day.

This form of riding, which suited their horses and the flat terrain where they were bred, had some influence over the lands to the south. Certainly Xenophon was well aware of the use of the forward seat when riding out across country. In 401, he joined up with a group of Greek mercenaries to assist Prince Cyrus in a bitter power struggle which led to a daring campaign into Persia. These adventures are recounted in his famous book *Anabasis* which deals with the long march home, through the wilds of Kurdistan and Armenia where he and his 10,000 men were constantly under attack, round the Bosphorus, and finally back to Athens.

Whilst always advocating a classical collected way of riding for battle, he does not neglect useful advice concerning the importance of letting the horse stretch himself into a more horizontal balance when galloping across country with the rider in a more forward position. Even jumping ditches and riding up and down hill is explained, particularly with reference to the varied head carriage as the horse balanced himself.

The Greek Warhorse

The American historian M. H. Morgan tells us that blood horses were an expensive commodity in Greece, and that the position and space devoted to the warhorses on the Parthenon frieze[8] signified their status in Attic life at that time.

Persian horses of 600 BC in stone bas-relief demonstrate a well-flexed head and neck position, obtained from a primitive form of curb bit. It was this flexion and subsequent yielding of the horse's mouth that was to become so important to the progress of collected riding for war and later pleasure. Xenophon taught that the hand must always be light on the rein.

[7] See *A History of Horsemanship* by Charles Chenevix Trench, also *The Horse through Fifty Centuries of Civilisation* by Anthony Dent.

[8] Part of this was brought to England (between 1802–12 by Lord Elgin), subsequently to be known as the Elgin marbles. The Parthenon was carved between 447–432 BC.

We read that the big Thessalonian and Madedonian horses were held in high esteem for their courage, whilst the Persians too owned magnificent warhorses. There is evidence that the very wealthy Greek equestrian classes also owned Iberian and Barb horses.

We know from the *Hellenica* that the Greeks, after colonising Spain and Portugal in around 700 BC appeared to adopt the Iberian method of skirmish, attack and retreat. This style of combat was used in the Pelopennesian Wars (431–404 BC). The warring Spartans, with whom Xenophon later aligned himself, were assisted by Iberian mercenaries who landed their own warhorses along the southern seaboard. Many of these horses would have remained and inter-bred, and it is particularly interesting that an ancient Greek word *zenete* meaning a light-armed cavalryman corresponds closely to the Portuguese and Spanish word *gineta* still used today in the Iberian Peninsula to describe a very distinctive form of ancient skirmish riding.[9]

Through its Macedonian, Thessalonian, Persian, Spanish and Barb blood, the ideal Greek warhorse would not have been so very different from those of later classical masters in the sixteenth, seventeenth and eighteenth centuries. Indeed this is indicated not only by pictorial evidence, but by the following excerpt from *Hippike* concerning the ideal war horse: 'The broader the chest so much the handsomer and stronger the horse, and the more naturally adap-ted to carry the legs well apart and without interference. The neck should not be thrown out from the chest like a boar, but, like a cock's rise straight up to the poll and be slim at the bend, while the head, though bony, should have but a small jaw. The neck would then protect the rider, and the eye see what lies before the feet.'

Xenophon also spoke of high-stepping parade horses, and horses with supple loins and thighs. 'Such a horse will be able to gather the hindlegs well in under the fore . . . Now when he has gathered them well in, if you take him up with the bit, he falls back on his hocks and raises his forehand so that his belly and sheath can be seen from the front.'

From this and other descriptions, it is obvious these warhorses were trained in levade, pesade and probably courbette as well as the trotting airs which would give way to the passage and probably the piaffe. Since Xenophon spent much of his youth either fighting in Persia, or with the Spartans against Athens[10] and Thebes (lying 30 miles to the north west), he was greatly influenced by the horsemanship of a number of cultures.

The Golden Age

For whom did Xenophon write his book of horsemanship? According to Morgan, Xenophon came from a well-to-do landed family; his writings show he was an ardent admirer of Socrates. *Hippike* would very naturally be studied by cultivated young men from a similar background, many of whom would attend one of the Athenian universities or agricultural colleges before entering military service. Since this was the age of Attic enlightenment, with its high moral tone, ethical ideals and the minute examination of the mysteries of the universe, so, even, a book on horses and riding had to conform. Thus in *Hippike* we find nothing in conflict with the laws of nature and unlike so many books today, every section whether on stable manage-ment or riding is clear-cut and logical. What sets the work of Xenophon apart, is his psychologi-cal approach to the training of horses.

From now on, all music, art, poetry, drama, philosophy, and literature connected however vicariously to this wonderful period of growth and discovery within Ancient Greece, would

---

[9] Research by Alfredo Baptista Coelho, Lisbon historian, sent to the author in a letter, 1986.
[10] This ended with the defeat of Athens which the Spartans ruled until 371 BC.

be termed by later scholars as classical. Equitation might so easily have been ignored, were it not for this one very educated, well-travelled and thoughtful man. Xenophon, for all his bellicose attributes, was able to embrace and develop the new idealism and make it applicable to riding. Thus was born the whole concept of classical equitation.

Xenophon's Psychological Approach

Let us now examine Xenophon's methods, all of which are quite simple. Undoubtedly, the cornerstone of his philosophy is summed up in the following sentence. 'The art of riding is based on rewards and punishments.' We have already briefly discussed this precept in the previous chapter, and according to Xenophon himself, the earlier Simon of Athens also promoted this fundamental.

Emanating from this, we can establish five basic principles for training the horse: those of tact, self-discipline, a constant quest for beauty and perfection, freedom for the horse and lightness. Since all these qualities are interrelated, the result of one, ensures the accomplishment of another. Xenophon provides us with a wealth of examples to follow. These were a source of inspiration centuries later, when the masters of post-Renaissance Europe began to study them.

Tact: Xenophon constantly practised this together with gentleness. 'When your horse shies at an object and is unwilling to go up to it, he should be shown that there is nothing fearful in it, least of all to a courageous horse like himself. If this fails, touch the object yourself that seem so dreadful to him, and lead him up to it with gentleness.'

Self-discipline: Xenophon stressed that we should never deal with the horse 'in a fit of passion for there is something blind in anger which makes us commit actions that will later be regretted.'

Beauty: Xenophon abhorred the use of force reminding us that 'For what the horse does under compulsion . . . is done without understanding; just as there would be no beauty if one should whip and spur a dancer. There would be a great deal more ungracefulness than beauty in either a horse or a man that was so treated.'

Freedom for the Horse: Xenophon believed submission must be achieved voluntarily otherwise it would spoil the noble nature of the horse. 'If you desire to handle a good warhorse so as to make his action the more magnificent and striking, you must refrain from pulling at his mouth with the bit . . . Most people think that is the way to make him look; but they only produce an effect exactly contrary to what they desire.'

To achieve real perfection, the horse must at all times be allowed to be himself, urged Xenophon. 'So when he [the horse] is induced by a man to assume all the airs and graces which he puts on of himself when he is showing off voluntarily, the result is a horse that likes to be ridden, that presents a magnificient sight, that looks alert. . .'

Lightness: 'If you teach your horse to go with a light hand on the bit, and yet to hold his head high and to arch his neck [collection] you will be making him do just what the animal himself glories and delights in.'

The technique of the yielding of the hand or 'giving him the bit' was not so much to impress others however, but to act as a reward and respite to the horse and encourage him to repeat the most difficult movements again and again. How convincing is the next passage on the same principle: 'Now if when his fire is thus kindled, you let him [the horse] have the bit, the slackness of it makes him think that he is given his head, and in his joy thereat he will bound along with proud gait and prancing legs, imitating exactly the airs that he puts on before other horses. Everybody that sees such a horse cries out that he is free, willing, fit to

A Portuguese mosaic from around the time of the Greek colonisation of the Iberian Peninsula from whence cavalry horses were later drawn to assist in the Pelopennesian Wars. Note the short-coupled, powerful body, the fine legs and strong upright neck – attributes much prized by Xenophon and other writers of the period. There is also a ceremonial plume.

ride, high-mettled, brilliant and at once beautiful and fiery in appearance.'

Some modern scholars seem to have missed the whole point of Xenophon's treatise. Yet just one of these quotations reproduced as a thought for the day on every advanced dressage test sheet might achieve wonders for the schooling of thousands of horses. It was this psychological element which after all inspired equestrian scholars after the Renaissance and was to prove the cornerstone of the philosophy of La Guérinière and the whole Classical School.

Love of the Horse

The lesson which shines out of Xenophon's book is that kindness will enhance training and discipline. A man of war with raw recruits to train, could not afford to use wishy-washy methods which might not work. Xenophon perceived that paying attention to the happiness and comfort of the horse reaped great reward. That is why throughout his text, he constantly encouraged lightness of hand, the sensitive approach. Reluctant converts should further read the section in *Hipparchicus* on the duties of a cavalry officer. This together with the *Anabasis* can leave no shadow of doubt that Xenophon was anything else but a man of iron will and self-discipline. Like all great leaders, however, he also possessed those valuable commodities of imagination and insight.

So much of Xenophon seems so modern that *The Art of Horsemanship* ought not to be neglected from the reading list of national riding examinations. How best to achieve a transition from trot to canter on a given lead is described in painstaking detail, how not to bang the horse in the teeth over a jump, and how, by caressing and getting to know your horse in the stable, his trust and friendship will be gained. In one small book, all the fundamentals are there.

Xenophon therefore gave us the Art of riding. Not only did he outline the important principles, he showed the path to further enlightenment. If a man of war, born two and a half thousand years ago could establish such close and clearly rewarding relationships with his horses, there is a lesson for all of us today.

THREE

The Historical Significance of Collected Riding

It is an accepted historical truth that classical equestrian philosophy lay dormant for over one thousand years after Xenophon. Only after the rediscovery of ancient writings in Renaissance Italy did equitation begin again to incorporate all Xenophon's ideals of lightness and the happiness of the horse, which reached its full flowering in the mid seventeenth and eighteenth centuries.

Macedonia

For the interim, the story of Alexander the Great of Macedonia (356–323 BC) with his stallion Bucephalus is important since again it reflects a humanitarian approach to horsemanship. Macedonia, a country of grassy plains and fertile river basins lying to the north of Greece, was noted for its beautiful horses. In 333 BC Alexander, son of King Philip II, raised 5,000 head of horseman and 20,000 foot soldiers to take on the mighty Persian Empire in a series of successful campaigns. A pupil of Aristotle the Greek philosopher, Alexander, like Xenophon had been brought up on ideals of refinement and reasoned logic. He had been taught that art should embody nature, only in a more perfect form and that the essence of beauty was order and symmetry. As a man of great perserverance, he endeavoured to incorporate these ideals into his riding.

The story of the fiery Bucephalus, tamed by Alexander as a boy when all others had failed, is significant because it incorporated vision and tact instead of force. Bucephalus was afraid of his own shadow, yet out of all the horsemen in the kingdom of Macedonia, it was only Alexander who was able to discover this.

Contemporary writers of the first century AD[1] mention the Numidian and Mauretanian tribes of North Africa who rode their desert horses without bridles using small switches, but there is no real evidence of classical reasoning so we must now look to the Roman period for some form of continuity after Xenophon.

Roman Cavalry

The Roman period is generally ignored by scholars of equitation since there remains not one single remaining treatise on the art of horsemanship. Yet, as we shall see, there are frequent observations in Roman literature to the suitability of differents breeds for cavalry, conformation and veterinary matters, together with undeniable archeological evidence of outdoor and indoor schooling rings.

Although they had long enjoyed a sophisticated form of charioteering[2] with the small swift horse from the plains[3] in the sun-swept amphitheatres of Rome and Naples, the Romans only turned to horses for use in cavalry after their wars with the Carthaginians when they encountered the much bigger, close-coupled horses of the Iberian Peninsula.

[1] Livy (Titus Livius), 59 BC–17 AD; Pliny the Elder (Gaius Plinius Secundus), 23–79 AD.
[2] See *The Horse Through Fifty Centuries of Civilisation*.
[3] Probably the Tarpan from the steppes north of the Black Sea. See *A History of Horse Breeding* by Daphne Machin Goodall.

PLATE 1

This painting by Meytens, entitled the *Damenkarussell*, celebrated on 2 January 1743, vividly
portrays the classic lines of the Winter Riding School, Vienna, and the grandeur of Imperial life
at the Austrian court. In the centre foreground, Maria Theresa leads the mounted quadrille, followed
by ladies of high rank. Note their proud riding positions and the intricacy of their gold embroidered
habits. The Archduchess Marianna heads the first coach quadrille followed by Princess Lobkowitz.
Above the imperial box hangs the famous portrait of Emperor Charles VI just as it does today (*see
Plate 3*). (*Courtesy Kunsthistorisches Museum, Vienna*)

PLATE 2

The English artist, George Hamilton's (1672–1737) fine portrayals of the Spanish Baroque horse are often presumed stylised. This is not so; these ancient blood horses are faithfully portrayed to show the deep, short-coupled body, long fine legs, proud, muscular neck and aristocratic mien, conformation which lent itself to the highly collected airs of the Imperial manège. (This was in contrast to that other blood horse, the sprinting, horizontally-built Arab of the desert.) These Iberian forerunners of the noble Lipizzan were generally black, dun, bay, spotted or the dominant grey. Under the patronage of Emperor Charles VI, a wealth of equestrian studies was completed, the best of which hangs in the Schönbrunn Palace and at the Winter Riding School. (*Courtesy the Spanish Riding School*)

In the Second Punic War (218–201 BC) when Hannibal marched into Northern Italy at the head of 6,000 head of horse, the pick of his Spanish and North African levies, the legions of Roman infantry suffered tremendous loss of life. In his book *A Short History of the Spanish Horse and of the Iberian Gineta Horsemanship for which This Horse is Adapted*, the historian Fernando d'Andrade describes the various manoeuvres of skirmish employed by these invading Iberian horsemen and their effect on the Romans. It was this, together with the agility and dexterity of their mounts, that caused the Roman leaders to rethink their tactics.

According to Anthony Dent in his book *The Horse Through Fifty Centuries of Civilisation*, the North African horses were less imposing than the Spanish, yet '. . . they could be employed with deadly effect.' Like most desert-bred animals, they galloped 'with their heads stretched out'.

This contrasted with the collected riding of the Iberian-Celts who had already discovered the curb bit[4] and used light armour, shields made of iron, and shod their highstepping horses with iron shoes remarkably similar to those of modern times. This combined cavalry daunted the Roman generals excessively, and a great victory was won by this army at Cannae in Apulia in 216 BC when 85,000 Roman foot soldiers were utterly defeated.

Finally, after twelve years bitter fighting, the Romans drove Hannibal back to Africa. As a result of wresting the Iberian Peninsula for Rome and subduing the rebellious tribes they converted many of their foot soldiers to cavalry. Polybius (145 BC, *Book XXXC*) described how the Romans not only copied the Iberian ways of combat, but also adopted their weapons, exchanging the calfskin shield and flexible lance for the short, two pointed iron lance and the *pillum* of the Portuguese and Spanish horsemen, as well as their strong oval shield.

By the end of the first century AD, the Romans were mounted. With their proud horses, and chain armour, they would never again be without the horse. Thus, the horses and equitation once so feared in adversity, was now turned to the Romans' own advantage. So respected was the Iberian horse as a warhorse, that his distinctive convex-shaped head came to be known as Roman-nosed, a term which has survived to this day.

Scipio (who invaded Africa in 202 BC) and Marcus Aurelius, Roman Emperor from 161–180 AD were two great cavalry leaders who typify the might of Rome when the transition from infantry to cavalry took place. They always rode Spanish horses.

Roman sculpture shows the absence of stirrups and the necessity for the horseman to be as balanced as possible, sitting into the strongest part of the horse's anatomy for the collected exercises of battle. Note the ancient way of holding the rein in the left hand, leaving the right hand for a weapon. The horse shows a noticeable yielding on the lower jaw.

[4] Remains of bits photographed in Andrade's book date back to the Iberian Celts of approximately 400 BC.

Ring Riding under the Romans

A system of large country estates around Lisbon and in Andalusia was organised from the first century AD. Here horsebreeding could be encouraged in ideal conditions to serve the Empire's growing needs[5] and remount depots were established. Twentieth century excavations in the Tagus valley have revealed the remains of carefully laid out stud farms and schooling areas. Roman ruins discovered earlier in this century at Mirobriga, near the Portuguese town of Santiago do Cacem, have only in this decade yielded up an exciting discovery. Described by Lisbon archaeologists as a *circo-hipodromo*, an area 76 metres in diameter and with seating for up to 25,000 spectators, has been unearthed. Authorities confirm that this was used for chariot racing and as an early riding ring for javelin practice and the schooling of Lusitanos.[6] Elsewhere, whole sections of mosaic floors have been preserved which show portraits of favourite horses reared there, their Latin names appearing alongside.

Pliny the Elder wrote: 'The cleverness of horses is beyond description. Mounted javelinmen discover their docility as they assist difficult passes with the actual swaying of their body . . .' Like the Greeks, the Romans rode without stirrups using weight aids with the seat to balance the horse. Portrayals of riders found on coins and pottery in the Peninsula dating from this period demonstrate a position which Xenophon could hardly have faulted. A fairly uniform, *classical* seat is shown in nearly all cases, the horse well in hand and back on his hocks. The rider's upper body is proudly upright, the seat deep from a relatively low slightly bent knee, and the lower leg hangs down long and relaxed. Over the rocky uncertain terrain, collection was a necessity not a mere extravagance for the parade ground.

The writing of Columella in the first century AD, and that of Oppian and Nemesian in the third century as well as Pelagonious and Palladius in the fourth century all confirm that disciplined riding instruction did take place. Pliny confirms, through other works, that he had written *De Iaculatione Equestri* (23–79 AD), but this has sadly been lost.

Lengthy accounts on the conformation of a suitable warhorse come from Virgil, Nemesian, Apsyrtus and Palladius[7] and are very similar to that of Xenophon, the emphasis always being on the strength, breadth and suppleness of the back and the ability of the horse to be easily aroused, light in the hand and to bring his hocks well under him.

Collected riding also played a part in the circus, an important facet of Roman life all over the expanding empire. Battle movements were developed into flamboyant steps for the amusement of the people and one of these involved a staccato beat of the hooves called the *Tripidium* from which the piaffe probably evolved. The Romans certainly enjoyed an affinity with their horses. They taught the Asturian horses to amble, by '. . . straightening the near and offside legs alternately', and there is an absorbing account of horses being taught to retrieve fallen weapons with their mouths from the ground, to save the rider dismounting. This would be hard to believe if it were not contained in some very weighty text about horsebreeding from Pliny.

A popular spectacle was the dancing horses of travelling shows which performed to the sound of brass and woodwind. Other ancient people who trained their horses to dance to music, were the luxuriant Sybarites[8] of Magna Graecia who came to their height of civilisation

---

[5] See *The Royal Horse of Europe* by Sylvia Loch.

[6] From articles published in *Jornal de Beja*, 26 June 1984; *Correio de Mantia*, 29 October 1984; *O Seculo*, 27 August 1986.

[7] Virgil, from the *Georgics*, published about 29 BC; Nemesian, from the *Cynegetica*, third century; Apsyrtus, a veterinary surgeon under Constantine in the fourth century, from his *Geoponis*; Palladius, from the *De Re Ruistica*, fourth century.

[8] From which comes sybarite – pleasure-seeing, hedonistic etc.

about 200 years before Xenophon. The most famous of the Roman riders appeared in the amphitheatres which lined the imperial route from Alexandria across the sea to Arles in France. Trick riding, vaulting and a form of High School riding were performed as well as charioteering. Constantine the Great (Emperor of Rome 306–337) was a great lover of the circus, and for many years Constantinople became the centre of circus riding.[9] This was quite separate from the sport of bullbaiting which was also introduced, the bulls reputedly coming from Crete and Thessalonica.

Roman Culture

With their love of order and discipline, reflected in their architecture, town planning, and engineering, it is sad that more is not known about the Roman period with regard to the schooling of horses. The civilised, cultural side to their character is too often overlooked amongst tales of cruel, crushing victory, persecution and the compulsive expansion of empire. The Romans conquered Greece in 146 BC and inherited much of their aesthetic love of beauty and symmetry, well reflected in the subtly tinted mosaics, tiles and pottery they left behind as well as the more obvious magnificence of their equestrian and allegorical statues, the bridges, columns and aquaducts.

Of especial significance are those southern lands of Europe, particularly round the Mediterranean, Sicily and Italy, deep into Baetica (today's Andalusia) and Lusitania (today's Portugal), to Saumur in France, a centre for horsebreeding and tournaments. Where the Roman influence was at its strongest, a very specialised form of collected riding based on lightness and agility, was practised long after the Romans had gone. This contrasts sharply with the later altogether stiffer form of collection displayed by the Frankish knights and Gothic peoples north of the Danube and the Rhine.

The Romanic Style

The term Romanic has remained to this day in relation to horsemanship. Little used in relation to other cultural spheres, riding masters throughout the ages recognised the term to indicate a highly collected, agile form of riding based on lightness in hand. Gradually people began to talk of the Romanic School, thus differentiating between this style and that of the heavier Germanic or Prussian influence. These national differences date back to the earliest times, and in the twentieth century the term Romanic continued still to be used by authors Podhajsky, Decarpentry[10] and Oliveira in a similar connection.

By recognising the importance of the Romanic period and its influence, it is easier by far to understand why Italy should emerge as the centre of equestrian cultural rebirth. History repeated itself as once again this influence crept westward and northward to the very heart of France where through the School of Versailles, it struggles to remain to this day.

When Rome fell at the hands of the barbarians in 410 AD, and the centres of civilisation were either destroyed, overrun or besieged, there was a complete abandonment of the real philosophical and moral influences on equitation.

---

[9] From *The Story of Riding* by E.M. Kellock.

[10] In *Academic Equitation* by General Decarpentry, first published in English by J.A. Allen in 1971. A footnote to the second edition states: 'We must regretfully state that, in 1964, no difference between Romanic equitation and Germanic equitation exists, in any case in international dressage tests.'

Carthaginian horseman mounted on an Iberian Barb charger. The surge forward into a semi capriole may seem a little stylised, yet horses of this strain use a similar movement today in the work with the bull.

The Dark Ages

The many excellent books on the history of riding which deal with the Dark and Middle Ages[11] indicate that once again, riding was influenced by methods of warfare and the type of horse involved. The Goths, Vandals, Huns and the Franks swept down from the north on their heavy coldblood cobs and sturdy ponies which were ridden with little finesse and with every form of iron contraption in their mouths to obtain some form of control. Gradually, the thickset, short-legged Teutonic breeds interbred and mingled with the hotbloods of the south, giving rise to the bigger chargers of peoples like the Lombards who came to Italy in the sixth century, and the smaller but spirited horses of the Normans who rose to power in tenth century France and followed southward in their wake. Around Italy, Yugoslavia, Austria and the lands of eastern Europe, there was also the influence of the Saracens, and later the Turks with their swift, finely built oriental breeds.

With different people of vastly contrasting cultures from Scandinavia to Armenia all jockeying for power, there was little time for the concept of equitation as an art. Later, under Charlemagne (died 814 AD) and throughout the Tournaments and Crusades (1096–1292), a generous element of chivalry at court returned but, on the field, with the introduction of plate armour, the necessity to breed a really big, coldblooded, weight-carrying horse took precedence over all other aspects of horsemanship.

During the fourteenth and fifteenth centuries, nearly all manoeuvrability was lost from the battleground since a fully armoured and accoutred cavalry soldier weighed somewhere between 24 and 28 stone and his horse could do no more that lumber towards the enemy at a slow and ponderous trot. The Greek and Romanic practice of single combat from the back of a fiery hot-blood charger was totally inappropriate during this period, yet ironically perhaps, it was the change to small firearms which rescued the practice from almost certain oblivion.

The Renaissance

It was the Renaissance, originating in Italy and gradually spreading across Western Europe which led to a very rich post-Renaissance period in France, Prussia, Austria, Spain, Portugal and England thus achieving the rebirth and recognition of equitation as an art. The Academies which sprung up to accommodate this revival for classical riding are discussed at length in the next five chapters.

---

[11] See *The Foals of Epona* by Anthony Dent and Daphne Machin Goodall, *A History of Horsemanship, op. cit.*.

This revival in the intricacies of advanced horsemanship was no mere coincidence. Riding had to be practical. It was the invention of small, handy firearms which heralded the return to the battlefield of a light, handy horse. Soon, the very heavy, coldblood horses of the plate-armoured knights were relegated to more mundane logistical tasks away from the front. The role of cavalry had taken a new turn.

In the same way that the ancient Greeks had developed agile manoeuvres for hand to hand combat with javelin and spear, so the European cavalry commanders were discovering that to take advantage of their small pistols and revolvers together with their slim cutting swords, they too must have absolute control of their horses. The whole training of the cavalry horse therefore had to be re- examined, and it became clear that a much more precise form of collected riding was necessary.

The Classical School Airs

Some modern writers have dismissed the idea of the High School movements playing a serious role in the execution of attack and defence; they are wrong. Single mounted combat whether with sword or a short range firearm requires a very high degree of horsemanship; tactical fighting will win, *ceteris paribus*, every time over muscle and brawn. Harnessing balance to assist the horse in his work rarely comes naturally; it has to be understood and taught as Xenophon and Simon discovered.

There was therefore a serious purpose behind the revival of scientific or academic equitation. Special movements such as the piaffe, the levade and the pirouette were again developed for battle. The piaffe was perhaps the most useful movement of all, it gathered the horse like a spring as he marked time on the spot for the sudden advance. The levade, used by the Greeks, developed from a highly collected half–halt, giving the rider a distinct vantage point from which to slash downward with the sword, or aim the pistol. It could also be used as a swift evasion from a low musket ball or a falling horse. Pirouette enabled the horse to wheel towards or away from the line of fire at a moment's notice. It gave the rider instant mobility of direction when confronted with the muzzle of a musket.

The courbette, when the horse rises up to over eight foot high, and takes a series of jumps along the ground must have been a terrifying sight for the infantrymen below and would easily disperse a small group. Since unarmed horses are still used today by the police for crowd control and generally treated with fear and respect, how much more effective they would be with their leaps and rears in battle.

The change of leg at canter or gallop were obviously vital in a charge, when confronted on every side with danger and opposition. A horse which could not be balanced and turned at speed was a sitting duck for rifle, sabre or lance. Only with constant changes of direction could the cavalryman get in and around the enemy without a head-on clash. Finally, the capriole was an effective means of escape above the heads of the infantry. Unlike a normal jump, it could be achieved from the standstill, but for this training the horse required tremendous gymnasticity and generous temperament.

It was this combination of natural talent that led to the favourite horse of the Romans, the Spanish, the Barb and the Lusitanian horse, spreading all over sixteenth century Europe in a sweeping revival of classical horsemanship.

FOUR

Academic Equitation: the Early Romanic School of Naples, Portugal and Spain

Naples has always been accepted as the centre of equestrian rebirth. As early as the thirteenth century learned men, charged with the spirit of the approaching Renaissance, began to write down their philosophies concerning the horse. When Xenophon was rediscoverd, the enthusiasm for antiquity knew no bounds, and with unashamed plagiarism, this work was copied almost word for word by the great sixteenth century Neapolitan riding masters. Now, with the influence of Leonardo da Vinci (1452-1519) and other great artists, philosophers and humanists, the world looked to Italy for its cultural inspiration for all art, sculpture, literature, landscape gardening, architecture, music and equitation.

Until the Renaissance, formal instruction had been passed on from father to son, master to pupil. Endless searching shows a dearth of early literature existed between the time of the Romans and the masters of the Renaissance, probably caused by the ravages of war. Italy had had more than her share of invasions. After the Gothic barbarian tribes came the Lombards, a Germanic race of people who brought their heavier chargers to these southern climes so that gradually the Greek and Romanic influence on equitation was virtually lost except in the extreme south.

Hotblood combat horses gave way to an increasing influence from the Teutonic, Gallic and Celtic peoples and their thicker-set horses, a very stiff form of equitation developed. This necessitated long-cheeked curb bits, sharp spurs and an inordinate amount of strength to drive the more cumbersome animals forward. Thus riding in north and central Italy was much akin to that of Germany, the Low Countries, Normandy and Gascony as exemplified by the Crusaders. What it lacked in finesse was compensated for by sheer weight and numbers.

A Mediterranean Culture

After 1200 Italy was divided into five separate self-governing republics which included the papal states and, standing somewhat alone, the kingdom of Naples and the island of Sicily. It was here in the south, close to the Mediterranean, that a recognisable Romanic influence had remained, with a struggle. From this background emerged a number of early equestrian manuscripts. The most important included *Hippatria* written in Sicilian around 1250 by Giordano Ruffo, and a detailed work by a farrier, Lorenzo Rusio, entitled *Hippatria Sive Marescalia* which alternates in advice from the refined to the crude. Later the Italian humanist Leone Alberti (1404–72) wrote *De Quo Animante*, thus setting the fashion for studies in horsemanship from all the philosphers of the day.

The sharp divide in the riding cultures of Northern and Southern Italy found a responding echo in France. Whereas central France had been influenced by the powerful Norman knights as they pushed towards the Pyrenees, one pocket to the south remained untouched. At Marseilles, where the great River Rhone divides and pours into the sea, the Mediterranean influence, shaped so formatively by the Greeks and Romans, had remained practically intact. Today, the Roman influence of horse and bull culture still thrives in that relatively unexplored region round the Rhone delta, known as the Camargue. Here, herds of white horses of ancient Villano,[1] Iberian and Celtic origin roam virtually free, and centuries old traditions of mustering and bull-wrestling take place near the once great Roman cities of Arles and Nimes.

Portugal and Spain, too, retained much of the culture of Roman times and before. Contrary to the myth of Arab horsemen sweeping in to enlighten the Iberian peoples with their stunning horsemanship, the fact is that *gineta* riding had been in existence for centuries prior to the Berber landing in 711 AD. Thus, while some Arab influences were naturally absorbed, the old Romanic practices remained firmly entrenched in areas of equestrianism despite the Moorish invasion and not because of it. Today's Arab[2] style of horsemanship could not be more deeply contrasting to that of modern Portugal and Spain.

It was the determination of the Iberian peoples to free themselves of this domination, that allowed traditions which otherwise might have died to be preserved. In Portuguese, the link with Rome also remains in the language which is often closer to old Latin than some modern Italian, but the further east one progresses into Spain, the greater the Moorish influence. In equitation, the Romanic influence has remained stronger in these two countries than anywhere else in the world today. There are probably two reasons for this.

The Moorish Occupation

First, in their struggles against the Moors (which continued in some areas for over seven centuries, a length of time which is difficult to imagine) the Portuguese and Spanish were fighting a subtle, internal and highly defensive war. The physical and geographical reality of the Iberian Peninsula virtually cut these peoples off from the rest of Europe. There were therefore few outside influences to disturb or change their approach to riding which remained controlled and collected and totally functional for their own particular environment. With cavalry employed as their best means of survival in a seemingly endless campaign over some of the most difficult and rugged terrain in the world, these Christian knights continued in the *gineta* tradition of their forefathers who had so impressed the Greeks and the Romans until they adopted it as their own.

El Cid and the legendary Santo Iago (St James) of Compostella were typical of the tough campaigning cavaliers of the day. Their high stepping, shortcoupled hotblood Iberian horses are still remembered by name, and there is a wealth of pictures to remind us of the riding style. This continued in the *gineta* mode (see Chapter 1) with bent knee, upright body and balanced seat. The difference between the Iberian form of riding and that of the straight-legged, somewhat perched, visiting English or Norman Crusader knights who called at the ports of Lisbon or Cadiz on their way to the Holy Land is easily distinguishable from contemporary art.

The Cult of Taurus

The second reason as to why equitation in Naples, Southern France and the Iberian Peninsula remained largely Romanic has, for some, a less acceptable moral basis. In Portugal[3] and Spain at least, that reason is still apparent. Despite intermittent bans imposed by the Church or successive governments of the day, the practice of tauromachy, first introduced by the Romans, continued to flourish in these southern regions. Tauromachy, initially bullbaiting, latterly came

---

[1] A heavier horse from the Pyrenees not recognised by the Spanish as a purebred but often referred to in ancient books.
[2] See *The Royal Horse of Europe*.
[3] In Portugal the bull is not killed, but eventually brought to a standstill by eight men with their bare hands.

to include bullfighting, bullturning, bullherding and bullwrestling, all of which, with the exception of the last, was conducted from the back of a horse. (Only in the mid 1700s was the pedestrian fight with a cape introduced to Spain).

Unlike the original Roman practice which took the form of a virtual free for all, bullfighting came to be governed by a formal code of conduct. A spirited fiery combat horse[4] was used; a horse whose courage, agility and obedience could be relied upon in the face of danger. Although bullfighting in those days lacked the chivalrous decorum of latter times, the horseman required more than an average feel for his sport if he and his horse were not to be gored.

Killer bulls with unprotected horns are deadly, and horses of the blood were an expensive commodity, therefore collected control was imperative and precise school or ring movements grew up around the practice of tauromachy to become an integral part of the region's horsemanship.

In Italy, bullfighting reached such a height of popularity under the infamous Cesare Borgia of the sixteenth century that inexperienced young noblemen began to indulge in the practice simply to cut a dashing, chivalrous figure and to establish themselves in high society. Such an irresponsible attitude without the expertise to back it up, resulted in many lives being claimed from the cream of Neapolitan youth. Matters reached such a pitch that in 1558, Pope Paul IV intervened and all bullfighting was banned from Italian soil. It was never to regain its hold in Italy, thus the art of High School riding slowly fragmented in this part of Europe, whilst being retained in the Iberian Peninsula.

Meeting Force with Force

When Italy was most involved in the Renaissance revival of academic equitation, it was undoubtedly the work with the bull which kept alive many of the same manoeuvres and the necessity for often exaggerated collection and preparation for the *sorties*, turns and retreats which was also associated with skirmish in war. This dangerous sport did little to reform ideas on the severity of bitting and bridling, a hangover from the Middle Ages.

Another contributing factor was the heaviness of the fourteenth, fifteenth and early sixteenth century Italian war horses. These are accurately depicted in the magnificent equestrian pictures of Uccello, Piero della Francesca, Gozzoli and other early Renaissance artists. Although clean-limbed and handsome, even the famous horses of St Mark's Square show a very thickset, muscular type of horse. No more

Donatello's great equestrian statue in Padua of Erasmo de Narni, completed in 1446, shows the thickset Italian warhorse which would within a century be much lightened by Spanish hotblood. Note in particular the severe, long-shanked spurs of the rider.

[4] Unlike the sad *picador*, the non-fighting, blindfolded horse of the Spanish pedestrian fight.

The influence of Iberian hotblood was radically to change the Italian horses of the south, particularly around Naples. Note in particular the longer legs and short-coupled body conformation which gave the Italians a more manoeuvrable battle horse.

stylised than the depiction of any art at that time, we know from the study of early Italian manuscripts that the Italian warhorse was indeed massive and often unwieldly, as indicated by the many schooling difficulties which arose. Hence the early Italians preoccupation with punishment is more understandable.

Enlightened Ideas

Around the time that the Italians were preaching their forceful methods of bitting and collecting, a more gentle approach to riding had been published in 1381, by a Portuguese monk, Mestre Giraldo. This was followed by two really important works by King Duarte l of Portugal (1401–1438) who stressed the need for tact and kindness to the horse, and was particularly concerned with the necessity for a good warhorse to be light on the hand. These books *Da Arte de Domar os Cavallos* (*The Art of Dressing Horses*) and *O Livro da Ensynanca de Bem Cavalgar – Toda a Sella* (*The Book of Instruction for Good Riding*) opened up the way for further enlightened ideas, and André Monteilhet, a twentieth century French historical writer placed King Duarte between Xenophon and Pluvinel in terms of importance.[5]

Spanish Domination

Horsebreeding in Italy took a dramatic step forward when the Spanish Crown formally annexed the kingdom of Naples, Sicily and Sardinia in 1502. Thousands of Spanish troops landed on Neapolitan soil, and within less than five decades the Italian horse had changed out of all recognition. The new-look Neapolitan, with his distinctively long Spanish convex head, lighter body and slimmer legs, became much sought after as a warhorse. Taller than the Andalusian, and of a proud, noble aspect, an English writer of the time, Thomas Blundeville described the breed in 1565 as 'both comlie and stronglie made, and of so much goodnesse, of so gentle a nature, and of so high a courage as anie Horse is'. The Sardinian also became popular.

Not only did the Spanish bring with them their hotblood horses, they also introduced a more refined method of riding. A wealth of Spanish equestrian literature appeared during the sixteenth century, all of which concerned the *gineta* style of riding. The best known of these is *Lo Cavaller* by Ponz de Menaguer, *Tractado de la Cavalleria de la Gineta* by Pedro Aguilar, *Libro de la Gineta en Espana* by Pedro Fernandez de Andrade and the still widely quoted *Teoria y exercicios de la gineta* by Vargas Machuca.

A modern writer, Don Diogo de Bragança of Lisbon (see Chapter 18) wrote in *L'Equitation de Tradition Francaise*,[6] 'It was then that the Renaissance Italians discovered the horses newly

[5] *Les Maitres de l'oeuvre équestre* by André Monteilhet, Odège, Paris, 1979.
[6] *L'Equitation de Tradition Francaise*, Le Livre de Paris, 1975.

Count Cesare Fiaschi on a Neapolitan horse with the typical long legs, powerful body and convex head of the breed which was to prove so popular all over Europe in the sixteenth and seventeenth centuries.

arrived from the Iberian Peninsula. Unable to obtain from their own horses what they saw accomplished with seemingly great ease by the Spaniards, they were led to invent rules bringing their mounts up to the degree of concentration observed in the Peninsula horses which, in that balance, handled themselves with the greatest of ease.' Although they swiftly adopted their horses, the Italians were slower to adopt the Spanish *gineta* style of riding.

Grisone and Fiaschi

The first civilian riding academy to be properly recognised outside Italy during those days of change and gradual awakening, was that of Federico Grisone, a Neapolitan nobleman. His Naples school was opened in 1532. Grisone is thought to have been a colleague of a Count Cesare Fiaschi from Ferrara, who in 1556 wrote an important manuscript *Tratto dell' imbrigliare, maneggiare e ferrare cavalli* (*A Treatise of Bridling, Schooling and Shoeing Horses*). The equitation side of Fiaschi's work concentrated on the exercises of the manège, especially suppling the horse on the circle. It also stressed the importance of the rider's seat to promote correct balance and the giving of invisible aids. Some understanding of cadence and rhythm is also apparent from Fiaschi's notes on the benefit of schooling horses to music.

As fellow Italians flocked to Naples to enjoy this new courtly pastime which benefitted both the soul and the constitution, Grisone's reputation abroad was assured for posterity when his lavish book *Gli Ordini di Cavalcare* (*The Rules of Riding*) was published in 1550. From this, came the title 'father of the art of equitation', yet but for the difference of six years, the bearer might well have been Fiaschi. A French translation of Grisone's book was published in Paris in 1559 and within less than a century, the book had appeared in sixteen Italian editions and fourteen editions in Spanish, Portuguese, German and English as well as French.

Grisone's methods have been much criticised, particularly for his use of punishment. His bits look formidable, but the numerous embellishments may not have been as cruel as they appear since they were there for the horse to play with (similar to keys on a modern mouthing bit) thus keeping his mouth moist. Whilst the long cheekpieces would be tortuous in the wrong hands, pupils of Grisone were taught to handle the reins with finesse, '. . . seek the gentle, good contact at the mouth, foundation of the entire doctrine . . .' as well as to reward the horse when he obeyed, '. . . you must also pat and caress him every time he comes willingly and does what you wish.'

There is a surprisingly advanced understanding of the interplay of equilibrium and impulsion, as well as the idea of the supporting and opposing aids to assist the horse through his own balance and the following passages appear quite modern: 'Do not think that the horse, no matter how well made, well proportioned and endowed by nature, can do things himself and go through his paces without help from a man and the proper discipline . . .

'In order to make you understand how to aid a horse with the spurs, at the beginning of the promenade, if you wish to turn to the right, you must aid him from the opposite side, with the left spur; and with the right, increase the pressure in order to make the turn a rounded one, so that the horse turns exactly on his track . . .'

The commonsense of the above is unfortunately marred by a later discourse on punishments. Too often there is a marked departure from Xenophon and a singular lack of understanding or sympathy about the mind of the horse: 'If the horse, either from fear of work or on account of obstinacy etc., does not wish to approach the mounting block in order to be ridden, you will hit him with a stick between the ears on the head (but be careful of the eyes) and on all parts of the body where it seems best to you, and also threatening him with a rude and terrible voice, so that, realizing that you are as obstinate as he, he will become as easy to mount as a lamb . . .'

Whilst no dressage rider would contemplate following Grisone's methods today, we should remember that sixteenth century Italian thinking was concerned as much with creating a grand illusion, as with seeking the truth. In drama, literature, art, and politics, rhetoric and spectacle abounded. So long as the final result was magnificent, the end justified the means. Thus, Grisone was able to echo the classical ideals of Xenophon without a single qualm of conscience. And the result required? That the horse be '. . . high-stepping in his walk, his trot easy and elegant, his canter vigorous and powerful, his jump elastic; and he must appear light, and his movements swift and sure.'

The Age of the Italian Riding Master

Two years after Grisone opened his school of equitation in Naples, a similar academy was founded in Rome and another in Ferrara. In 1573, Claudio Corte published an important book entitled *Il Cavallerizzo* which was dedicated to the Earl of Leicester who was instrumental in arranging his visit to England during the reign of Elizabeth I to advise on this 'courtly education'. By this time it was fashionable all over Europe to import

Frederigo Grisone of Naples is generally remembered for his harsh methods of training horses. Yet, without his influence, the Italian School might never have flourished as it did in the sixteenth century, bringing the concept of the art of equitation to France, England and Germany.

not only Italian riding masters but also dancing, music and painting masters. Leicester, favourite of the Queen, was particularly interested in the art of the manège and probably through his influence, the English court enjoyed the benefit of another Neapolitan's teachings, one Prospero d'Osma, a colleague of Pignatelli.

Pignatelli is important since he taught the Frenchmen Pluvinel, La Broue, Saint-Antoine and the Spaniard, Vargas, and probably the German von Löhneysen whose own weighty book echoes all the discipline and the severity of the Italians. Unfortunately however, little is known of Pignatelli's background. There are two schools of thought as to who taught him. Whether it was Fiaschi or Grisone or both is immaterial, of far more importance was his effect on so many future masters.

According to E.M. Kellock's original research in Naples for her *History of Riding*, Pignatelli was first influenced by the circus riders who landed in Naples from Constantinople and whose methods, disdainful of severe bits and spurs, were based on weight aids, voice control and constant reward. Pignatelli taught close to or within the old cavalry barracks, on the site of today's Naples Museum. 'Professional soldiers sat in the saddle, 'calm, sword in hand, and by slight movements of hand and heel caused the horse to dance aside, rear up, charge, stop, turn, pirouette without giving a hint to the adversary.' It sounds as if Pignatelli initiated lateral movements and work on two tracks; the oblique piste was used to perplex the enemy and was performed by a whole squadron of mounted men as the caracol.'

Gregoria de Tapia Y Salzedo's book, published in the early seventeenth century, shows the *gineta* style of riding with bent leg and shorter stirrup which the Spanish brought to southern Italy.

To Pignatelli is also attributed the introduction of the pillars, which Pluvinel was to use with enthusiasm. He was the medium through which enlightenment grew and his pupils spread the art of the Italians far and wide. Gradually the rigidity and austerity of the Renaissance period began at the very end of the sixteenth century to give way to the Baroque and a gentler form of Classicism. The Baroque School which we shall now follow, was noted, particularly in art and architecture, for its fantastic ornamentation coupled with convoluted and exaggeratedly wavy or billowing outlines, styles and borders.

The Birth of Baroque

The word Baroque is thought to come from the Spanish *barrueco* which means an intricate or irregular shaped pearl – and later the same derivation led to the word rococo, to indicate sumptuous intricacy of design. For almost two hundred years until 1707, the south of Italy was to continue under Spanish rule. It was inevitable that the wealth and foreign gold which was pouring into the Spanish-Hapsburg empire from the recently conquered Americas and Indies was at least partly responsible for a general preoccupation with lavish ostentation, pomp and ceremony which heralded the Baroque period. This extravagance was to permeate every aspect of art, architecture, sculpture, literature and finally equitation.

The Noble Art

Under this influence, equitation was to flower into the most resplendent period of its existence. To understand such a phenomenon, we must remember that in those days, the riding of good horses was very much the prerogative of the king or emperor and his noble born courtiers. With this new sophisticated era came a preoccupation with etiquette. Soon the courtesies and conventions of the manège became their own artform. From simple skirmish manoeuvres therefore evolved elaborate school movements, bound by rules and principles. A leap could no longer be a haphazard affair, from now on there would be a prescribed height, with the body of the horse held at a certain angle, preparatory necessary flexions worked out in a logical and scientific way.

Since the art of horsemanship had become a noble pursuit, the idea of the noble horse evolved. (Unfortunately the nobility of the horse himself did not necessarily reflect man's appreciation of the equine character, but rather that the horse was enobled through the nobility of his rider).

Every court had its royal *écuyer* with other lesser *écuyers* under him, and during the Baroque period the quest for learning and improvement was also coloured by the desire to display everyone and everything, king, princes, nobles, horses, and palaces to their richest and best advantage irrespective of the poverty and squalor that might lie without the courtyard walls. The art of manège riding was of course to reach its height under Louis XIV at the Court of Versailles and this will be discussed in Chapter 6.

Before we leave the Italians to examine the horsemanship that was simultaneously developing under the Austrians and the Germans during this same period, we should remember that had not the Italians been imbued with a romantic, enquiring preoccupation with the past, and had they not combined this with the Spanish love of flamboyance and ceremony, equitation would never have so evolved, leaving us so very much the poorer.

FIVE

Academic Equitation in Austria and Germany

THE AGE OF BAROQUE

Extraordinary as it may seem, the immediate and permanent future of classical riding and the classical horse was assured when one very powerful Austrian family, headed by the Archduke Habsburg, rose to immense power in the sixteenth century and through marriage linked their vast central European territories to those of the Spanish crown. We shall shortly explore the effect this mingling of culture made on equitation, but first it is important to understand the breadth and depth of the huge empire which resulted.

The Holy Roman Empire under the Habsburgs

For generations, the dynastic lands of the Habsburgs which included Friesland, Burgundy, Artois, part of Alsace, Bohemia, Hungary and the jewel in the crown, Austria, whilst all retaining their individual identity had been joined to the Holy Roman Empire which comprised the bulk of modern East and West Germany[1] and beyond. The title of Holy Roman Emperor had been handed down to successive Frankish claimants since the time of the first Emperor, Charlemagne (742–814) who had knelt before the Pope on Christmas Day, 800 AD to receive this honour. But now it was the turn of the Austrian claimants, the Archdukes Habsburgs, whose family name sprang from their original home, the castle of Habsburg, built in 1028 on the River Ahr close to its junction with the Rhine.

The Spanish Connection

In 1516 Emperor Charles V succeeded through his Spanish mother to the Spanish throne. Thus King D. Carlos I of Spain and Holy Roman Emperor Charles V of Austria were one and the same. This joining of two powerful royal families created the dynasty known as the Spanish Habsburgs (which much later would crumble and make way for the Austro-Hungarian dynasty or Dual Monarchy of the mid nineteenth century), an empire of immense proportion and wealth. In Europe, the Spanish dominions eventually included Naples, Sicily, Milan and Sardinia, the Spanish Netherlands, and of course Spain itself, whilst abroad, the very rich Spanish possessions in the Indies and Americas, produced the raw materials and gold to swell the Empire's coffers.

Through the Spanish link, the Spanish horse began again to make an impact on the civilised world. From Naples, the demand for this breed so suited to the battlefield and to High School training, spread quickly throughout the Empire to the distant courts of Dresden, Saxony, Hanover and Brunswick. In the latter, the court equerry, von Löhneysen wrote in 1588, 'It ought to be recognised moreover, that of all the horses on earth, the Spaniards are the most intelligent, the most likeable and the most gentle.' Such was his physical and mental aptitude for the intricate battle manoeuvres now being taught that other countries followed suit. Spanish

---

[1] The German Imperial Crown remained with the Habsburgs for three centuries, until 1806. (The term 'German' is of course a modern word, used here for purposes of clarification.)

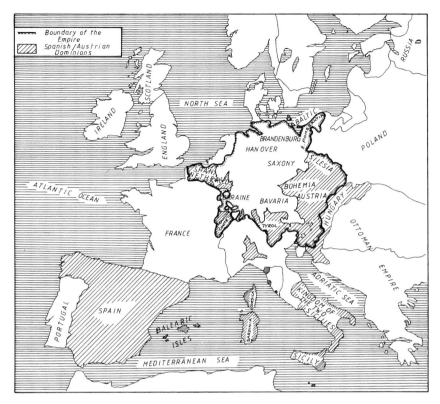

Map of Austria, Germany and the Imperial principalities at the height of the Holy Roman Empire around 1650. Note the shaded areas depicting the Spanish mainland and Spanish possessions.

horses were imported for the royal manège by King Frederick IV of Denmark in 1562, King Henry VIII of England (1491–1547), and Louis XII (1462–1516) of France. These importations continued until the mid eighteenth century when the English Thoroughbred influenced or eclipsed all other breeds.

The Origins of the Lippizzaner

The prestige of the Spanish horse was given further impetus when in 1580 a large shipment of purebred Andalusian stock was sent to start a foundation race of manège and carriage horses at the Imperial Austrian Stud. Twenty-four Spanish mares, three stallions and six colts were sent to the Karstplateau of Lipizza (now part of north-west Yugoslavia) where the harsh conditions and sterile limestone soil had been favoured for the breeding of a hardy race of horses since the time of the Romans. Although climatically colder than their native land, the hardy Iberian horse flourished on the rough hillsides of this outlying corner of the Empire, and breeding commenced successfully.

Further to the north, an earlier importation of Spanish stock in 1572 for the Imperial Kladruby Stud (now in modern Czechoslovakia) had created the renowned Kladruber horse, a breed selectively produced for carriage driving, with jet black or snow white being the only acceptable colours for the Emperor's coaches.

But it was the Lipizza which provided the Hofburg with the proud, high-stepping progeny of initially grey, black, dun, coloured and spotted horses so favoured at that time. These forerunners of the Lipizzaner were extravagant movers, of noble mien, and mentally and physically attuned to the airs of the High School. Together with their magnificent plumes and jewel encrusted trappings, these splendid

German warhorses of the fifteenth century prior to the introduction of Spanish and Neapolitan hot blood. Note the more horizontal conformation and short stocky legs which would gradually give way to a taller, shorter-coupled, more elegant cavalry horse.

mounts of the early manège reflected all the glory of the Imperial Court. Today's Lippizaner is equally distinctive with his often slightly hawked face, and muscular robustness, changing little in appearance from the early portraits. The late Colonel Podhajsky always maintained he had some Lipizzan from that original stock which were closer to the Spanish horse of the sixteenth century than the modern Spaniard, although the old type still exists in parts of Andalusia and Portugal.

The Spanish Riding School

The first reference to the name *Spainischer Reithsall*, (later the *Spanische Hof-Reitschule*) came in a document dated 1572. Previous to this, court riding in Imperial Vienna had been conducted in an open courtyard enclosed by ornamental gardens close to the Hofburg Palace. As equitation began to blossom into a highly complex art form, attempts to build a suitable riding hall were made. By the time of the Emperor Leopold I who assumed the Austrian throne in 1658, a substantial wooden structure had been erected.

This was a difficult period for the Austrians who had been fighting back against warring Turkish invaders that intermittently had held their capital under siege. The last invasion took place in Leopold's reign in 1683, but despite sustaining desperate bombardments against her city walls, Vienna was saved. Together with his Spanish wife, the Infanta Margaret Theresa, Leopold, a great lover of the arts, now encouraged the Baroque style of life properly to flower in Vienna. Despite the damage by the Turks, Leopold instructed his architects in 1685 'to rebuild the Imperial riding school and outfit it in such a way that His Imperial Majesty may be able to ride the whole winter through . . .'

By the early eighteenth century, Vienna was a city in love with beauty and romance. Lavish architecture, glorious music and art, and general pomp and circumstance abounded. An imperial wooden opera house with seating for over five thousand was built. Expensively staged musical horse ballets, copied from the Italians, were arranged. During the Emperor's wedding celebrations a contemporary description of one such spectacle runs, 'The Emperor, decked out in festive robes and carrying his crown and sceptre, entered at the head of the procession on a dark brown Spanish horse. His mount's bridle was studded with gold clasps and diamonds,

These eighteenth-century engravings from a rare book *Remarks on Cavalry* by the Prussian Major General of Cavalry, depict (*left*) a typical Austrian Hussar of the period and (*right*) a Bavarian Hussar. Note a bent knee position in the saddle in contrast to the earlier fixed position shown on page 47.

PLATE 3

This imposing equestrian portrait of Emperor Charles VI by George Hamilton dominates
the interior of the Winter Riding School. Still today, the tradition of saluting the Emperor
is continued by every rider who enters the manège, in homage to Austria's great imperial
past and to the man responsible for the final inauguration of the Spanische Hof-Reitschule
in 1735. (*Courtesy Kunsthistorisches Museum, Vienna*)

PLATE 4

This dashing equestrian portrait of the ill-fated French Queen Marie-Antoinette in hunting costume, was painted by Louis–August Brun at Versailles in 1783. The queen had been taught to ride astride in the classical manner of the day, and cuts a fine figure on her prancing hot-blood probably of Turkish or Arab origin. Interestingly, the horse wears the accoutrements of the Imperial Hungarian Guards to the Court of Austria. (*Courtesy Musée de Versailles*)

Emperor Leopold I of Austria under whom the initial work of the Winter Riding School was inaugurated. This leader was renowned for his love of ceremony and personified the Baroque age of elegant and extravagant living.

a tuft of blue and white feathers was fitted on its head, and his saddle-cloth was worked with pearls and precious stones.'

Charles VI (1697-1745), who ascended the imperial throne after his father Leopold's death was, like his ancestor Charles V, a very gifted horseman. Work had ground to a halt on the imperial manège, but under the new Emperor much of the work initiated by Leopold came to fruition.[2] The Schwarzenberg and Belvedere palaces, masterpieces of Baroque architecture were completed by 1732. In 1735, the Imperial Manège, brilliantly designed by Joseph Emanuel Fischer von Erlach was complete. This magnificent new classical building, fitting to the age, yet sufficiently austere not to detract from the magnificence of horse and rider, would henceforth be known as the Winter Riding School. With its four storeys, and impressive range of slender columns supporting the galleries above, this palatial structure reflected discipline coupled with graciousness. Today, we are reminded of its original purpose from the words above the proscenium: 'This Imperial Riding School was constructed in the year 1735 to be used for the instruction and training of the youth of the nobility and for the schooling of horses in riding for art and for war.'

There are many excellent and beautifully illustrated books devoted to the history of the Spanish Riding School; of more importance for this book is the equitation which developed and the nature of the original foundation horses from Spain.

The Baroque Horse

Today's Lipizzaner breed is the product of careful selective breeding over the centuries for gymnastic performance, a patient yet willing temperament and a natural aptitude for this specialised work. The original Iberian blood remained undiluted over many years, but due to historical events and the problems of importation, vital additions of fresh blood from the Neapolitan (see Chapter 4) and the Arab took place from 1765. With the exception of the Siglavy line which commenced in 1810, the original sires of the six main branches were either pure Spanish or Neapolitan. The names, now used as prefixes, run in order of date of birth as follows: Pluto (1765), Conversano (1767), Favory (1779), Neapolitano (1790), Siglavy (1810) and Maestoso (1819). Interestingly enough, although all today's Lipizzaners eventually turn white, of the original sires Conversano was a black, Favory a dun and Neapolitano a bay.

Climate and environment at the stud at Lipizza and later Piber has also wrought certain changes within the breed, but physically and temperamentally, the Lipizzaner horse today is

---

[2] The architect was Lukas von Hildebrandt. The Belvedere was built for the dashing cavalry commander, Prince Eugene of Savoy.

remarkably close to his sixteenth century ancestors and for this reason, the Austrians have consistently adhered to the term *Spanish* Riding School long after the Spanish alliance was broken.

Apart from his agility and his adaptability for war, what made the Baroque horse, the Imperial Horse, or the Classical Horse so esteemed, and stranger still, why did such a horse continue to last in Vienna, this much fought-over, intrinsically central European city until the present day? First we must remember the Spanish and the Barb horse were the only hot-blood widely available at this time. The passage of Arab horses into Europe was virtually impossible because of the wars with the Turks.[3] The English Thoroughbred did not fully evolve until the mid eighteenth century, and it took another twenty years or so before this new race was exported to the Continent in any number.

Second, the Baroque horse suited the imperial grandeur of the day. Anthony Dent sums it up very well, 'We can see him [the Andalusian] painted as the throne of royal models for equestrian portraits scores of times over – by Velasquez in Spain, Van Dyck in England, by the Clouets in France. It was the only European hotblood, shortcoupled, with a superb outlook, around 15 hands, very massive powerful sloping croup and superbly arched neck.' (*See Plates 2 and 3.*)

Third, the Iberian and his descendant the Lipizzaner was hardy. Coming from the poor grazing lands of the Peninsula, he thrived on land which was fit for no other agricultural purpose. A contemporary document sent to the Emperor at Vienna in the late sixteenth century confirms this: 'These are the most select and soundest horses to be found; they run and graze where there is practically nothing but rocks, and very little forage.'

Indeed, the Spanish horse seemed to have been custom made for the Imperial House of the Habsburgs. Since the Austrian Empire continued magnificently into the early twentieth century, a permanent stage was provided for the living spectacle represented by these horses, a constant reminder of the age of splendour.

The Early German School

Historically, the development of the Prussian or German school was inseparably linked with that of Vienna and of Hungary, bound as they mainly were under the same Imperial Crown. Even devastating interruptions such as the Thirty Years War could not destroy the sense of continuity between those early schools whose passionate ideals of beauty, art, chivalry and splendour prevented those early foundations being lost. The first German riding master of note, Engelhart von Löhneysen, mentioned earlier, was born too early to study at Vienna. As *écuyer* to the Elector of Saxony, he studied in Naples and acknowledged Pignatelli as a great master. His substantial book *Die neu eröffnete Hof-Kriegs-und Reitschule* published in 1588 was concerned with both court and tournament riding, as well as how to cure difficult horses; it had a detailed discourse on bridling and bitting which illustrates complicated mouthpieces similar to that of the Italians. Although this was still the age of certain barbaric practices to achieve the leaps and airs above the ground, von Löhneysen was more lenient than Grisone whose ideas he nevertheless copied in no small proportion. The logical excuse for many of these excesses was that the Germans, like the Italians, still used many coldblood local horses which showed little aptitude for refined manège work. As the breeds lightened however, first with Spanish hotblood, later with the prized Arab and Thoroughbred, horsemanship improved

---

[3] A good example of this degree of difficulty in bringing just one Arab horse to England was sustained by Oliver Cromwell in 1655. (See *The Royal Horse of Europe*.)

Horses of the Royal Danish Manège at Fredericksborg Castle, painted around 1680. Manège horses were continually interchanged through the Courts of Europe at this time.

out of all recognition. Even in the early days however, there are glimpses of enlightenment. This one from von Löhneysen is worthy of repetition and is reminiscent of Socrates. 'One of the chief rules should be that the art of riding never takes a stance in opposition to nature, for one should rather seek to imitate nature and follow it, even to improve upon it wherever possible.'

The same author's remark on saddlery, 'It cannot be denied that a good deep, well-made saddle should be prized . . . but a rider should not let himself become spoiled by such deep and comfortable ones, or he will find that he can no longer ride a horse without one, but must learn all over again . . .' suggests a move away from the immobile seat inherited from the old Frankish knights. Their deepcut tournament saddle had fixed the rider against the cantle in such a way that the lower leg was thrust forward and bending at the knee was virtually impossible.

Von Löhneysen was followed by Johann Wallhausen who was in service to Prince Maurice of Nassau of the House of Orange, and who wrote the *Art of Chivalry* in 1616 and later a useful thesis entitled *Military Art*. Both books became important milestones during the sixteenth century when Germany was being ravaged by the Thirty Years War (1618–48) which had begun with a revolt of the Bohemians against the Habsburgs. Germany was overrun first by the Swedes, and later by the French who fought a bitter war against the Emperor's Spanish allies, and it became vitally important to create a really versatile German cavalry horse.

A More Artistic Approach

As more and more hotblood was introduced, Germany's own breeds began to blossom. With the translation of Pluvinel's book *L'Instruction du Roy* into German in 1628, a change in technique developed. The German School was only able fully to develop however when peace was restored in 1699.[4] Under the influence of Emperor Charles VI, the arts now had an oppor-

[4] Under the Treaty of Karlowitz.

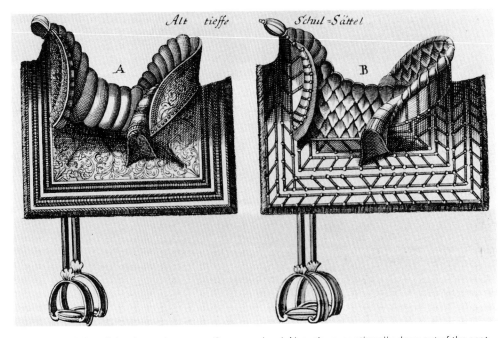

Manège saddles of the sixteenth-century German school. Note the exceptionally deep cut of the seat, which held the rider in a very fixed position, and the forward sling of the stirrups. This would change under the influence of La Guérinière.

tunity to flourish. Fifteen years later the Elector of Hanover became King George I of England and this established Hanover as a central pivot in German life. André Monteilhet wrote in *A History of Academic Equitation*, 'Vienna and Hanover became the two great poles of the equestrian upswing in Germany, and so, despite wars and revolutions, they have remained to this day.'

The Baroque era in Germany was to prove as lavish by the mid eighteenth century as Classicism was in France. There was something more grandiose about the Prussian system however, and whereas the French were preoccupied with lightness and artistry, the Prussians were concerned more with discipline and accuracy. A superbly illustrated book translated to mean *The Court and Military Riding School* appeared in 1729, the author one Valentin Trichter, who held the influential position of first instructor at the University of Göttingen riding school. This showed lavishly plumed and caparisoned horses of the manège, their fine heads, clean legs and compact conformation showing that a complete transformation had successfully taken place in the military horse which compared noticeably with the days of the armoured knights.

In 1727 a German *écuyer* to the Court of the Habsburgs, Baron von Eisenberg travelled to England and produced a sumptous book entitled *Description du Manège Royal* which was published in London in 1747. One edition of this book was dedicated to King George II and a subscriber was Eisenberg's British contemporary, Henry, 10th Earl of Pembroke (see also Chapter 9). The original gouache illustrations produced by this talented German riding master have remained as an entire collection in the possession of the Herbert family at Wilton House. Fifty-five magnificent pictures colourfully depict all the various exercises, the leaps and airs, caprioles and courbettes of the Imperial High School, leaving no doubt of the Prussians' dedication to these disciplines. Von Eisenberg, a former pupil of Master Regenthal of the Spanish Riding School, travelled extensively through Europe and his book reflects all the different breeds of horse he encountered. The engravings for this book were made by B. Picart.

Johann Heinrich Ayrer (1732–1817) was another horseman from Göttingen who furthered his education in Vienna. Interested in physiological and anatomical matters, he founded a famous German veterinary college in 1784. Around this time, many important equestrian figures were becoming more aware of equine locomotion[5] and how correct training could improve muscle tone and function. This general awareness led to the term 'scientific equitation' which received a further impetus when, in France, La Guérinière's great *Ecole de Cavalerie* was published in 1729.

The Influence of La Guérinière

This important book translated into German, Italian, Portugese and Spanish was soon considered the epitome of enlightened thinking: nowhere more so than in Vienna and Hanover. It laid the path for the true classical school, and its ideals and teaching have held dressage scholars enthralled to this day.

During the second half of the eighteenth century, an important German *écuyer* emerged in the service of the Elector of Cologne. This was Baron J. B. von Sind (1709–76), a student of La Guérinière in France and of Regenthal at Vienna. He published *Art du Manège* first in Germany and later in Paris, and his work shows many progressive ideas particularly in the work with the pillars and the exercise of shoulder-in. A telling excerpt from the writings of von Sind show that some horses, having achieved a very high standard in one particularly difficult exercise, were to remain schooled exclusively for these movements. 'Those horses destined only for public functions should be exercised only at the Passage and the Courbette so that they will not mix them with other airs.' How different this idea is to our philosophy of a pleasant all round mixture of training today!

Probably the last of the great German Baroque masters at this time was Louis Hunersdorf, sometimes referred to as the first of the German Classicists. *Ecuyer* to the House of Hesse, he was later in service to the King of Württemberg who knighted him. Cavalry training in Germany was again undergoing enormous change as the War of the Austrian Succession (1740–48) loomed with Prussia, allied by France, struggling for power against the Austrians, allied by Britain. Convinced of the value of classical movements such as the piaffe and the levade, Hunersdorf was able to harness the art of dressage based on La Guérinière's principles to the practicalities of training cavalry horses which must also perform swiftly and freely across country. In his book *Guidelines to the Training of Horses in the Most Natural and Best Manner* published in 1791, he also described today's balanced seat and defined self-carriage and how to achieve lightness of the forehand.

Maria Theresa

Meanwhile in Austria, Empress Maria Theresa (1717-80) defied political opposition after a complicated, debilitating war,[6] and finally established herself at Vienna as Archduchess of Austria and Queen of Hungary and Bohemia. The connection with Spain had been lost after the death of her father, Emperor Charles VI, but although now more inward looking, Austria's own prestige had grown. It was under this powerful personality, beloved by the Viennese, that the Baroque period developed into an excess of rich ornamentation throughout the arts.

---

[5] English books of this time dealing with veterinary medicine, anatomy and locomotion include William Gibson's *A New Treatise on Diseases of Horses*. 1751; George Stubbs's *The Anatomy of the Horse*, 1766; Strickland Freeman's *Mechanism of the Horse's Foot*, 1796.

[6] The War of the Austrian Succession was followed by the Seven Years War 1756–63.

Under Maria Theresa ceremony and ostentation pervaded every aspect of court life. Architecturally and artistically, Austria was at her richest.

A connoisseur of equitation, Maria Theresa's mounted carousels at the Winter Riding School became the talk of Europe. The most resplendent of these was probably the *Damenkarussel* with which she celebrated the recapture of Prague from the French. This was organised for the high-born wives of princes and cavaliers, who were rewarded for their participation in the mounted and carriage quadrilles with priceless gifts or 'prizes' of jewels as souvenirs of the occasion (*See Plate 1*).

Other gala festivities, involving complicated tournament games such as Moor baiting which involved knocking wooden Turkish heads off their posts by galloping at speed and using lance or pistol, to commemorate the defeat of the Turks. There were also lance quadrilles and the usual displays of High School, the more elaborate airs bringing horse and rider closer to heaven.[7]

After Maria Theresa, the important, classical airs were retained at Vienna, but gradually a more military approach was adopted with the emphasis on technique rather than pure splendour.

Tournament games required as much control and precision with the horses as hand to hand combat.

POST BAROQUE AND MILITARY INFLUENCES

Until 1804, when the title of Holy Roman Emperor finally came to an end, and Francis I assumed instead the hereditary title of Emperor of Austria, the Spanish Riding School had enjoyed a succession of *bereiters* steeped in the tradition of the classical art or riding. By far the most influential of these was Chief Rider Johann von Regenthal who died in 1730. Another important figure was Adam von Weyrother who was created Knight of the Empire in 1733

[7] An idea expressed in *Manège Royal* by Pluvinel.

under Charles VI for his responsibility in moving the School into the newly completed Winter Riding School.

It was his descendant, Maximilian von Weyrother, who was to make such an impact when, having first served at one of the prestigious Austrian cavalry schools, he rose to the position of Chief Rider in 1825. As a purist and disciplinarian, Weyrother was more occupied in teaching and running the School than in writing books. Nevertheless he left a very useful treatise on bridling and bitting, and notes made during his lifetime were published posthumously under the title *Fragments and Unpublished Writings*. These are still highly regarded at Vienna today.

The most important legacy that we derive from von Weyrother, was the laying-down of firm guidelines. He defined the purity of the gaits and stressed that the young horse must be totally established in all three before attempting more complicated work. An example of this was the walk, where the horse must take 'solemn steps', maintaining the four beats of the gait. It must not be allowed to deteriorate into a diagonal or pacing movement. Weyrother's invaluable notes, together with the later work of Meixner and Holbeinsberg, still constitutes the basis for today's *Directives* which all riders at the School must follow.

Von Weyrother was first and foremost a devoted disciple of La Guérinière. His task at Vienna was clear: to consolidate and make practical for conditions at Vienna, the theory, principles and ideals of the great French Master. This he achieved with remarkable success, thus ensuring the unswerving future of enlightened methods at the Imperial Spanish Riding School.

German Expansion

Germany's greatest contribution towards our understanding of modern dressage undoubtedly came about at the end of the eighteenth century. The great age of the Baroque and the extravagant had ended with the meteoric rise of Napoleon and the niceties and ceremonies of the manège which had been so pronounced when the Holy Roman Empire was at its height quickly faded. All around there was change. Whereas England had completely abandoned the concept of art in equitation, the German military commanders sought to modernise and improve upon it. What resulted was an all round form of horsemanship which suited their horses and their military requirements. Collection was still encouraged to teach the horse accuracy, but at the end of the reign of Frederick the Great of Prussia (1712-1786) the emphasis was on *campagne*[8] riding made up of three vital ingredients:

Speed: attacks at the gallop
Obedience: total collection and agility in face to face single combat
Safety across country: the ability to negotiate any form of country or obstacle

Frederick's greatest Generals, Ziethen and Friedrich von Seydlitz (1771-73) trained their men out of doors, in formation and with a natural seat. Many of the light cavalry were drawn from Poland. Their job was to be fast, handy, efficient and safe, working always as an integral part of a huge military operation, in harmony with artillery and infantry.

By now the Germany cavalry horse was tall, streamlined, relatively big-boned and clean-limbed. Cold-blood horses were relegated to logistic or agricultural duties, and the short-coupled, smaller Baroque horses which had earlier contributed so much to breeding, gave way to the more horizontal frame of the modern cross-country horse. The East Prussian (today's Trakehner) was the most popular riding or cavalry horse displaying not only speed and ver-

---

[8] Defined in the official German Instructors Handbook, *Richtlinien für Reiten und Fahren, Band II*.

satility, but courage and hardiness in drawn-out campaigns.[9] For Hanover, the studs of West-phalia, Mecklenburg and Pomerania were producing strong artillery horses which also displayed much stamina. Breeding in Germany had been much advanced by the introduction of Arab and Thoroughbred blood. The presence of a Hanoverian king sitting on the throne of England, must have helped speed the transformation which took place at the end of the eighteenth century.

The Austro-Hungarian Period

Throughout Austria and Hungary too, the cavalry turned to *campagne* riding. Cavalry horses with clean thoroughbred lines filled the stables of the illustrious cavalry schools of Budapest, Salzburg, Wiener-Neustadt, Schlosshof and Vienna. Dressage became more practical and less artistic, but horses were still expected to pirouette on a 'space the size of a plate',[10] and the Baroque horse was retained in diminished numbers at imperial establishments where the cream of the cavalry might be taught the High School airs.

Through the Lipizzaner, therefore the spirit of Imperialism was preserved. Gradually, as the map of Europe continued to undergo traumatic change, with the redefinition of borders, and whole principalities and small countries losing their identity, people began to regard the Spanish Riding School as a last precious link with Austria's dazzling past.

As Europe prepared for war, Austria became inextricably involved with Napoleon who successfully contrived to marry the Emperor's daughter. In 1813, together with Prussia, Austria declared war on France and eventually, after victory at Leipzig, Napoleon was driven back to Belgium. Throughout this time, Austria was still linked to Hungary which was later con-solidated in the Dual Monarchy of 1867–1918, but her predominance in Germany was lost forever. This period had coincided with the end of the Baroque. Austria's huge empire was crumbling, but together with Hungary,[11] her great culture had been slow to relinquish the love of grandeur, ceremony and stirring romance which can still be found in modern Vienna, and parts of Budapest. The last Imperial riding carousel held in the Winter Riding School took place in 1894 recalling the Baroque brilliance of an earlier day; there was scarcely a dry eye in the house.

From thenceforth, work at the Spanish Riding School continued quietly and the Chief Instructors von Nadosy, Niedermayer and Meixner all made their mark during the period of the Dual Monarchy. Together with Meixner, that great Director Holbein von Holbeinsberg (from 1898-1901) wrote his *Directives*. These, like Weyrother's, defined the gaits, concentrating on their purity and regularity. Definitions were also given for suppleness, impulsion, lightness and harmony which summarised all that had gone before, giving it a logical and understandable form for the future.

Another great product of Vienna, not from the Spanish Riding School but from the military, was Baron Borries von Oeynhausen (1812–75) who had been Chief Instructor at the Imperial Cavalry School of Salzburg in 1844. His *Guide to the Finishing of Horse and Rider* was based on his observations at Vienna, and forms one of the reference books in use today. General Sigmund von Josipovitch (1869–1945) was another product of the Imperial system. A most distinguished horseman and the teacher of Waldemar Seunig (see Chapter 16) he served as

---

[9] See *The Flight of the East Prussian Horse* by Daphne Machin Goodall.

[10] The words of King Freiderich II of Prussia.

[11] Hungary still today has retained the Lipizzaner, recognising their cultural importance. Stud stallions are housed in the old stables of Szilvasvarad Castle, north of Egra.

instructor at the *Militär-Reitlehrerinstitut* of Vienna before going on to teach at the Military Institute of Equitation in Budapest. A well-travelled man, who like Seunig, taught in America, the height of his career was achieved when he went to Orkeny where he taught for almost fifteen years until his tragic death during a bombing raid on Vienna in 1945.

He and many like him, highly educated and distinguished officers of Czech, Polish, Romanian and Hungarian descent, too numerous to mention, made a stunning contribution to this period and their all-round equestrian performance was incomparable in the world at that time. The *Militär-Reitlehrerinstitut* in Schlosshof was the last important cavalry school of the empire and provided a brilliant background for all the disciplines until the glorious Austrian cavalry came to an end with the *Anschluss* in 1938. The Vienna Cavalry School, the *Reitlehrer-institut*, which was separate to the Spanish Riding School, had ended in 1919.

Three Great Men

Meanwhile, in Germany, Louis Seeger (1794–1865), Seidler (1798–1865) and Gustave Steinbrecht (1808–85) are the three great names who influenced Central Europe most directly at this time. In 1817 an organisation was set up in Berlin which was 'to teach the training of horse and rider according to uniform principles'. Initially, this operated from the Military School at Schwedt; from 1867 onwards it was based at the Cavalry School in Hanover and gave strength and solidity to cavalry instruction throughout the realm.

Seeger, whose motto was: 'Never forget that riding forward is the soul of the art of riding, and that the necessary impulsion must come from the hindquarters', was an ardent pupil at Vienna under Weyrother. In his highly acclaimed *System der Reitkunst* (*A System of Equestrian Art*) published in 1844, he suggested crookedness in the horse was due to the horse being narrower at the shoulders than in the hips. Later Colonel Podhajsky was to agree with this theory. The teacher of Steinbrecht, Seeger understood his art very well but too much of his time was taken up with writing pamphlets against Baucher, a product of the French School whom we shall meet in Chapter 10. It was he who coined the phrase still used at Vienna but not at Saumur that Baucher was the 'gravedigger of French equitation'.

Seidler on the other hand was an ardent Baucherist, although he disapproved of some of his circus movements, such as cantering backwards. Nevertheless he was able to apply Baucher's better methods to training the cavalry horse. As Master of the Horse in Berlin and Director of the Schwedt Military School, he wrote two important books, the translated titles of which are *The Dressage of Difficult Horses and Correction of Ruined Horses* (1846) and *The Systematic Dressage of the Field and General Purpose Horse*.

Of the three great 'S's', Steinbrecht is thought to be the finest and his *Gymnasium of the Horse* has become the German classical rider's bible. There is little here that clashes with Vienna and some random quotations from Steinbrecht show a writer who is straightforward, full of commonsense and who places much emphasis on impulsion.

'Ride your horse forward and hold it straight . . .' is his first instruction at the beginning of the book; a phrase which Colonel Podhajsky called the *leitmotif* of the Spanish Riding School. Then he goes on to pursue Xenophon's theory of reward and punishment, the reward often constituting the cessation of the aid.

'The limit to clarity of the aids is the point where they begin to cause pain. Pain only produces unwanted tension in the animal's muscles.' How saddened Steinbrecht would have been by the constant use of the spur which so often we observe today. To him this would have been unwarranted and unclassical; the spur was to be reserved for quick pricks to give precision to a specific movement – never to be used incessantly with every stride.

'The flexion of the neck, thus its permeability, may not be obtained except by impulsion propagated by the hindquarters which convey it on through the horse's body. These two phenomena, the compliance in the neck and the bend of the hindquarters, go together as a pair . . .' shows his understanding of locomotive power and muscular control, as does 'The counter canter will assure us of a decisive strength in the horse', and it perhaps comes as no surprise to learn that before he became an instructor, Steinbrecht was a veterinary student. Steinbrecht's advice to obtain piaffe[12] was to teach the horse immediate departures in trot from halt, and then methodically, little by little to reduce the strides of the trot between halts until the horse started to piaffer.

It is often forgotten that, like Baucher and Fillis, Steinbrecht was involved with the circus. For a time he ran his own school at Dessau, and sold many High School horses to the great Russian circus. He exhibited his horses all over Europe and in America.

Like Baucher, he admired the English Thoroughbred and believed the breed quite suitable for the advanced airs. 'If the English breeder, being of the best in Europe, could improve his riding and schooling to the same standard,' he pronounced, 'he would be impossible to beat in horsemanship.' This was echoed by a German breeder, Baron G. Biel who much impressed by conversations with Max von Weyrother at Vienna wrote: 'The equestrian art is a valuable most important ally of the breeder. I would consider myself very lucky if I could breed horses for an institute following the principles of the Spanish Riding School. Nobody would then dare to maintain that the noble English horse was not suitable for the art of riding.'[13]

For Steinbrecht, lightness must never be obtained at the expense of straightness or impulsion, and the following passage sums up much of his writing: 'The rider has achieved his aim and fully trained his horse when both forces of the hindquarters – the propulsive force and the weightcarrying power – coupled with elasticity, are fully developed, and when the rider can then use and balance the effect of these forces exactly.' This idealistic approach has formed the basis for German dressage riders ever since.

In Conclusion

Steinbrecht and Holbeinsberg therefore bring us up to the twentieth century in the development of equitation in Germany and Austria. The importance of the old traditional German school is often overshadowed by the French and many people tend to consider Germany only in a modern light, i.e. asssociated with her brilliance in successive Olympic games in all three riding disciplines. Certainly it was the French influence which was to inspire *écuyers* all over Europe which enabled those of Vienna and Prussia to make their contribution to equestrian literature. Nevertheless it would be wrong to assume that the principles of lightness, collection from a soft rounded frame as well as the importance of flexions and suppling were not sought after by all connoisseurs of the time, whether Germanic or Romanic.

Although today there exist those who have cast aside the ideals of the classical school in an effort to obtain quick results in the competitive field, there are still, fortunately, those who continue on the lines of the great classical Masters. The Germans have a strong tradition of application at whatever cost; they are also perfectionists. Their strong historical link to Vienna has left enough dedicated adherents who will continue to explore that gift from the past – in short the classical heritage.

[12] Also prescribed by Nuno Oliveira of twentieth century Portuguese equitation.
[13] From *The Noble Horse*, published in Dresden 1830.

SIX

Glorious France and the School of Versailles

The age of academic equitation in France owed its inception to the spirit of classicism which achieved its full glory at the Court of Versailles under Louis XIV. This classicism, born of the Italian Renaissance, based its ideals on certain predetermined laws of strict order, symmetry and traditional beauty. Where in Italy, equestrian ideals had been true to this spirit, but the methods had not, in France, the message of classicism became all-pervading. This enlightenment was reflected in art, architecture, sculpture, music, landscape gardening and equitation. Here, the often convoluted and complicated Baroque embellishments never truly took root. Instead, the French Classical School of the seventeenth century developed an essential lucidity, best described as art in its purest form.

The Age of the Riding Academy

Under Henri IV (1533–1610), known affectionately as Henri the Great, a number of magnificent buildings were completed throughout Central France. These included the great gallery of the Louvre, the Hotel de Ville, the Place Royale, the Pont Neuf and the Tuileries. This king's love of horses together with his interest in architecture, led to the inauguration of a comprehensive system of riding academies across the land, the oldest being at Toulouse. Their purpose was to encourage national interest locally; they relied on royal patronage and the King's Master of the Horse held the purse strings. Thus at the more provincial academies, the noble art became available to the sons of country gentry and one no longer had to be a prince to be versed in the art of High School.

The Court of the Sun King

Under Louis XIV (1638-1715), French classicism blossomed into its most brilliant epoch. A lover of fine horses, Louis filled his stables with the most prestigious mounts money could buy. By 1682 he had moved the entire royal court from Paris to Versailles where he undertook a programme of reconstruction and landscaping on an unprecedented scale. Whilst Le Nôtre planned the magnificent terraced gardens, with its fountains, bronze sculptures and wide boulevardes, Mansart (born 1598) designed the Orangery, the Trianon palace and the famous Royal Stable.

These magnificent twin structures were divided into the Petite Ecurie for the coach, carriage, post and hunting horses; the Grande Ecurie housed the horses of the manège and the parade, also the School of Pages. Presided over by a *Premier-Ecuyer* with over 100 *écuyers* under him, the French court had the benefit of the best of all the breeds for the various purposes required. Spanish and Italian horses were the favourites for the Royal Manège, Warmblood horses from the German and Austrian principalities for carriage and coaching, and lighter English and French saddle horses for sport in the forest. The *crème de la crème* of the school horses were promoted first to the ranks of silver bridles, and finally to the highest accolade of gold bridles. No other country in Europe could equal, in sheer size, diversity and magnificence, the contents of the Sun King's stables.

To understand a little better the atmosphere of Versailles, such an important milestone in equitation history, try for a moment to imagine yourself in that almost allegorical atmosphere. In a wide ornate courtyard, ringing with the sound of blacksmiths' iron, echoing with the clatter of hooves over the cobbles, the whinnying and stamping of scores of horses and the shouts and cries of the runners, grooms, pages, you awaited your horse. As the stately steed approached in the care of a liveried yardman, his new padded buckskin saddle specially commissioned from Paris, with its gleaming silver studs and mountings, was noted with satisfaction. After removing a speck of dust from a cuff, you prepared to mount from the stepped block. By and by, after a decorous arranging of your coatskirts, you proceeded in the company of others, all elegantly attired, towards the manège. Astride a high-stepping stallion whose skin had been burnished like beaten gold, you could pause halfway down a sandy avenue between the fountains and the huge imposing Versailles trees to collect the horse a little more. Here, before a statue from Greek mythology, conscious of the eyes of lesser mortals, you would set the noble steed on his haunches and practise a gentle piaffe or levade, before going on to enter those lofty portals, taking care to remove your hat before taking up a place in the Royal Manège.

Already, you felt in a suitable frame of mind to pursue the strict disciplines that lay ahead in the morning's lesson. From early childhood you had learned that this was the most noble of pastimes. The nobility and beauty of the horse, the sheer staggering grandeur of the gardens, the perfect lines of the statues, the austerity of the riding hall, now all combined to thrill and inspire the senses so that you happily conformed to the dictates and doctrines of the wise écuyer to whom one had been assigned. Imagine . . .

The Classical Approach

The preoccupation with academic riding appealed greatly to the French mind. The Italians had played their role in rediscovering equitation; with their great feeling for antiquity, they had tried to preserve the ideals of the Greeks and Romans in the best way they knew how. Then came the mixed influences of the Holy Roman Empire, Spanish and Austrian – a curious amalgam – combining to produce a sense of the grand and the ornate which culminated in a flamboyant but sometimes self-important excess of grandeur. But it was the French who loved to reason and would eventually discover that simple rules could be applied to equitation in a way that would cleanse, refine and gently hone all that had gone before. With this reasoned logic they brought a dimension of lightness and freedom to the riding academy from which art could flourish.

As we have seen with architecture, the French preoccupation with beauty and harmony was no haphazard affair. Nothing could be achieved without planning and order. Thus the French School set about laying down a set of principles which prohibited any form of force but concentrated instead on the positive side of training. They believed that the horse could be enticed to cooperate through balance, ease of movement and enjoyment. Only through a picture of harmony, man and horse working as one, could true beauty be derived.

To create this perfect picture, the French were prepared to discipline themselves and work hard. In those days of hedonistic excess, there would have been a refreshing contrast about the toughness and honesty of the work within the riding hall as well as the strict discipline of the men who ran it. Apart from swordsmanship and hunting, there were insufficient facilities in those days for the taking of exercise, apart from the obvious indoor kind. Equitation offered

Louis XIV, the Sun King, portrayed in his youth by Simon Vouet (1590–1649) outside the Chateau de Versailles. This picture, with its careful attention to detail – note the bit, stirrups and spurs – sums up the spirit of French classicism.

a challenge, an opportunity for physical and mental exercise, and the French embraced it with fervour.

Literature

France is far richer in equestrian literature than any other country we have discussed so far. Yet a twentieth century French writer bemoans the fact that this golden period did not produce more books. Michel Henriquet writes in *L'equitation*, 'It is thanks to a cultivated and curious man that we know nearly all the equestrian authors. J. Huzard (1755–1838), veterinary and bibliophile, dedicated his life to following the trail of all the books, handwritten or printed, devoted to equitation. On this subject it is a known fact that he owned *everything* that was published before 1837. The catalogue of his collection (1842) is an irreplaceable source of documentation.'[1]

The general assumption must be that during the richest period of equitation, knowledge was gained first and foremost by practical experience. All the conditions in Europe at this time were right for true scholars of the equestrian art to take themselves to a Master, or enrol at one of the great academies, and remain there for a number of years until truly versed in the practical art of the manège. Only the very great *écuyers* would consider writing a book. These theses, with their wealth of engravings to explain each stage in the training of the horse, were extremely expensive to produce and were normally paid for by subscription.

This was undoubtedly vital in equitation. It immediately removed the risk of mediocrity and ignorance being perpetrated on paper and confusing later generations. As Henriquet goes on to point out: 'Nowadays, a flowering of publications coincides paradoxically with a great *poverty* in worldwide equitation.'

Our story of France therefore will now concentrate solely on a small handful of equestrian authors and teachers whose work has made the greatest impact on classical riding as we know it today. The period with which we are concerned is approximately 1590–1790, the latter date being the year when hereditary nobility and hereditary titles were abolished in France. Those who reject and object to this period of history and scorn it as being a profligate period of money-wasting at the expense of the poor, must consider the achievements. The pictures, the buildings, the sculpture, the incredible landscaped gardens and parks – all are legacies of those Bourbon kings whose rich pleasures are now ours to ponder over and enjoy. Out of extravagance has come common good. The ideas, the philosophies, the rules and the science of the one small area of equitation, has secured a better life for countless horses, and given those of us who ride, a true and worthwhile goal at which to aim.

[1] *L'Equitation* by Michel Henriquet and Alain Prevost, Editions du Seuil, Paris 1972.

The Great Master: Salomon de la Broue

The title 'Father of French equitation' is invariably accorded to Antoine Pluvinel (1555–1620) but his earlier contemporary Salomon de la Broue (1530–1610) published the first important French book of equitation, *Le Cavalerice François*, in 1593 which breathed a breath of fresh air to manège riding, displaying a marked departure from the harshness of the Italian school where he had originally studied under Pignatelli.

De la Broue's concern was to achieve an effortless, light quality in all school work. 'The lightness of the mouth of the horse precedes the lightness of the horse himself . . .' he wrote, and he deplored '. . . those little secrets which have been invented for lack of skill' – an obvious referral to the barbaric techniques discussed earlier.

De la Broue was the first of his generation to recognise that the young horse made mistakes not out of cussedness and temper, but from real fear and lack of proper preparation. He stressed the need for moderation and kindness and what makes his work outstanding was his progressive method of schooling.

This was divided into three stages before the horse might be allowed to work in the full bridle. The first stage involved the use of the cavesson only; the second stage recommended the use of the snaffle (with or without draw-reins); the third allowed the curb bit with the snaffle, but without the curb chain. Only when the horse was happy and accepting of the bit in all three stages could he then be 'placed in a normal bridle with a curb chain' from which de la Broue concluded 'he will move beautifully, freely and without causing any difficulties.'

De la Broue also introduced flexions of the neck and lower jaw to supple and entice the horse to yield to his rider. This could only be achieved with good hands, the all important requisite of the true horseman. His definition '. . . those which know how to resist and how to yield at the proper moment, and to control with precision the action produced by the legs . . .' could have been written today.

As with the Austrian and Prussian school, he disliked the over-use of the spur. 'Horsemen should remember that big, sharp spurs are not appropriate to the training of young animals. The punishment these give can frighten a horse and make him suspicious and timid, and, as a result, even more skittish, while those animals that are hot-blooded or choleric may be easily driven to desperation instead of learning obedience.'

De la Broue recommended the value of riding out across country without spurs when a horse showed reticence or rebellion in the manège; he stressed the importance at all times of retaining the horse's good spirits and happiness of mind. An interesting aside to this is that our top British dressage competitor gives her Grand Prix horses ample riding out in the fields and the forest,[2] whereas others on the international circuit believe the dressage horse must always be confined to the schooling arena. Perhaps the latter should take a lesson from de la Broue.

Starting in life as a page to the Count d'Aubijoux, and returning to France from his five years of study in Italy as *écuyer* to the Duke of Epernon, de la Broue should have enjoyed an illustrious career. Like so many great riding masters of the time however, his existence was often precarious and depended too much on the generosity of his royal patron and a sufficient number of wealthy pupils. Sadly, he ended his days first in prison (for a crime of which he had no knowlege) and finally in abject poverty.

[2]Jennie Loriston-Clarke (from an interview with the author, 1988).

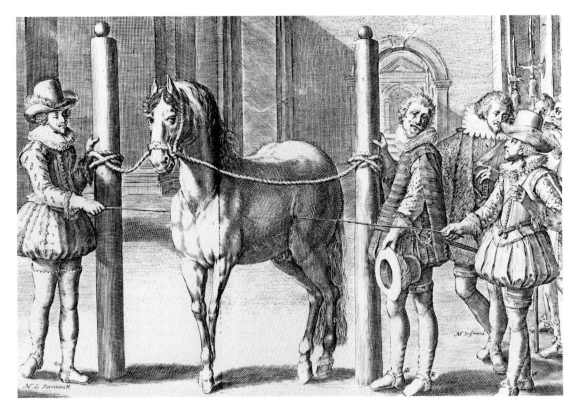

Antoine Pluvinel is generally acknowledged as the father of French equitation. He explored the use of the pillars and is here seen to the right, instructing the 26-year-old Louis XIII who stands in the foreground, a switch in his hand.

Pluvinel

Antoine Pluvinel fared better. According to one source[3] he spent six years studying and riding under Pignatelli in Italy, before being brought back to France by M. de Sourdis, royal *écuyer* of Charles IX. He immediately went into the service of the Duc d'Anjou, who later suceeded his brother as King Henri IV. Under this royal master, he automatically became the *sous-governeur* of the young Dauphin who would eventually succeed to the title of Louis XIII.

Pluvinel's important posthumously published book *L'Instruction du roy en l'exercise de monter a cheval* appeared in Paris to much acclaim in 1625. The engravings are by the Flemish artist Crispian de Pas. The most popular of these well-known prints depict Pluvinel on the ground, instructing the young Louis splendidly mounted upon a Spanish horse. An earlier, but incomplete edition of the same work appeared in 1623 and was entitled *Manège Royale*, but this was a result of a confusion between the artist and Pluvinel's great friend Menou de Chernizay. Menou had been entrusted with the task of publishing the writings, but de Pas had pre-empted him, and unfortunately the earlier engravings in the incomplete book are superior to the latter ones. It is not altogether clear however if the second book was not partly rewritten by Menou.

Pluvinel's book takes the form of a constant dialogue between himself and his royal pupil. If one disregards the fact that Pluvinel is required to flatter the royal pupil, this book is rich in substance. His work lays the basis for discipline through gentleness and the understanding of the horse's mind, in particular making use of the horse's excellent memory which if filled with bad experiences could spoil the horse forever. 'Let us beware of upsetting the young

[3] Michel Henriquet.

At the Court of Louis XIV extravagant equestrian carousels, which had orginated in Italy, became extremely popular. This engraving by Chauveau in 1670 displays the king dressed in Roman costume in 'a corset of silver brocade embroidered in gold'.

horse and robbing him of his friendly temperament because this is like the scent of a fruit's blossom which once departed, never returns.'

Like de la Broue, Pluvinel exhorted the patient, humane approach. He took definite steps to change and improve upon the long-cheeked, highly restrictive curbs, still popular all over Europe. Nevertheless he felt the use of curb to be important '. . . for the horse can learn more quickly to tolerate and obey a mouthpiece and a curb chain, thereby becoming lighter . . .'

He is also generally regarded as the first person to explain adequately the use of the pillars with which he liked to assess the horse, his temperament and his movements, without the weight of the rider: 'All this I do much more easily in a place where the horse is restricted, for one has the advantage of being able to see all his movements, far better than if he were mounted . . .'

Pluvinel was convinced that one-sidedness or crookedness in the horse, stemmed from the position (usually to the left) the foal had lain in the womb. One of his cures was further work on the pillars to supple not only the neck but also the hindquarters – a factor generally over-looked by the Italian school. 'The horse learns, through combining these means, how to walk, trot and canter; how to go on a single track and to move back and forth. He also gives himself more punishment,[4] because of the cavesson, than any man would, should he go off the track.' From the lesson of the pillars, three important things would be achieved '. . . first, they [the horses] are never strong in the mouth; second, they are never restless; and third, they rarely turn stubborn or wilful or resist, turning to the right and left, which is the most common fault one finds in unschooled horses.'

The saddle of Pluvinel's time, although much improved from tournament days, still tended to wedge the rider into position from a very high pommel, and (to a lesser degree) high cantle. This encouraged too straight a leg, although Pluvinel advocated pushing forward with the stomach and inwards with the loins in keeping with the later La Guerinière and other classical masters. He also recommended that the horse be taught to round the back '. . . which gives grace to the Horseman as well as to the horse and which makes the horse place his haunches under his belly.'

In the span of his sixty-five years, Pluvinel lived under four French monarchs and actually served three. Such was the esteem with which they held him, not only as a riding master

[4] The idea of making the horse responsible for his actions is similar to a concept of training used by the twentieth century American professional horse-breaker Monty Roberts.

Monsieur de Nestier (1684–1754), royal *écuyer* mounted on Le Florido, a Spanish horse given to his patron, Louis XV by the King of Spain. The accomplishments of Nestier are still remembered in France. To this day, a really exceptional manège rider is referred to as 'a veritable Nestier.'

PLATE 5

(*below*) This glorious, finely tapering head of an early Lipizzaner from a study by George Hamilton reflects all the gracious nobility of the horse. Note the pronounced convex profile of the Baroque horse, giving a proud, hawked appearance. (This look was bred out to some extent with the later introduction of Arab blood.) The eye is liquid, forbearing and full of intelligence.

(*above*) Henry Herbert, 10th Earl of Pembroke, not only taught the classical airs of the High School but wrote in his *Military Equitation* of crosscountry riding, jumping, lunging, long-reining, flexions and the extended gaits. He recommended the extended trot to encourage the sluggish horse to move straight and freely forward, the collected trot to improve suppleness. (*Courtesy the 17th Earl of Pembroke, Wilton House, Salisbury, Wiltshire*)
(*below*) A fine piaffe. This unusual oil painting by Thomas Parkinson dated 1766, an exhibitor at the Royal Academy, demonstrates an unknown English horseman on an English horse. The indoor manège, with pillars, is similar to that run by Philip Astley at Lambeth in London around this time. (*Courtesy Arthur Ackermann & Sons*)

PLATE 6

but as a diplomat, that he received many trusts and benefices which gave him the security to practice his equitation coherently and in a way fitting to a great scholar.

In 1593 he opened his own academy at the rue de Faubourg Saint-Honoré in Paris where the arts and literature were taught as well as equitation. He may also have instructed at one of the provincial academies. There were now twenty of these operating throughout France and they attracted visitors from England, Germany, Austria, Portugal, Italy and Spain. Much later, we know that the young future Duke of Wellington studied at the academy of Angers, whilst that of Marseilles attracted visitors from along the Mediterranean.

The School of Versailles

This was the name given to the whole philosophy of French court equitation. By 1685 there were ten academies around Paris and Versailles where a hard core of professionals enhanced the work of the Royal Manège through enlightened ideas and shared dedication.

Perfecting the art of the *rassembler* (collection) was the hallmark of the Versailles School. The constant theme of slow cadenced work with the horse light in hand and absolutely obedient to the leg permeated (as we have seen) through to the schools of Germany and Austria as the only way for a horse to work once fully dressed. Pluvinel's definition of collection had been simple and clear. 'This lesson, properly applied, lifts and lightens the horse, fuses and sets him on his haunches, and gives him sureness in his cadence, making him freely receptive to the aid of the hands and the heels, which renders him more agile in performing all that is desired of him and consequently, makes everything easier.'

Other Lights

Before we proceed to a new chapter to discuss the methods of the most famous of all the French masters, François Robichon de la Guérinière, a number of masters of the period are worthy of mention. They include Menou de Charnizay (1578–1651), Pierre de La Noue (beginning of seventeenth century), Delcampe (end of the seventeenth century), Jacques de Solleysel (1617–1680), Imbotti de Beaumount (mid seventeenth century), Gaspard de Saunier (1663–1748) and François Alexandre de Garsault (1692–1778). Each of these *écuyers* who either ran their own acadamies or served a royal master, left books which echo the revolutionary work of de la Broue and Pluvinel with the emphasis always on classical lines of lightness and refinement.

Solleysel's book *Le Parfait Mareschal*, published in 1664[5] was particularly highly regarded since he included much of his knowledge of veterinary work with horses. With 5000 horses under his charge at the royal household of Versailles alone, he wrote enthusiastically of the different breeds and their aptitude for the manège. Garsault, who was captain of the French stud farms published a book of similar title in 1741, *Le Nouveau Parfait Mareschal*, and like Solleysel favoured the Spanish horse above all others.

The French stage was now set for the grand entry of France's greatest and most illustrious Master of the classical period. Through the hard efforts of innovators like de la Broue and Pluvinel, a point of enlightenment had been reached which would banish for ever the use of force and cruelty. The spirit of classicism with its magnificent achievements at Versailles was the perfect backdrop for the flowering of the art. In short, as so often happens in history, de la Guérinière was the right man appearing at the right time, and such was his importance that he must rightly occupy the lion's share of another chapter.

[5] This was translated into English by Sir William Hope and was published in 1717 under the title *The Compleat Horseman*.

The Classical School

SIEUR DE LA GUERINIERE

If the word greatness is to be accorded to only one of the individual Masters whose work is reviewed in this book, François Robichon de la Guérinière (probably 1688–1751) must achieve this accolade. This committed equestrian artist inspired the world of classical dressage; it is to him that the great Schools of Vienna, Saumur and Hanover have bowed over the centuries. His beautifully illustrated definitive book *Ecole de Cavalerie*, first published in 1729 in Paris, has become the authoritative bible of the dressage world.[1] It is a lucid compilation of all the methods and principles of the French Masters to that date, written in the elegant style of a great academician. To this day, it is still widely quoted, and remains the source by which most, if not all, equestrian arguments may be settled. Before the turn of the century, translations of this work and a later tome, *Elemens de Cavalerie* (1768) were available, at least in part, throughout Europe.

Although La Guérinière personifies the classical School of Versailles, he himself was never truly based there. Born in Essay, the son of a lawyer, he trained under M. Geneval Monpoint Vendeuil and immediately had to earn his living by teaching commercially. He received his *provisions d'écuyer* from the Count of Armagnac in 1715 and ran his own academy at the Rue de Vaugirand. As news of his brilliance spread, he was eventually appointed *Ecuyer-Royale* and entrusted with the running of the Manège des Tuileries in 1730, which led to worldwide recognition within his lifetime.

The real value of La Guérinière's writing is that he preserved in an understandable form all that was good from the past, whilst ruthlessly discarding all that was harsh and artificial. The two authors whom he truly admired were de la Broue and Newcastle whom he referred to as real 'connoisseurs' of the art of the manège (see Chapter 8), but we also find much from the Greeks, the Italians, and his French predecessors,[2] but only that relevant to the Versailles spirit of classicism.

La Guérinière's interpretation for example of Xenophon's reward and punishment theory is uncompromising: 'Praise as much as possible, punish immediately, and only as much as necessary: the severity of the punishment must be matched to the horse's temperament. A

The frontispiece of La Guérinière's *Ecole de Cavalerie* (1729–30), his great *oeuvre* which went through a 1736, 1751, 1756, 1766 and 1769 edition, as well as being translated and retranslated in almost every European country within less than a century. (*From the Paul Mellon Collection, Upperville, Virginia*)

[1] Translations from *Ecole de Cavalerie* (with further editions in 1733, 1736, 1751, 1756, 1766 and 1769) have been taken from three sources: A.J. Fox, 1989–90 (excerpts); G. Gibson, 1986 (excerpts) and from Captain William Frazer's full translation of the Equitation Section, dedicated to Viscount Wellesley and published in Calcutta, 1801.
[2] Surprisingly Pluvinel is rarely referred to in his text.

gentle remonstrance applied at the proper psychological moment will often suffice to regain obedience. A horse so treated will perform his task with cheerful acceptance, verve, and brilliance rather than with resistance and resignation; he will also remain at his peak of excellence longer. If a horse disobeys it is generally because he has simply not understood what the rider wants or because of some physical deficiency.'

Nowadays, La Guérinière is best remembered for his work on the exercise of shoulder-in and the half-halt. Previously, many masters had made use of sudden halts and departs with their horses which Guérinière condemns as being too harsh for all but the hardiest of horses. 'This is not the case with the half-halt' which does not 'cause such apprehension as the stop . . . It makes the contact with the mouth light; it can be repeated frequently without interrupting the pace, and as the horse by this aid is brought back into balance and his forehand is slightly reined in, he consequently is obliged to lower his quarters which is exactly what you wish him to do.' Later on La Guérinière advocates that a correct half-halt must be followed by a momentary yielding of the rider's hand.

Longitudinal softening and suppling was also of paramount importance, and he stressed that whatever its later role in life '. . . a horse which is not absolutely supple, loose and flexible cannot conform to the will of man with ease and carriage.' This would be achieved through voltes and lateral movements on straight lines.

The Shoulder-in

La Guérinière was the first to acknowledge that it was that 'great Master', the English Duke of Newcastle who had invented and laid all the groundwork for the shoulder-in on the circle. This tended however to place too much weight on the shoulders of the horse so La Guérinière developed it to its present form as an exercise along the perimeter of the school and through the corners. This would supple the whole body of the horse and indirectly combat crookedness. It also taught the horse to move away from the leg: 'This same lesson disposes a horse to move away from the heels [legs] because with each movement, being obliged to cross and pass the legs the one over the other, as much those in front as those behind, he acquires, by this, the facility to cross over the forelegs and hindlegs on both hands [reins] which it is necessary for him to do, to go easily sideways.'

The above description shows us that La Guérinière's shoulder-in was made on four tracks or traces (as with Newcastle) although the angle made by the horse to the side of the school is relatively oblique.

Today, although the FEI surprisingly makes no stipulation about the number of traces, an angle of roughly 30 degrees is defined in the rules. In a very supple horse this would allow for La Guérinière's 4-trace shoulder-in as still faithfully employed at the Spanish Riding School and in the Portuguese School,[3] but the majority of competition riders interpret the modern rules to imply a 3-trace movement.

Because of these practical differences, some theorists have argued that the original Guérinière text is not in keeping with the superb engravings by Charles Perrocel. In a highly academic article 'The Shoulder-in Yesterday and Today',[4] the author, Jean-Claude Racinet, refutes this claim and warns of the futility of these arguments since so much depends on the size and shape and of course the lateral suppleness of the horse. 'It is likely that the original shoulder-

[3] Although Nuno Oliveira prescribed a more acute angle of 45 degrees.
[4] Published in *Dressage & C.T.*, USA, October 1986.

in of La Guérinière was on four tracks . . . One should not however emphasize this issue too much, for the number of tracks is basically dependent on the proportions of the rectangle formed by the four feet of the horse.'

The real importance of La Guérinière's shoulder-in is the proof of a well balanced horse who is displaying good suppleness in the back with a well-flexed thigh, hock and fetlock. As La Guérinière pointed out, this fundamental exercise 'supples the entire horse, and allows him perfect freedom in every part.'

Compare La Guérinière's description to that of the FEI concerning the benefit to the horse of the shoulder-in exercise! The FEI is almost pure Guérinière.

Guérinière: '. . . the shoulder-in prepares the horse to put him on his haunches, because with each step that he takes in this way, he advances under his body the inside hind leg, bringing it in front of the outside hind, which cannot be executed without a lowering of the inside haunch.'

FEI: Shoulder in, if performed in the right way . . . is not only a suppling movement but also a collecting movement because the horse at every step must move his inside hind leg underneath his body and place it in front of the outside, which he is unable to do without lowering his inside hip.'

La Guérinière also defined the role of the rein of opposition, an area which has been well explored by the German and Austrian schools, and which supports his theories of working the horse into the outside hand with the inside leg.

Pesade, Piaffe and Passage

Let us now examine some of the more advanced movements as seen through La Guérinière's eyes. His definitions are still in use at Vienna today: 'In the pesade, the horse elevates his forehand. The hindquarters remain motionless in place with the haunches deeply bent. . . the horse has now grown accustomed to carrying all his weight on his hindquarters, to lifting himself elegantly, and to bending his forelegs in a graceful manner. This is the movement upon which all the jumps are developed.' Later he reminds the reader not to confuse the pesade with a rear: 'There are significant differences; in the pesade the horse stands in perfect obedience on the rein and bends his haunches.'

More practical to today's dressage riders are his definitions for passage and piaffe which have been incorporated in modern language into today's FEI directives. The following excerpt from a detailed explanation of both movements relates to the piaffe, which alters little from today's rules, except that La Guérinière required more height with the front legs.

La Guérinière: '. . . the piaffer should be regarded as a passage on the spot neither advancing nor moving backwards . . . In the piaffer, the knee of the foreleg which is in the air should be level with the elbow of the same leg and should be flexed in such a way that the front of the shoe is raised to the height of the middle of the knee of the leg which is on the ground. The hind leg should not be lifted so high as otherwise the horse would not be on its haunches. The front of the shoe which is in the air, is raised to the height of the middle of the cannon bone of the other leg.'

FEI (BHS) definition of Piaffe: 'The piaffer is a highly measured, collected, elevated and cadenced trot on the spot. The horse's back is supple and vibrating. The quarters are slightly lowered, the haunches with active hocks are well engaged, giving great freedom, lightness and mobility to the shoulders and forehand. Each diagonal pair of feet is raised and returned to the ground alternately, with an even rhythm and a slightly prolonged suspension.

'In principle, the height of the toe of the raised foreleg should be level with the middle of the cannon bone of the other foreleg. The toe of the raised hind leg should reach just above the fetlock joint of the other hind leg . . . etc.'

Setting aside the matter of height plus the inclusion by the FEI of the attitude of the horse's back, haunches etc., which are described in great depth elsewhere in La Guérinière's book, the two definitions are virtually the same. The requirements for the passage (which are not included here) are also identical.

Today, with less emphasis on training for these slow, elevated movements, there are few horses, even at Grand Prix level, which can perform passage and piaffe even to the FEI standard. In those days, they were part of the normal education of a gentleman's horse.

English Horses

A feature of La Guérinière's writing is his understanding of horses in general. Wisely, he pointed out that not all types and breeds could be trained to the same standard and that different results must be expected of different horses. He was obviously familiar with English horses and admired their ability to hunt all day without losing condition (see Chapter 9). He advocated that the gallop of the hunting horse should be 'more extended than raised', recognising that a horse travelling at speed must be allowed to stretch his neck and enjoy more liberty with the head in order to lengthen the frame and breathe more easily.

What he criticised in the English hunter was the near absence of any preliminary schooling or suppling which, he wrote, would have saved their forelegs since it was well-known that hunting horses at the time broke down after two or three years. 'The reason for this weakness,' he explained, 'is doubtless because the snaffle is always used, whereas it should only be employed in the beginning to school them. As this instrument is not made to supple the forehand nor to give the horse proper *appui* he is not helped in his gallop.' The young hunter should not

be galloped in full extension to start with otherwise they will
bear upon the hand and lose balance.'

It is a tragedy for the English-speaking horse world that
no modern translation of La Guérinière's work is widely
available today. Whilst his work on the various exercises is
universally remembered and made available through FEI
rules, other fundamental principles particularly concerning
lightness and the psychological aspect of training are invariably overlooked.

One of the shrewdest, which could well have been written
for the composers of dressage tests today is, 'Those riders
who seek exactitude and absolute accuracy destroy the
courage of a brave horse and ruin the gentility which Nature
has given him.' This from a man who expected the highest
degree of training from pupils and horses alike must surely
make the majority of us stop and think.

This engraving of the horse in
croupade by J. E. Ridinger
illustrates the bold, straight-
legged fixed position of the
French manège rider which
changed under the influence of
La Guérinière and Marialva.

Descente de Main

It was La Guérinière who fully developed the precept of the *descente de main et des jambes*
(inadequately translateable as the yielding of the hand and the legs) of which we have already
spoken. Developing the concept of reward and punishment, La Guérinière believed that once
a horse had reached a higher level of training, where he could be easily collected, was happy
in the mouth and supple through the back and flexed in the hocks, there came a point where
he might, as General Detroyat[5] of Saumur once put it, be put 'on parole'. Once this pleasant
state had been reached, the pressure of the leg and of the rein was completely eased whilst
the horse continued in the same flexion, in the same degree of collection, without losing impulsion, cadence, rhythm or outline. The act of relinquishing the hand and the leg, momentarily
– or with a really exceptional Master – for a sustained period of time within a particular exercise
– was an invaluable way of thanking the horse, thus encouraging him to further brilliance.

La Guérinière's description of this yielding is somewhat long and complicated so for reasons
of space we shall use certain quotations from *Ecole de Cavelerie* to illustrate in what context
La Guérinière used this valuable aid. The first quote, however, is the only adequate definition
I have found in English of the exact meaning and spirit of the *descente de main* achieved by
Henry Wynmalen in his book *Dressage* published in 1953. In the interest of scholarship, this
should be read in its entirety by every thinking rider. For now, probably, the most relevant
excerpts are as follows:

'Surrender of the Hands *(La descente de Main)* . . .'
'This can only be done on the very well-schooled horse, who is so fully confirmed in
his balance and paces that he will continue the work which he is doing in his best form,
and without alteration, whilst completely free, for a time, from all perceptible control.
'The *descente de main* . . . has inestimable value as a means of calming the horse, keeping

[5] A brilliant dressage rider (and later judge), he took command at Saumur after Colonel Blacque-Belair in 1914.

his mouth fresh and happy, or even overcoming slight disturbance in the mouth. Even the very slightest degree of irritation felt by the horse will set up some stiffening of the jaw; the complete surrender of the hand described is usually fully effective in restoring complete harmony; the horse will at once flex with a smile and champ his bit. The quintessence of this surrender of the hand is that the horse *shall not alter his head carriage or his speed by one iota.*'

The italics are mine since this is the point which is very often misunderstood by scholars who are not familiar with the teachings of La Guérinière. It remained however one of the most important principles of the French School which set the Versailles approach in a higher plane in terms of gentleness and refinement. For those who understand it, its practice constitutes a clear line of definition when working at more advanced levels, between the conventionally schooled dressage horse, and the brilliantly schooled dressage horse.

In the former, accuracy of work is obtained through the continual interaction of positive aids, the horse being retained – a willing, or unwilling partner as the case may be – between the constant use of hand and leg. The latter comprise those horses which, having passed beyond this point to total self-balance, give themselves freely to the rider, without loss of accuracy, the merest weight aids being sufficient to elicit each response.

Having defined this most important precept, we now return to La Guérinière's own text. 'Care must be taken not to yield the hand or make the *descente* when the horse is on his shoulders; the proper time for either is after making a half-halt, and then, when the rider feels that the horse is upon his haunches, he must gently give the bridle or make the *descente de main*. The timing, which must be exact and is difficult to catch, [makes this] one of the finest and most useful aids in horsemanship; . . . as the horse bends his haunches at the moment the *appui* [contact] is taken off, he must necessarily become light in hand, since he has no support for his head.'

This idea of freedom was first advanced by Xenophon, albeit somewhat rudimentarily, and therefore was not new. It took a Master of Guérinière's capacity however to explain and make it relevant to the complicated airs of the Versailles School, thus rendering the work expressive and truly beautiful.

As already stated, the doctrine of *la descente de main* (or *de jambes)* is not widely taught nowadays (except in France and Portugal) and therefore there is no FEI passage on the subject to which to refer.

The Classical Seat

None of this progression would have been possible had not La Guérinière contributed towards a more balanced position in the saddle. The old saddles, as discussed, afforded little movement; the rider remained in a fixed position, quite unable to use the subtle weight aids so necessary for adjusting to the horse's balance according to what he was doing. La Guérinière thus made several improvements to the manège saddle, flattening it in front so that the rider could sit closer to the horse's centre of balance, and dispensing with the high protective rolls left over from the days of tournament riding. From a broader based, more balanced position, the rider could now draw the leg further back with a slightly bent knee. With the lower leg closer to the horse's sides, the aids became more effective and there was no longer any need for the monstrous spurs of Grisone's time.

Captain William Frazer's *A Treatise of Horsemanship – translated from the original French of Monsieur de la Guérinière*, written at the turn of the eighteenth century and published in 1801,

The classical seat of the eighteenth century. Note the shoulders are set back and down, the loins or lower back is slightly hollowed, whilst the waist or abdomen is pushed forward and down into a snug contact with the saddle. The thighs are low, the knee bent and the legs generally relaxed. (*From Arte de Cavallaria (author's collection)*)

gives us a clearcut definition of the ideal position of the saddle in the section entitled 'Of the Horseman's Seat'. This description, which appears to come from a much later edition, was much copied by contemporary authors Claude Bourgelat, the English Richard Berenger[6] and in part, the Portuguese Marquess of Marialva. Clearly, La Guérinière was at pains to point out that the foundations of a correct seat should be the same for riders of all nationalities.

> 'The Italians, the Spaniards, the French, and in a word every country where riding is in repute, adopt each a posture which is peculiar to themselves; the foundation of their general notions, is, if I may so say, the same . . .

'The body of a man is divided into three parts, two of which are moveable, the other immoveable. The first of the two moveable parts is the trunk or body down to the waist, the second is from the knees to the feet, so that the remaining immovable part is that between the waist and the knees.

'The parts which ought to be without motion are the fork or twist of the horseman and his thighs; as these parts should be kept without motion, they ought to have a certain hold and centre to rest upon, which no motion the horse will make will disturb.

'This point or centre is the basis of the hold, which the horseman has upon his horse and is what is called *the seat*; now if the seat is nothing else but this point or centre, it must follow that not only the grace but the symmetry and true proportions of the whole attitude depends upon those parts of the body that are immoveable.

'Let the horsemen then place himself upon his twist sitting exactly in the middle of the saddle, let him support this posture in which the twist alone seems to sustain the weight of the whole body by moderately leaning upon his buttocks, let his thighs be turned inwards and rest *flat* upon the sides of the saddle, and in order to do this, let the turn of the thighs proceed directly from the hips. Let him employ no force or strength to keep himself in the saddle, but trust to the weight of his body and thighs.

'This is the exact equilibrium, in this consists the firmness of the whole building [structure], a firmness which beginners are not sensible of, though it is to be acquired and will always be attained with practice. I demand but a moderate stress upon the buttocks, because a man that sits full upon them can never turn his thighs flat upon the saddle and the thighs should always lie flat, because the fleshy part of the thigh, being insensible [insensitive], the horseman would not otherwise be able to feel the motions of the horse.

'The horseman should present or advance his breast; by that his whole figure opens and

---

[6] The Frazer translation appeared also in Berenger's book of 1771.

displays itself; he should have a small hollow in his back and push his waist forward to the pommel of the saddle, because this position corresponds with and unites him to all the motions of the horse. Throwing the shoulders back, produces all these effects . . .

'The arms should be bent at the elbows and the elbows should rest equally upon the hips; if the arms were straight, the consequence would be that the hands would be infinitely too low or at too great a distance from the body, and if the elbows were not steady, they would of consequence give an uncertainty and fickleness to the hand, sufficient to ruin it for ever.'

This was the seat later to be pursued by Baucher and all the main adherents of the Romanic school. It is still to be seen in Vienna, Portugal, Spain, and by certain but by no means all dressage riders in France and Germany.

La Guérinière warned his pupils to guard against sloppiness. A further passage incorporating the concept of yielding or letting go, is again quite modern in context.

'Grace is a great ornament to a rider . . .

'By grace, I understand an air of ease and freedom. This must be conserved in a correct and supple posture, whether while maintaining one's seat and controlling the horse as necessary, or while purposely letting go, yet still retaining – through all the horse's gaits – that exact balance which comes from properly applying the counterpoise [weight aids] of one's body. Furthermore, the rider's every move should be subtle, so that each one serves more to complement his seat and his aids to the horse. Since this concept has been neglected, and nonchalence together with a certain air of slackness, now attracts the attention of the man who in the past might have been concerned to acquire and maintain that beautiful seat – . . . it is not in the least surprising that riding has lost much of its lustre.'

Strong words and a sharp reminder that even in La Guérinière's day, the art of horsemanship lived under continual threat. Careless attitudes, lack of discipline and a desire for quick results are not the exclusive characteristics of the twentieth century. They had been upsetting perfectionist Masters since the time of Xenophon.

Masters All

Followers or colleagues of La Guérinière under the School of Versailles are too numerous to be listed individually. Of the best remembered, M. de Nestier (d in 1754), who became *écuyer* to Louis XV, was remembered as a taciturn disciplinarian who rarely spoke to anyone other than the monarch thus earning the name of '*Le Grand Silencieux*'. A contemporary description of the horsemanship he displayed out hunting with the King at Versailles runs thus: 'His thighs and legs formed a vice which kept the the horse from any disorder; he rode *à la française* shunning the English fashion. I have often admired the way he would gallop off, then rein in his horse without forceful movement; you would have believed man and horse to be one as he had his horse race on at will and at other times made him perform passades as though in the manège.'[7] Still today in classical circles, the expression 'a veritable Nestier' denotes a truly remarkable rider. (*See Plate 5*.)

Claude Bourgelat (1712–1760) directed the manège at Lyon, and later published numerous books on veterinary science as well as his celebrated reworking of the English Duke of Newcastle's methods, which appeared under the title *Le Nouveau Newcastle* in 1744.[8] Bourgelat was

---

[7] From the memoirs of the Comte de Chevernay quoted in an article by Lily Powell, *Equi*, Jan/Feb 1984.

[8] Berenger made an English translation of Bourgelat's book in 1754 entitled *A New System of Horsemanship from the French of Monsieur Bourgelat*, before publishing his own book on the subject.

able to take all that was valuable in Newcastle whilst dispensing with the longwinded, extravagant and often conceited asides. Ahead of his time, he developed the idea of the three trots (see Chapter 9) long before the Count d'Aure, who usually takes the credit for developing the extended trot in France. For his description of the seat, Bourgelat unashamedly lifts that of La Guérinière, word for word. It was therefore Newcastle and La Guérinière seen through Bourgelat's eyes that clearly influenced the English Richard Berenger, Master of the Horse to King George III, since many of the same descriptions appear in his book published in 1771 (see Chapter 9).

Montfaucon de Rogles (1717–1760), *écuyer* to the Dauphin in 1751 and the author of a concise manual, the principles of which are still used at Saumur, was followed by Dupaty de Clam (1744–1782), another royal *écuyer* and author of three important books the last of which, *La Science et l'Art de l'Equitation*, describes the mechanics of equitation. Other influential figures included the Prince de Lambesc, the last *Grand Ecuyer*, M. de Neuilly, Lubersac, the Marquis de la Bigne, and finally Viscount d'Abzac who became a royal *écuyer* at the age of nineteen.

It is ironic perhaps that at the very time when France was producing her most talented Masters who under the umbrella of Versailles all promoted ideals of kindness and lightness and were able successfully to achieve a highly collected form of riding so different from the forced methods of an earlier age, that the reality of life outside was pulling equitation in other directions.

First, there was the threat of *Anglomania*, as the French called it (see Chapter 9); the temptation to throw away all the old principles and charge across country in a haphazard free for all.

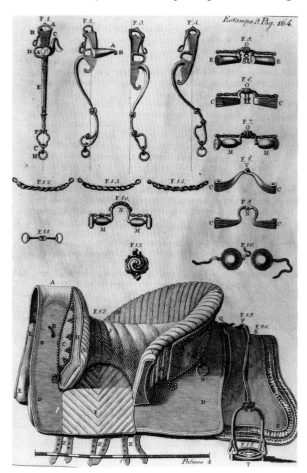

An eighteenth-century Portuguese manège saddle modelled on similar lines to that of La Guérinière. The broad, flattish seat encouraged a deep all-round contact of the entire seat of the rider, allowing his weight to be carried as close as possible to the horse's centre of balance. Still in use in Portugal, ceremonial saddles at Saumur and Vienna are similar in concept but have over the years lost the protective leg guards of the fighting saddle. (*From Arte de Cavallaria (author's collection)*)

Second, there was the challenge from the military which started in Germany but quickly spread throughout all the armies of Europe. Even in France, this reached a point where manège riding was no longer seen as a useful contribution, but rather as an impractical extravaganza even to some extent by the *chevauxlegers*, noble born cavalry officers such as the Comte d'Auvergne and Drummond de Melfort[9] in 1750 who were familiar with the manège.

La Guérinière himself was forced to defend his love of the High School, insisting that his was still the best way to prepare horses for war, instead of admitting more truthfully perhaps that art for art's sake should be preserved. As we have seen in the days of Grisone, High School training of horse and rider had made sound practical sense for hand to hand combat and short range firearms; by the mid eighteenth century however, the role of cavalry had changed drastically with the invention of long range guns. Instead of small, often semi-private armies led by noble-born officers, each country now recruited from all the ranks in the systematic build-up of militia by the superpowers which preceded the Napoleonic wars. The refined methods of La Guérinière therefore had little real place in the military scheme of things to come.

Realistically, it is little short of a miracle that the art of classical riding was not lost forever in a Europe torn apart by the proletariat fervour of Bonaparte's revolutionaries. Certainly, the Fall of the Bastille in 1789 and the days to come, changed the whole history of French equitation. Fortunately for us, the greater part of the teachings of the disbanded School of Versailles[10] have found, as we have seen, a firm and permanent place within the portals of the Spanish Riding School of Vienna. It has also constituted the basis of all serious equitation in Portugal, and parts of Spain, that most ancient home of ring or manège riding.

THE MARQUESS OF MARIALVA

Whilst the work of La Guérinière made a lasting impression on the French, Austrian, and to a great extent Prussian, Danish and Swedish schools of riding, another great eighteenth century master would have a similar effect on the Latin-speaking nations of Portugal and Spain which would spread across the Atlantic to much of Mexico and South America.

Sometimes referred to as the Guérinière of the Iberian Peninsula, Dom Pedro de Alcantara e Meneses, 4th Marquess of Marialva was born near Lisbon in 1713, and entered the Portuguese royal household as *écuyer* under the patronage of the Duke de Cadaval, Master of the Horse during the reign of King Jóao V (1706–50).

King Jóao, who had founded the important Alter Real Stud in 1748 from a foundation line of Spanish horses brought over by the Bragança family, was succeeded by his son Don José I in 1770. Both monarchs were ardent horsemen, and since Portugal was now constitutionally separate from Spain, a strong defensive cavalry was required.

With a centuries old tradition of training horses for war, the breeding of Lusitanos enjoyed a great revival in the eighteenth and nineteenth centuries. At the King's instigation, selective breeding based on performance and courage in the manège or the bullring was to take precedence over every other form of equestrian sport. On his accession to the throne, King José's first step towards this end was to create Marialva, Royal Master of the Horse.

[9] An officer of Scottish Jacobite descent who wrote in 1776 that it was sufficient for the troop horse to advance, rein-back, halt, turn, trot and gallop.

[10] The School of Versailles was partly re-established in 1814 under Louis XVIII, but once based on miliary lines, lost its continuity from the past and was disbanded in 1830. Baron d'Abzac was the last Director.

Terra à terra to the right (see Glossary). The Marquess of Marialva demonstrates the exaggerated flexion in the horse's hindlegs which although hard to credit is necessary for the impulsion required for this important battle air. (*From Arte de Cavallaria (author's collection)*)

The Art of Marialva

In the style of La Guérinière, Marialva set out to devise a method which embraced all that was good from the past, but which excluded all that was crude, damaging to the horse's mentality and unnatural to his way of moving. We know little about his early training, but at this time there were close links between the aristocracy of Portugal and that of Austria through intermarriage and diplomatic channels, and it is possible Marialva visited Vienna and may have studied at the Spanish Riding School.

Unlike La Guérinière, he was fortunate enough to come from a wealthy background and from his early days in the royal household, enjoyed immediate access to the horses of the Royal Stud. This afforded him that precious commodity of time and it is well recorded in the Portuguese royal archives how at Alter he was to be seen schooling for up to ten hours daily until the age of seventy-six, often succeeding with a difficult stallion where younger men had failed.

Through a progressive system of exercises, always exhorting his pupils to be content with a very little at a time, Marialva's aim was to achieve lightness in all movements, with the horse always rounded with supple loins and quarters. Contemporary illustrations of his riding, show an almost exaggerated engagement of the hind legs, but we must remember that for the Iberian breeds, this is not difficult.

Marialva laid down a set code of rules for mounted bullfighting which are still used today. These concentrated not only on training technique and a proper procedure for the attack and retreat, but also clarified the chivalrous aspect, where at every turn the bull must be given a fair chance. His refinement of the art is still known today as the Art of Marialva which to the Portuguese is synonymous with the national preoccupation for High School riding.

In the eighteenth century, unlike today, the *cavaleiro* faced a bull with unprotected horns. Yet it was considered the height of disgrace if a horse ever was touched by the bull. Nevertheless accidents occurred. To his eternal sadness, Marialva's son the Count dos Arcos, a respected amateur horseman was killed in 1762 at the small town of Salvaterra de Magos, an ancient Roman site, in the Ribatejo province, which boasts one of Portugal's oldest bullrings, still in use today.

Luz da Liberal e Nobre Arte

Marialva's lasting contribution to modern classical riding is found in the pages of a famous book in which his method is explained by his own *écuyer* Manuel Carlos Andrade. Entitled *Luz da Liberal e Nobre Arte de Cavallaria* and published in 1790 in Lisbon, this impressive volume is divided into 10 *livros* (books) and covers every aspect of horsemanship from ailments to bitting; the section on the senses, anatomy and muscle function of the horse as well as the effects of the rider's seat on the spine are of particular interest. How to use the manège to the full through intricate suppling exercises is explained, and much emphasis is placed on the protocol and courtesies expected of each rider whilst entering that hallowed enclosure.

The equitation section, taking up seven books, covers the schooling aspect of every movement from the pirouette to the ballotades, caprioles and courbettes. A wealth of magnificent copperplate engravings show horse and rider in every attitude from highly collected and elevated for mounted work as well as in-hand between the pillars, to full extension in the gallop. Ninety-three in total, these are mainly full page (modern A4), or double length pullout engravings which depict a platoon of horses working together.

Like La Guérinière, Marialva and Andrade recognised the importance of liberty for the head and neck of the horse when riding out across country. The book emphasises the need for the hunting horse to remain in equal equilibrium, taking a firm contact on the hands whilst still obedient to the legs.

For the collected exercises however, the weight must be transferred to the haunches and the horse should become lighter and lighter on the hand until the reins become as silken threads. To facilitate collection, the use of voltes, half-halts and the shoulder-in and haunches-in on the circle and straight lines is prescribed.

A detailed description of the seat similar in all aspects to that of La Guérinière is given. Similarly, the author warns against too much movement in the seat, and looks always for elegance and quietness.

'. . . The rider should keep his face high, always looking between the ears of the horse whether the horse is going straight or turning. When the horse is bent, the rider must turn the same way so that he continues to look between the ears of the horse . . . The Master should recommend his pupil to keep his shoulders down and to put them backwards, firm and straight, since the shoulders control the movements of the breast, kidneys and waist. The rider should carry his breast forwards, although not exaggerated, and the kidneys [lower back] should also be carried forward since this will achieve the best equilibrium.'

Lightness of hand and leg are essential for the classical horseman. Overall, he urges his reader to understand how everything is connected to everything else, and that unless everything is balanced and in alignment, true security and harmony of posture will not be achieved.

The *Picadeiro Real do Palacio de Belem*

As well as supervising the Royal Stud at Alter, Marialva oversaw High School work within the newly completed Royal Manège in Lisbon. This beautiful building at the Palace of Belem on the banks of the Tagus was designed by an Italian, Giacomo Azzolini, in the neo-classical style, and richly decorated by local craftsmen working under Francisco de Setubal in 1777. With the bitter Peninsular

Pirouette to the right. Note the pivotal foot around which the other three legs must turn. Horse and rider look in the direction of the movement. (*From Arte de Cavallaria (author's collection)*)

Ballotade. The importance of this battle movement is that the horse shows the back of his heels but does not strike out as in the capriole, the most final of the airs. (*From Arte de Cavallaria (author's collection)*)

Wars, riding in the new building never had a chance properly to flourish, and soon the practice of High School returned to the provinces where it is still practised today in private *picadeiros* up and down the land. Today, Belem has become the National Coach Museum, housing a sumptuous world collection of private and state coaches which has become a large tourist attraction. As this book goes to print, we hear that the Portuguese Government has bowed to public pressure promising that the Picadero Real, second only to the Winter Riding School of Vienna in terms of architectural magnificence, should be restored to its original purpose in the near future.

Portugal's last royal Master of the Horse, Mestre Joaquim Goncalves de Miranda, who continued to practise his art even after the reigning King and Crown Prince were assassinated in 1910, was able to pass on the classical ideals of Marialva to a number of pupils. Outside Portugal, the best known of these was Mestre Nuno Oliveira (see Chapter 18) whose colleagues and pupils continue to preserve the Art of Marialva.

Marialva's Stud of 'royal horses', the Alter Lusitanos, continues still at Alter do Chão despite some alarming interruptions during the course of its history and today form the nucleus of breeding for the resurrected Portuguese School of Equestrian Art. Until recently, this classically based School of matched dark bay stallions ridden by unpaid gentlemen riders have practised and exhibited mainly at the Campo Grande and in the outdoor manège of Queluz Palace, Portugal's official royal residence just outside Lisbon. (*See Plate 9.*)

Under the direction of the national *chef d'equipe*, Dr Guilherme Borba, the School has also given outstanding displays of High School riding in France and in England, the latter taking place in 1986 at Osterley Park, Windsor and Goodwood House, near Chichester, their visit chosen to celebrate the historic Treaty of Windsor (1386) marking six hundred years of friendship between the 'oldest allies in the world', Great Britain and Portugal.

Eight horses and riders take part in the School Quadrille which is similar in content to that of Vienna, but marked by the very rich colours of the burnished bay Alters and the eighteenth century frocked vermilion coats of the riders with their tricorn hats trimmed with gold. The airs above the ground, including the courbette and the capriole, both ridden and on the short and long rein, are impressive, as are the exercises between the pillars. Here, the School's most brilliant stallions mark time with most superb cadence in the lightest of piaffes, giving way to the athletic levades at which the Baroque horse of Portugal and Spain excels.

The Art of Marialva, or riding in the classical Baroque manner has also now returned to Spain. This contrasts sharply with the faster, less stately, but dashingly agile *Doma à Vaquerà*[11] which took over in national popularity when Philip of d'Anjou succeeded to the Spanish throne and banned mounted bullfighting from Spanish soil. As many Spanish hidalgos who favoured a more classical approach exiled themselves (and their horses) to Portugal, the *vaquero* style

[11] Literally dressage for the *vaquero* (or cowboy) horse.

with a more common touch, became the national style of the Spanish horseman. Still apparent today at the great horsefairs and shows of Southern Spain, *vaquero* riders practise their own form of specialised 'dressage'. To those who do not understand it, this ancient form of *gineta* riding (see Chapters 2 and 4) may seem reckless and crude, recalling an ancient age of cross-country mounted games with the bull, yet in his way, the *vaquero* rider requires as great a sense of feel and precision with his horse as any modern dressage rider.

Despite their differences, both the classical and the *vaquero* schools of the Iberian Peninsula pride themselves on horses which are easy to collect, light in hand and laterally very supple. The ground was laid for the Andalusian School of Equestrian Art when in 1973 Alvaro Domecq, head of a branch of the famous sherry family set up an important establishment to complement his magnificent stud of Spanish and Hispano-Arab horses. The Portuguese Dr Borba was brought in to school and train horses and riders in the Marialva style of court riding, and today the School gives elegant displays of classical horsemanship on the famous Domecq greys.

In 1982 a magnificent site was constructed for the the School in the grounds of a Spanish Baroque palace at Avenida Duque de Abrantes in the centre of Jerez. With government backing, performances are given weekly in the spring and summer season and the riders wear a distinctively Spanish Goya costume. The School earned the right to call itself 'royal' after a glittering official inauguration in the presence of King Don Juan Carlos and Queen Sofia in 1987. Thus together with the Portuguese School of Equestrian Art it strives to preserve not only the Baroque horse, but the essential ingredients of traditional Court Riding.

Note

Although many dressage establishments in the main body of Europe claim to adhere to the letter of La Guérinière and certain guidelines are incorporated into today's dressage definitions, the overall spirit of the Versailles manège is rarely seen to be the case except at Vienna and Saumur. By contrast, the Art of Marialva is not only practised at the national schools mentioned above, it is generally read, studied and understood by almost every educated rider in the Iberian Peninsula. Thus those precepts of seventeenth and eighteenth century court riding (now lost to most of us) are still generally incorporated into the practical everyday horsemanship of those particular countries.

EIGHT

England and the Duke of Newcastle

It is often said that the development of academic equitation which took place in post-Renaissance Europe was never really given a fair chance to become established under the English. A singular, independent, national character and a love of freedom and open spaces is often quoted as the root cause. It is probably all best summed up by the phrase 'Fog in Channel, Europe isolated.'

There was a time however when the English had embraced a more European way of life and the important groundwork for the art of equitation was laid. High School riding was only abandoned as a way of life at court when Parliament ousted the Catholic monarchy in 1688 when the Old Pretender, son of James II, was finally driven from English shores. The ties the English court had enjoyed with their French and Italian counterparts were thus effectively broken, and with the banished House of Stuart went much of the artistry, the love of extravagant spectacle and even the hitherto court languages of French and Italian.

Nevertheless, one English figure survives above all this change. Indeed it was under the ill-fated Stuarts that England's greatest ever exponent of High School riding, William Cavendish, Duke of Newcastle (1592–1676) made his contribution. His great book, generally known today as *A General System of Horsemanship* was written whilst in exile during the English civil wars from 1642–1652.

Early Court Riding

Long before Newcastle, the tastes of the earlier Tudors and Elizabethans show us that the High School airs were already fashionable, and formed part of the education of the British aristocracy. When Henry VIII ascended the throne in 1509, he enthusiastically embraced music, poetry and the arts. At this time, a number of books were beginning to appear on the craft of venery, and although an ardent follower of hounds, it was Henry's appreciation of beauty which drew him to the work of the manège. In the words of an adviser, Sir Thomas Elyot,[1] in 1531, the art of the manège was 'the most honourable exercise' for kings and princes. Henry installed Robert Alexander, a riding master fresh from the Neapolitan school of Grisone, in the royal household at Hampton Court, the site of one of his three major studs[2] for the breeding of hotblood horses. Henry is given insufficient credit for the fine contribution he made to English breeding. Although not everyone applauded him for raising the height of the average saddle horse, he was one of the first to import extensively, recognising the need to differentiate between horses for hunting, parade and war and accordingly breed selectively for purpose.

The Elizabethans

After Henry, Elizabeth I (1558–1603) was the monarch who actively shared her father's enthusiasm for beautiful horses. It was her Master of the Horse, Robert Dudley, Earl of Leicester

---

[1] See *A History of Horsemanship*.

[2] These were based at Hampton Court, Tutbury Castle in Staffordshire and Malmesbury in Wiltshire. See C.M. Prior's *The Royal Studs of the Sixteenth and Seventeenth Centuries* and *The Royal Horse of Europe*.

PLATE 7

(*above*) This post-revolutionary French painting by Alfred de Dreux (1810–1860) of a Thoroughbred schooled by a groom exemplifies changes at the reinstated (1825) Royal School of Cavalry at Saumur. General Oudinnot had 25 Irish horses with full English tack. (*Courtesy Arthur Ackermann & Sons*)

(*below*) Waloddi Fischerström was equerry at the Swedish Court in 1868, and here demonstrates the the piaffe on his powerful Swedish cavalry horse, ancestor to today's Swedish Warmblood which has proved so successful in modern dressage.

PLATE 8

At Saumur, the airs above the ground, or *les airs reléves*, form an important part of traditional training. Unlike Vienna, mainly Thoroughbred horses are used for these *sauts* or leaps. Here the horse demonstrates the courbette with a lively impulsion and even a certain violence which is much admired. All this, according to the French, merely confirms the true depth of the rider's seat and emphasizes the requirement for *la souple elegance*.

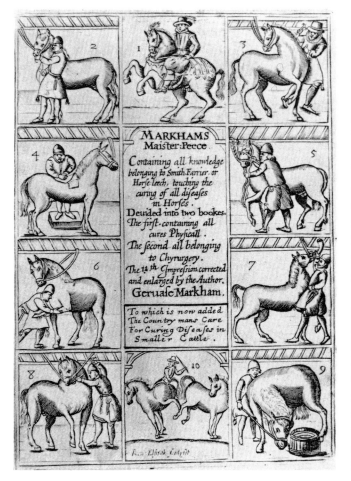

MARKHAMS
Maister-Peece

Containing all knowledge
belonging to Smith Farrier. or
Horse leech, touching the
curing of all diseases
in Horses.
Deuided into two bookes.
The first containing all
cures Physicall.
The second all belonging
to Chyrurgery.
The 11.th Impression corrected
and enlarged by the Author.
Geruase Markham.

To which is now added
The Country mans Care
For Curing Diseases in
Smaller Cattle.

The frontispiece of one of the Englishman Gervase Markham's several books concerning the art of horsemanship. This one, Markham's *Maisterpiece*, appeared as a revised edition in 1688. For that time, Markham was a comparatively enlightened exponent of the manège, although he was soon to be superceded by Newcastle. (*From the Paul Mellon Collection, Upperville, Virginia*)

who brought to London two Italian riding masters, Claudio Corte and Prospero D'Osma. The former's book *Il Cavallerizzo* was dedicated to the Earl; it laid down in a scientific and co-ordinated way the basic principles for preparing the horse in the manège for battle.

By now, Federico Grisone's book had been translated into English, as *The Art of Riding and Breaking Great Horses*, which was incorporated into a book published in 1565 by Thomas Blundeville in Norfolk entitled *Fowre Chiefest Ofyces Belonging to an Horseman*. Amidst the illustrations of cruel bits and spurs, some encouraging signs of finesse began to appear. Blundeville wrote of 'the stroke of the spur', and defined the aids as 'helpes' to assist the horse in his understanding of the rider's requirements.

Like Xenophon, he recognised the importance of a strong back and loins particularly for the collected exercises and there are interesting notes on how to supple and engage the hindquarters by stopping and advancing with impulsion up and down hilly ground. The language of some passages including the section 'How to Ride a Horse before a Prince' is archaically quaint: 'Ride first, fair and loftily towards the Prince to make your reverence; that done, depart with a good round trot towards the farthest end of the career, bearing[3] your rod with the point upward towards your right shoulder . . .' A series of suggested stops and turns to show off the horse to advantage follows to include '. . . entertaining His Highness with the Capriole and Curvette' which should be made with 'a livelier courage.'

This set the scene for a fine display of horsemanship. Blundeville emphasised the necessity for a good seat, horse and rider in harmony. 'See that you do not only sit him [the horse] boldly and without fear, but also conceive with yourself that he and you do make as it were one body. And that you both have but one sense and one will. Accompany him with your body in anticipation of any movement that he maketh, always beholding his head right between his ears.' Later he advises 'keep your thighs and knees close to the saddle, holding your legs straight as you do when on foot.'

This book was followed by similar tomes from John Astley in 1584 who wrote *The Art of Riding*, and Christopher Clifford, a year later, whose *Schoole of Horsemanship* was published in London. Another Englishman concerned with falconry, hunting and all aspects of horsemanship including the work of the manège was Gervase Markham,[4] whose *A Discource of Horseman-*

---

[3] This is still practised in some classical schools where in the old manner the curb reins are still held in one hand.

[4] Famous for allegedly bringing the first Arab stallion (the Markham Arabian) to England.

shippe appeared in 1593. In 1607, the same author produced *Cavalarice* of which the sectional subtitle on equitation reads: 'The Arte and knowledge belonging to the Horse-ryder; how horses are to be handled, ridden, or made perfit, eyther for service [military] or pleasure.' Like Blundeville, Markham also instructs us how to ride before a Prince, and whilst much of his advice seems crude to our modern minds, his books are generally based on practicality and commonsense. Of particular note is the advice on the application of 'helpes' (aids) and 'cherishes' (rewards). 'Now for your Cherishings, they must be used at no time but when your Horse doth well and hath pleased your mind with his cunning and tractableness. Although the time for the same be when he hath finished his Lessons, yet there is a secret pleasing and cherishing of a Horse with the Bridle which must be exercised in the doing of his lessons, and that is the sweetening of his mouth by a little easing of your bridle hand . . . letting it come and go with such unperceiving motion that none but the beast may know it.'

Corrections were fairly mild for those days. The rider must give a 'little check in the mouth' if the horse suffered from 'forgetful passions', the rod was used sparingly. In teaching the rein back it was helpful for the groom to tap the horse on the chest, and only if the horse showed complete disrespect for this was a sound stroke applied. Here, there are none of Grisone's harsh beatings between the eyes, which proves the point that the English have generally respected their horses.

Markham recommended the use of the pillar[5] for suppling. He was also cognisant of the use of voltes and demi-voltes for developing collection and obedience. The terms for the exercises are given in Italian, the various turns including the *Terra Terra, Carragolo, Serpeigiare* (probably a serpentine), and the airs consisting of the *Incavallare* and the *Chambetta*.

Under the Stuarts

By the time of King James I (1603–1625), the Italian influence had permeated the French courts and a contemporary of de la Broue and pupil of Pignatelli, the Chevalier Saint-Antoine came to England as court riding master. His enlightened thinking would pave the way for Thomas de Grey who wrote *The Compleat Horseman and Expert Farrier* in 1639, dedicated to King Charles I (1625–49), followed by England's greatest equestrian master of all time, the Duke of Newcastle. Newcastle's tome, translated into French from the original English text and first published in Antwerp in 1658, far outweighed in detail and importance any book from an English author before or since. Magnificently illustrated with 43 plates of engravings and 50 woodcut diagrams, its early title *Methode et Invention Nouvelle de Dresser les Chevaux*, gave way to the title *A General System of Horsemanship in All Its Branches*[6] when published in English in 1743.

A devoted Royalist, and appointed tutor by Charles I to his young son (later Charles II), Newcastle was a real child of the Renaissance. A man of letters as well as a horseman, he delighted in foreign travel and the arts, and was fluent in Italian, French and Latin. Clearly influenced by the strong links which, as a prominent member of the English Court he was able to enjoy with the rest of Europe in the seventeenth century, the fashionable Baroque mode of life appealed to his character which we know to have been enthusiastic and expansive. He read avidly, he wrote poetry and he claimed to have studied equitation under every great master in Europe.

Born into a family which gave him tremendous power and position, he not only inherited

---

[5] This came to England from the Italian School and was referred to by Markham as a 'post'.

[6] This original edition contains in addition to Newcastle's text, an English translation of Gaspard de Saunier's *La Parfaite Connaissance des Chevaux*.

William Cavendish, 1st Duke of Newcastle, demonstrating the Ballotade on a Spanish horse at Bolsover Castle. Note the somewhat fixed position in the saddle, together with the straighter leg which differs from the later teaching of La Guérinière and Marialva (see previous chapter). (*From the author's collection*)

great riches, he also enjoyed the perfect pastoral setting for his ample stud both at Welbeck Abbey in Nottinghamshire and Bolsover Castle in Derbyshire. An avid importer of foreign horses, we are told his favourite was the Spanish horse, '. . . the lovingest, gentlest horse. . .much more intelligent than even the best Italian horses, and for that reason the easiest dressed.' His book also shows a number of Neapolitans, Barbs and the occasional rare Turk which was taller and more shortcoupled than the Arab.

With all these advantages, Newcastle was able to pursue his chosen science of equitation in a setting and manner which echoed the luxury of the courts of France, Italy, and the Imperial Habsburg states. At Welbeck he built a lavish stable block (now demolished) in addition to existing facilities, and the master craftsman, John Smithson, completed his famous Riding House[7] in 1623 which can still be seen today. A true innovator, Newcastle arrived on the equestrian scene early enough to secure a permanent place in the history of classical equitation.

Yet whilst his name is better known abroad than it has ever been in his own country, this noble duke is still today insufficiently read or appreciated. Too often, critics have allowed his undoubted high opinion of himself to cloud their judgement of his ability, yet Christopher Falkus, the historian, tells us that, 'The Duke of Newcastle was courteous, kindly, optimistic and supremely conscious of the qualities which went to create a gentleman,'[8] and that he never allowed scholarship to stand in the way of manners. Certainly, the celebrated French master, La Guérinière, recognised in Newcastle the quality of greatness, and unstintingly credited him with many of the ideas which were subsequently explored in *Ecole de Cavalerie*. In 1733, he wrote: 'The names of the great riding masters are without doubt connected with the glorious times in riding. Unfortunately, only few left guidelines and gave us their lifework. Of many authors the two I most greatly admire are de la Broue and the Duke of Newcastle. Some

[7] The Riding House today forms the Welbeck library and chapel. The Horseman's Dressing Room still contains however the panelled wall and stone vaulting of Newcastle's time including the Cavendish coat of arms.
[8] Christopher Falkus, *The Life and Times of Charles II*.

French, Italian and German tomes are either too short to be of any help or are written in such a chaotic manner that they stifle the simplicity and truth. Thus, we are conclusively left with only the two authors I have mentioned. I believe in method and correct guidelines. I have therefore explained the most instructive thoughts of both these authors in my book.'

Guérinière then proceeded to lay down the teachings of La Broue and Newcastle in a more understandable and less repetitive form. Unfortunately, much of this has largely been overlooked so that nowadays La Guérinière takes all the credit for work which he himself acknowledged to be that of Newcastle.

Tragically, even in England there are thousands of riders who have never heard of Newcastle, and millions who have never read even a fragment of his works. Perhaps this reflects the British habit of being unable to recognise genius from within their own ranks.

A Man at odds with his Countrymen

Even in his own lifetime, Newcastle was fully aware of the growing reticence of Englishmen towards the art of High School riding. The subtitle of his book clarifies this point: 'A Science peculiarly necessary throughout all Europe, and which has hitherto been so much neglected, or discouraged in England, that young Gentlemen have been obliged to have recourse to foreign Nations for that Part of Their Education.' Even Blundeville had begun to question the point of court riding and had asked drily who needed a horse which 'falls a-hopping and dancing up and down in one place?'

With the shift towards Puritanical ideas which would find a champion in Oliver Cromwell, the new middle classes of England were unimpressed by the practices of court riding and were moving swiftly in other directions. Despite the Restoration in 1660, social change ensured that a rift remained between the aristocrats of the manège and those hard-riding men who galloped their horses across country. Newcastle was not unaware of the critics. Passages from his book however, did little to help and much to alienate: '. . . I presume those great wits [the sneering gentlemen] will give Kings, Princes and persons of quality leave to love pleasure horses, as being an exercise that is very noble, and one which makes them appear most graceful when they show themselves to their subjects . . .'

Setting aside his personal conceit, Newcastle's work is thorough and thoughtful. A bold outdoor rider, he used the confined space and the advanced exercises of the manège to concentrate the horse's mind, to supple him and to make him utterly obedient in the field. Both Newcastle and his later French contemporary, La Guérinière, advocated galloping and jumping the warhorse, as did the earlier de la Broue. The advantage of teaching the school airs first was this: that the horse would be '. . . much fitter for galloping, trotting, wheeling or anything else which is necessary.' Furthermore, '. . . curvettes and other airs settle a horse mightily upon the hand, make him light in front and put him on his haunches which are all useful especially for a man in armour.'

Civil War

Because of his ardent royalist sympathies, the noble Duke lost Welbeck Abbey and was forced to flee to the Continent when Civil War broke out in England. Undeterred, he opened his own riding school while in exile in Antwerp and attracted the nobility of Europe. One of his pupils, Prince Rupert, nephew of Charles I, was to prove a brilliant crosscountry rider simply because he followed the guidelines laid down by this Master. On return to England he fought valiantly as a Cavalier against the Roundheads, making his charges at the gallop

A plate from *The Anatomy of a Horse* published in 1693 by Andrew Snape. This engraving was designed to explain to the reader the position and function of the muscles in the horse's chest and neck, important to understand for the teaching of flexions and achieving suppleness of the forehand. (*From the Paul Mellon Collection, Upperville, Virginia*)

and confounding the enemy by sailing over hedges and ditches with the greatest of ease. Out of many bloody confrontations, Rupert only lost one battle, proving Newcastle's point that a well-dressed horse was essential to cavalry at that time.

Newcastle's 'New Method'

Since Newcastle is so often quoted out of context and his respect for the horse totally disregarded, let us now concentrate on those aspects of his book which not only show him in a more accurate light, but are still relevant for horsemen and women today.

Primarily the Duke was a man who disliked force and whenever possible sought a solution based on a gentle, psychological approach. For him a horse was not born good or bad. Bad horses, or 'jades' were the result of bad handling: 'It is altogether the ignorance of the horseman that makes jades, and not nature; wherefore if the horseman studies nature, and the dispositions of his horses, he would know better how to appropriate them to the uses for which they were created, and consequently they would become good horses.'

On Difficult Horses and Vice

Unlike the early Italians, he saw the futility of force even with the most difficult animals. Since vice was the result of man's bad training, one merely had to start from the beginning again. 'I have never yet seen that force and passion have prevailed the least upon a horse . . . if the rider begins to beat and spur, the horse will resist; it is not the beast which is vanquished, but the man, who is the greater brute of the two.' His advice for dealing with a runaway horse is sound. 'One must not give a rough bit to a passionate runaway horse, for that makes him worse and his mouth the harder. Such a horse should never be spur'd . . . the spur indeed but aguments his vice.' Instead he recommended working the horse forward and not asking for halts for a long time, but '. . . when you do, let it be very gently, and by degrees upon a slow walk, and win him in this manner. By which you will see that is an excellent thing to have a gentle hand (it is one of the greatest secrets we have in managing horse) even so sometimes to let it be quite slack.' To this he added that the clever horseman's contact would be 'light as a feather,' whilst still securing the position of the horse's head with firmness.

Many have attacked Newcastle for the use of the drawrein and for the fact that in many of his illustrations the horse's neck looks contorted. It is possible indeed that his suppling methods were carried too far, yet he showed great dislike of other gadgets and condemned over-use of the pillars, since he believed them to be very punishing for the horse. What is commendable is his understanding of working the horse freely forward, always asking for a little more impulsion than he would normally give until that impulsion becomes natural and immediate.

On Grisone

Grisone's constant use of reinbacks and halts to put the horse on the haunches are condemned. Newcastle abhorred the cruel nosebands of the Italian school; he insisted that the cavesson should be made of soft, doublesided leather, and took immense trouble with the fitting of his bits, respecting the delicate skin at the bars of the mouth, '. . . for I would not hurt his mouth nor his nose nor anything else about him if I could help it.' Gadgets such as the martingale were also frowned upon, for when taken away, 'the horse is not better than before'.

The Shoulder-in

Newcastle's contribution to work on the shoulder-in[9] has been much underrated. We are often told that he was only interested in suppling and freeing the shoulders. What he said was that it was more difficult to supple the shoulders correctly than the haunches, but he maintained always that the rider 'must give an entire ply to his [the horse's] whole body from the nose to the tail'. He taught that the rein and leg of the same side worked the shoulders, i.e., bending the horse around the inside leg; whereas the rein and opposite leg worked the croup. In his book there are many exercises on the volte for suppling the quarters and careful diagrams illustrate the footfalls. From these, we can determine it was Newcastle who invented the use of the shoulder-in on the circle and La Guérinière who developed it on straight lines.

Newcastle recognised also that true collection could only be achieved when the horse's hind legs stepped well underneath the body and worked close together.

The Seat

Newcastle was a stickler for position. He insisted that the rider remained as quiet in the saddle as possible although his saddles with their padded kneerolls still encouraged a somewhat fixed straight leg. Newcastle chides the rider who sits only upon the buttocks 'though most people think they were made by nature' to do this, recommending the rider to sit 'upon the twist'[10] . . . leaving a hand's breadth between his backside and the arch of the saddle . . .'

He wrote of the use of the thigh aids 'which is the most gentle aid you can use' and insisted that both knees and thighs be turned inwards towards the saddle, keeping them as close as if they were *glued to the saddle . . .*', an expression still used in countless dressage books today. Further on in the same passage, he writes: 'The rider's breast ought to be in some measure advanced, his countenance pleasant and gay . . .' an aspect of instruction too often omitted today. 'Moreover I venture to affirm, that he who does not sit genteely upon a horse, will never be a good horseman.'

Happiness of the Horse

Contrary to popular thinking about Newcastle, the overuse of collection was not advocated. Newcastle was a hundred years ahead of his time by advocating more freedom for the horse. 'To keep a horse in perpetual subjection and slavery, makes him either desperately or stupidly restive. Divert him therefore sometimes, give him liberty, riding him large upon a piste in walk, trot and gallop, finishing quietly, and you will find good will result from it.'

Generally rejected by his fellow countrymen as being too early in the history of equitation seriously to count, Newcastle's work is still appreciated abroad. If we set aside the flowery and self-adulatory language of the seventeenth century, the writing is generally direct and easily understood. According to the French chevalier, von Solleysel, who translated Newcastle's

[9] Some time after I completed this chapter I was heartened to find the following quote from Vladimir Littauer in *Commonsense Horsemanship* (revised edition), New York 1976: 'The invention of shoulder-in is usually erroneously attributed to . . . de la Guérinière . . . But in essence it was described a good 80 years earlier by an Englishman, Charles Cavendish, Duke of Newcastle.'

[10] Medieval English term for fork or crotch.

An interior view of the Duke of Newcastle's indoor manège at Bolsover, measuring 30m by 10m, sufficient space for the High School work of the time.

book into French, 'The Duke of Newcastle . . . may quite justly be called the pre-eminent horseman of his time.'

After the Restoration

Whilst Newcastle wrote his book, proud and productive in exile, Englishmen at home were pursuing a form of riding which could not be further removed from the aims of those Royalist cavaliers. England was far ahead of the continent in developing a free society not bound by court etiquette and regal favour. Since the Wars of the Roses had diluted the powers of the great noble families, a new breed of landed gentleman had appeared. Largely unpolitical, they enjoyed the healthy pursuits of the countryside in a way which their continental cousins, bound into a rigid class system, had never been able to explore. Hunting and racing became the rage. At the same time, by happy coincidence, the introduction of Arab blood was helping to create a completely different type of horse from the former popular highstepping animals of Spanish or Neapolitan descent. The English Thoroughbred had appeared on the equestrian scene.

With the Thoroughbred came the snaffle bit. This light, forward-going horse had no need of the curb; collection was obsolete and irrelevant to riding across country – argued this new breed of ardent sportsmen. For those whose one ambition was to cover as much ground, with or without obstacles, in as fast a time as taking a line would allow, this was arguably logical. Stag hunting, once the sport of kings, now gave way to hunting the hare, and later the fox. As the great forests of England were being cut down to provide timber for a growing navy, the land was opened up for agricultural and sporting purposes. Charles II, a real king of the people, may have ridden in the manège under his mentor Newcastle with the lightest of hands, but his real love was galloping across Newmarket Heath on a sleek coursing horse which extended itself close to the ground – the antithesis of the proud, prancing horses of the manège.

To understand the way in which modern riding has evolved and particularly how this has affected dressage, we must now leave the halls of academic equitation and appreciate what was happening elsewhere.

NINE

A Time of Change and of Controversy

If it was the English who led the way for a complete revolution in riding style all over the world, it was the powerful influence of the Arab and Turkish horse from the orient which made this possible. Without the Arab hotblood, that dramatic genetic transformation from the plump, rounded lines of the Van Dyck, Velasquez and Wootton horses to the sleek, streamlined equine elegance of the paintings of Stubbs, the Herring family (father and son) and Munnings, would not have taken place.

The evolution of the English Thoroughbred with its three foundation sires, the Darley Arabian, Godolphin Barb and Byerley Turk,[1] may have been an accident of fate, but to the racing and hunting world, it was the *coup de grace* to the bad old days of expensive importation. Now the hustling over borders, the bribes on a foreign quayside and the often humiliating knowledge that only foreign was best, could be forgotten. English nobility and commoner alike were now able to enjoy their own hotblood. National breeding allowed small provincial studs to exist alongside those of the great country houses. All that mattered was the propagation of a race of stamina and great speed which bred true. Aesthetically beautiful with fine limbs and delicate head, sensitive, exciting to ride, hotheaded and brave, the Thoroughbred had come to stay.

Performance on the track and across country led to selective breeding. Early names like Flying Childers, Eclipse and Gimcrack became legendary and soon there was an established hierarchy of breeders although the first volume of the *General Stud Book* did not appear until 1791. Horses which did not win races became relatively cheap, and by the mid eighteenth century, every country squire had his English hunter and the first English Thoroughbreds were established in America.[2]

Anglomania

With the Thoroughbred came a complete change of riding style. Academic study had no place in the lives of most sporting gentlemen, although there were still a number of classical devotees particularly amongst those at court or who travelled abroad. Nonetheless, former principles of balance, collection and control were happily abandoned by the majority, seen widely as counterproductive to goals of speed and freedom.

In England, writers such as Philip Astley (born in 1742) of circus fame,[3] who also served in the 15th Light Dragoons and was as bold a rider as any, wrote in his *System of Equestrian Education* that there was a real need to return to a proper study of riding technique since 'the many fatal accidents which daily happen, sufficiently prove the necessity of acquiring some knowledge of equestrian education, of which a pliability and command of the body on horseback, certainly forms a most essential part.' He went on to comment with obvious firsthand

[1] See *The Royal Horse of Europe.*

[2] The most famous early horses were Bull Rock, son of the Darley Arabian, arriving in the 1730s and Jason, grandson of Godolphin Barb, in the 1750s.

[3] His manège was in the London borough of Lambeth, but he performed all over England and was renowned as an exhibition High School rider.

Part of the index from Philip Astley's *System of Equestrian Education*. Amongst the technical terms, special attention is drawn to enlightened entries such as 'Pears or apples, by way of reward . . .'; 'Quarrelling with horses, reprobated . . .'; 'Rewards . . .'; 'Sounds, necessary to direct the horse in obedience . . .'. An interesting indication of thinking at that time. (*From the author's collection*)

experience on the many gentlemen who, having 'purchased Commissions in the Cavalry, merely because they can ride a fox chase or a horse race . . .' soon discover, after a little active service in the field, 'the necessity of being taught to ride on pure scientific principles and under able professors. Certainly the more requisite in a country so much admired by all Europe for its breed of excellent horses . . .'

Across the water, Frenchmen shook their heads and called this resistance to discipline *Anglomania*, but they also could find no fault with the English horse. La Guérinière admitted '. . . English horses more than any other European have this quality. . .[they] are often out for a whole day without being unbridled, and always they are on the tail of the hounds in their foxhunting, jumping hedges and ditches . . .'

Captain L. Picard of the French cavalry remarked in his *Origines de L'Ecole de Cavalerie*, 'The English school made a complete revolution in the equestrian world. It founded speed racing and regenerated the breeds of horses. . .' And a modern writer, Etienne Saurel remarked in his *Histoire de l'Equitation* (1971), 'Aside from Newcastle, equestrian art owes little to England, but due to her creation of the Thoroughbred, king of horses, breeding and equestrian sport owe her their very essence.'

It is extraordinary how historical events often appear to complement each other to bring about a major change. Whilst a powerful middle class was growing up in England, whilst the English Thoroughbred was evolving, whilst an English king[4] was promoting the sport of racing, a major act by the British Parliament known as the Enclosures Acts had transferred to private ownership vast tracts of common land which previously had been used by mediaeval serfs for grazing sheep and cattle. This resulted in the erection of stout fences and walls, the planting of hedges and the digging of ditches which made excellent hunting obstacles.

Books which previously had dealt almost exclusively with the manège now promoted riding across country. Early hunting books included *The Hunter* by Gerard Langbaine (1685), *The Gentleman's Recreation* by Nicholas Cox (1686) and a popular title for a number of eighteenth century books, *The Compleat Sportsman*,[5] replaced in popularity the theme of a byegone age, namely *The Compleat Horseman*.

Prior to the Restoration, the only jumps known had been the leaps and airs of the High School. Now, young gentlemen of fashion took to jumping across country with zest and enthusiasm as though they had been doing it for centuries. Priding themselves on a lack of formal

[4] Charles II, known to his people as 'Father of the Turf'.

[5] The title was used by Giles Jacob in 1718, Thomas Fairfax in 1760, followed by *The British Sportsman* by William Osbaldiston in 1792 and by Samuel Howitt in 1800.

Before the Start, a nineteenth century engraving by Samuel Alken. With the English Thoroughbred horse came a complete change of riding style, the 'backward seat', which, originating in the race track, then permeated the sports of hunting and chasing until it influenced almost every aspect of British riding life.

riding style compensated by their own daring, natural ability and the excellence of their horses, the proof of a good day out with hounds for the average hunting man was to chase at breakneck speed over every manner of obstacle in any country and close the day with himself and the horse caked in a profuse lather of sweat and mud.

The Hunting Seat

Those more academic horsemen who were able to see the value of classical training prior to riding across country, were mostly disregarded or ignored in England. The balanced, classical seat of the manège so necessary for achieving collection, was fast becoming outdated. Saddles changed drastically to complement a new position; the English hunting saddle was lengthened in the seat to accomodate a shortened stirrup which afforded riders an easy passenger seat when walking or standing at a cover, but gave upward mobility for the faster gaits.

The thinking behind the new hunting saddle was basically good. In 1805, John Adams, an advocate first and foremost of manège riding, recognised that for hunting a completely different balance was required. Long before Caprilli made equestrian history by introducing the forward seat to the world, Adams was advocating a mobile forward approach in the English hunting field. In his book *An Analysis of Horsemanship*, he wrote: 'The hunting seat is that of riding in the stirrups. The intention of this style of riding is to relieve yourself from that friction and heat which the bottom would receive from such a strong and continued gallop if seated close down on the saddle.' Frank words which signified, more importantly of course, that the horse's back would also be relieved from the bumping effect of a seat which struggled to remain in contact with the saddle.

Unfortunately for the horse, at this stage the forward seat prescribed by Adams never really

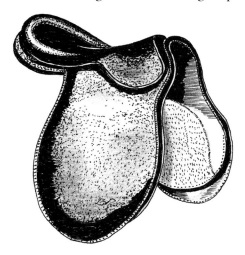

A nineteenth-century hunting saddle allowing some knee support. Whilst some hunting saddles of the period were excellent in design, others were webbed up in such a way that the twist was high and narrow, pinching the rider uncomfortably in front. This promoted a backward seat which pushed the rider towards the loins and necessitated too much dependence on the stirrups and reins or support.

Going to Cover by Samuel Howitt (1756–1822). This engraving epitomises the poor posture of those Englishmen whose riding style so aggravated writers like Astley and Adams and invited the derision of Continental riders who dubbed it *Anglomania*.

caught on. More often than not the new English saddle encouraged inexperienced or unathletic riders to wedge themselves against the cantle, too close to the horse's loins. Sporting prints of the period show hunting gentlemen leaning backward rather than forwards, drawing support from the reins, their feet rammed home in the stirrups, and Jove help you if you broke a leather! Years later, Colonel M. F. McTaggart described this as 'the old gentleman's seat – in which the body was back and the feet forward at the canter . . . however pleasurable to the rider, it is very much the reverse to the horse. It is in fact a travesty of riding, it is not horsemanship.'

Some attempt to adopt a forward posture was made, however, when people began to 'post' or rise to the trot. The energetic lengthened strides of the Thoroughbred proved hard to sit to, so out of self-preservation, riders learned to rise, and this in turn encouraged the horse to a freer, faster gait. As a result the slow collected trot hitherto used for riding out virtually disappeared and horses were increasingly ridden on the forehand. The word 'post' probably comes to us from the appearance of post-chaises around the mid- eighteenth century, when those employed as post-boys rode in the new forward style. This word is little used today in England, but is still popular in North America where it was introduced by the English settlers.

These various modifications of style all added to the Continentals' viewpoint that the English now mimicked their servants. Even John Adams, was forced to write despairingly: '. . . they [his fellow countrymen] ridiculed the idea of learning to ride at a school, but preserved, or sought to copy, a hunting groom, or racing jockey.' This condemnation was echoed by Colonel Dodge in nineteenth-century America who wrote that there were few English cross-country riders of that time who could 'hold a candle' to the natural horsemanship of the American cowboy.

The majority of the English however seemed blithely happy with their new style. Ceremony and protocol had vanished with Catholicism and with the Hanoverian kings came a puritanical love of the great outdoors. The day was not far off before it would be quite normal to see the Prince of Wales riding neck and neck across a stubble field alongside the local butcher; even acceptable for the two to arrange a wager as to whose horse would clear the next bullfinch.

The Last of the Old School

Nevertheless, the arguments on style continued for the classical school in England was not yet dead. Although diminished in importance and number, there remained those masters of

Sir Charles Blunt Boar Hunting by James Ward RA (1769–1859). This surprisingly modern illustration shows that some riders had discovered the forward seat for themselves long before Caprilli, but they were greatly outnumbered by those who refused to take their weight off the horse's back when riding across country.

the manège who argued that a gentleman's horse should be fully schooled before he was taken hunting. Richard Berenger, Gentleman of the Horse to George III translated Bourgelat's great tome on Newcastle in 1754 and then produced his own, *A History and Art of Horsemanship*, in 1771, in which he repeated almost word for word La Guerinière's definition of the classical seat. This, as we have seen, was the complete antithesis of the hunting seat.

In 1778, Berenger's contemporary, Henry Herbert, 10th Earl of Pembroke[6] (*see Plate 6*) wrote *Military Equitation* which dealt with the more difficult airs of the High School as well as crosscountry riding and jumping. Like Adams, he believed the secret of all successful riding was a feeling for the correct balance, and wrote 'No man can be either well or firmly seated on horseback unless he be master of the balance of his body.' The recruit must be 'seated neither forwards, nor very backwards, but with the breast pushed out a little, and the lower part of the body likewise a little forwards; the thighs and legs turning in without constraint, and the feet in a straight line, neither turned in or out. By this position, the natural weight of the thighs has a proper and sufficient pressure of itself, the legs are in readiness to act . . . they must hang down easy and naturally, and be so placed as not to be wriggling about. . . but always near them [the horse's sides] in case they should be wanted . . .' – a description which can hardly be faulted today.

He made the wise remark that 'A raw man is much easier taught to do well than one who has learnt ever so long on bad principles for it is much more difficult to undo than to do, and the same in respect to horses.'

Whilst he recommended the snaffle bit for novices, it was important that 'men use their snaffles delicately; otherwise, as a snaffle has not the power, which a [full] bridle has upon a horse's mouth, they will use themselves to take such liberties with it, as will quite spoil their hands and teach the horses to pull, be dead in hand, and quite upon their shoulders, entirely deprived of good action.'

Like Berenger, Pembroke wrote of the three trots, first explored by Bourgelat in his *Nouveau Newcastle*, and these are described as the extended, the supple, and the even, which in today's terms may be defined as medium, collected (with suspension) and working. It is again generally forgotten that these differentials of gait were understood in England at this time, and Pembroke regretted that less and less cavalry horses were first schooled in the manège to improve and establish the nuances of gait.

A man of great practicality, he wrote that *epaule en dedans* (shoulder in) was 'the very touchstone in horsemanship, both for man and horse' but whilst useful for suppling, it must never ever be practised in the field. Chapter 7 of his *Military Equitation* contains some evocative and rather moving subtitles which read: 'The method of teaching horses to stand fire, noises, alarms, fights, etc., of preventing their lying down in the water . . . to stand quiet to be shot off from

[6] His home, Wilton House, near Salisbury, houses the famous Riding School collection of gouache pictures by von Eisenberg (see Chapter 5).

. . . to go over rough and bad ground . . . to leap hedges, gates, ditches etc., standing and flying . . . to disregard dead horses . . . to swim, etc.'

By the turn of the eighteenth century, however, army commanders throughout Europe were rejecting all High School work as being too time-consuming. Captain Robert Hinde recommended in his *Discipline of the Light Horse* (1778) that it was sufficient merely for every soldier to be taught to turn, rein-back, canter serpentines and wheel with ease. This was understandable with so many raw recruits being enlisted into the army, but the aspect of riding

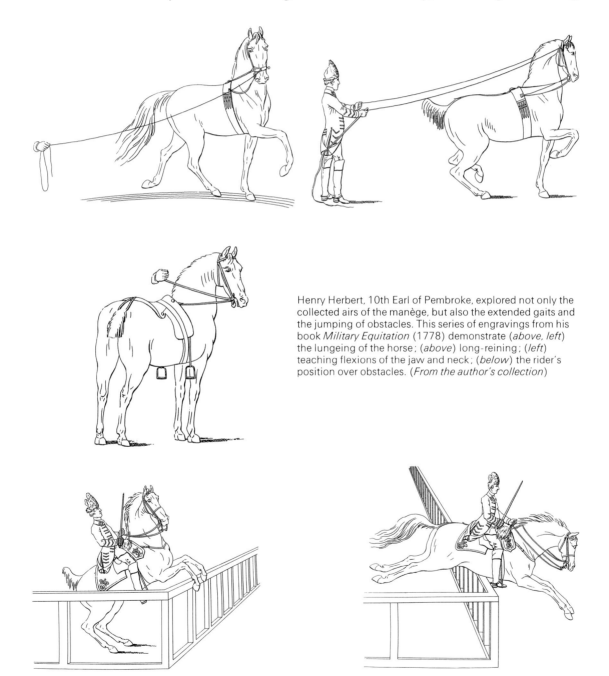

Henry Herbert, 10th Earl of Pembroke, explored not only the collected airs of the manège, but also the extended gaits and the jumping of obstacles. This series of engravings from his book *Military Equitation* (1778) demonstrate (*above, left*) the lungeing of the horse; (*above*) long-reining; (*left*) teaching flexions of the jaw and neck; (*below*) the rider's position over obstacles. (*From the author's collection*)

which was totally neglected, unlike Europe, was how to acquire a good seat. From now on it seemed that the hunting seat was the established seat of the English army.

By the nineteenth century, only those scholars who had had the benefit of active service or training abroad, raised a lone voice from time to time. Colonel J. G. Peters, an expert cavalryman and Commander in Chief to the British Forces just prior to the publication of his book *The Art of Horsemanship* (1835) warned, 'The more the rider lays back his body from the above lines [i.e. the perpendicular] of his proper balance, the more he is forced to seek strange aids to support himself by the force of his knees, or the strength of his hand, on the pull against the horse's mouth . . . which will take away all grace, ease and elegance.'

F. Dwyer, who wrote and published *Seats, Saddles, Bits and Bitting* in 1869, returned to England inspired by the work he had seen in Vienna but depressed by what existed at home. He warned against the hunting saddle which caused so many riders 'to sit almost on the loins of their horses, where they seriously impede the action of the propellers and are then obliged to throw the body forward in the most inconvenient and unsightly manner.' His particular argument, a most sound one, was based on the fact that the stirrup leathers of the English saddle were generally slung too far forward from the lowest point of the seat. This prevented the rider ever being able to sit over his stirrups and use 'the elasticity of the legs . . .' since '. . . the equilibrium is never permanently in the right place.'

Dwyer advanced his argument by writing that no amount of teaching would help a man attain a quiet, balanced seat if he had not the right tools, therefore the real responsiblity lay with the saddler and not the instructor. (This is as relevant today as it was then.) For precision purposes, particularly for the military rider, '. . . the stirrups must be placed in the centre of the saddle directly under the rider's seat; there is no alternative.' With such a seat, there would be greater control and many less broken down horses.

Even future sporting journalists like Nimrod would see the limitations of the English style. In a series of articles written for *Horse and Hound* in 1893, he warned that the short stirrups of the English hunting seat placed the rider too far back, even although this seat had originally been designed to help the horse. McTaggart, whom we will meet again in Chapter 14, wrote: '. . . the shorter the stirrup, the more it throws back the weight on to the horse's loins at the walk and stand, and the more cramped the rider becomes.'

Yet such was the rage for hacking and hunting in the eighteenth and nineteenth centuries that there existed no alternative seat. How sad for British horsemen that more notice had not been paid to Newcastle, Berenger, Astley, Pembroke, Adams, Peters, Dwyer and others. Their influence would not have detracted from the crosscountry seat; rather it would have given riders a stable start from which they could later diversify for whatever purpose. For dressage riders of the twentieth century it would also have given some form of continuity from the past.

Abroad, the notoriety of the English seat grew apace. This often led to unfair comments about English horses. In comparing these to the Spanish, Italian and Hanoverian horses, even Berenger had written: 'the English horses are accused, and not unjustly, of being obstinate and uncomplying in their tempers, dogged and sullen, of having stiff and inactive shoulders and wanting suppleness in their limbs which defects make their motions constrained, occasion them to go near the ground, and render them unfit for the manège.' For this he completely blamed the rider's seat.

Picard, of whom we have spoken before, whilst admiring English horses complains that although the British once had great masters and a method of schooling, it had disappeared.

These illustrations from the English master Philip Astley's book demonstrate movements which are generaly only associated with the Continental School. Here we see a series showing how to ride (*above*) the capriole, (*above, right*) the pirouette, and (*right*) the piaffe. (*From the author's collection*)

'A very developed taste for horses exists in this country,' he writes, extolling the enthusiasm and love for horses of the British, but he goes on '... as to equestrian principles, they have completely disappeared. Horsemen have an incontestable boldness but no method.'

France and Germany

As we have seen, change had also taken place in Europe as Prussian cavalry leaders such as Seydlitz (see Chapter 5) prepared their young recruits outside in the field, having neither the time or the space for work indoors. 'One who cannot gallop for a long time is useless as a rider!' was one of Frederick the Great's favourite maxims. This wisdom had been proved before the eyes of all Europe on 5 November 1757 at Rossbach when 38 Prussian squadrons charged at the gallop, 2000 swords drawn and quivering, as Seydlitz' cavalry broke like lightening through the French lines and claimed a huge victory.

With the emphasis now on speed and extension, much of the artistry and finesse was lost, but the Continentals never lost their basic seat. Generally, the military saddle – unlike the English hunting saddle – did not disturb the balance of the rider, so the rudiments of the central, upright seat were still taught and valued. Years on, far into the twentieth century English people still comment in amazed admiration at the seats of the Continentals.

It was the Napoleonic Wars which struck the final death-knell for the art of the manège as a way of life for the average European. Even in France, the home of classical riding, there was no place for the courtesies of the manège amongst Bonaparte's egalitarian revolutionaries. One aristocratic *écuyer* who had not yet flown the country, was the Marquis de la Bigne from the School of Versailles. Desperate to save the royal manège horses, he persuaded the authorities to let him establish a national school of equitation. In 1798 this became *Ecole d'Instruction des Troupes à Cheval* (School of Instruction of Mounted Troops), but the men or *piqueurs* who ran it had large ideas and little understanding. Within a decade, suddenly and shockingly, French equitation suffered a complete breakdown. Those who could have saved it were either in exile or guillotined; many horses suffered as a result. According to the great French general, Murat, French cavalry could only 'walk on the march' and at best 'trot in the presence of the enemy'.

England of course had already rejected classical training, but her people had always been noted for their love and care of the animal, so in other ways hunting was a good preparation for campaigning across Europe. At least her horses were fit. Not everyone agreed however with their slapdash style, including Wellington,[7] brought up in the classical style, who remarked that the French cavalry was 'more manageable and useful than the English, because it is always kept in hand and may be stopped at a word of command.' From the other side came the remark from the French General Excelmann who pronounced, 'Your horses are the finest in the world . . . The great deficiency is in your officers – who seem to be impressed by the conviction that they can dash or ride over everything, as if the art of war were precisely the same as the art of foxhunting!'

With the rough and tumble, the lack of adequate training, and so many unbalanced riders on unbalanced horses, it became increasingly clear by the end of the wars that some form of organised cavalry training must be reintroduced, however simplified. The toll on horses and men had been horrendous, too often because of a lack of agility in the field, but too often also because of unsoundnesses during the march. This was blamed on saddlery, unbalanced equipment and sloppy riding. It was time to look again to the discipline of the past.

A New Dawning

With the coming of peace therefore, there was almost a second Renaissance in classical riding, particularly in France and to a lesser extent Germany. Figures from exile reappeared; old masters such as D'Auvergne and d'Abzac left a number of pupils, and names like Baucher, d'Aure, Fillis, von Holbein, Hohenloe, Steinbrecht, Plinzner, Raabe, Faverot de Kerbrech, Lenoble du Teil, Guerin, Gerhardt, L'Hotte, Saint-Phalle and Beudant came to the fore. The majority of their ideals were based on former principles from the School of Versailles, which had been maintained throughout this time at Vienna, but now there were certain modern interpretations. Since horses themselves had changed dramatically with the coming of the Thoroughbred, these modifications were probably necessary and to be expected.

Now that the chain of continuity had been broken, it was inevitable that strong arguments would break out between the more prominent figures all jockeying for recognition in a time when the economy of the countries concerned could no longer support their work unless they were attached to a military establishment.

One of the most interesting of these controversies which resulted in huge personal rivalry was the on-going clash between François Baucher and the Count d'Aure, whose methods we will come to in the next chapter. At the same time, an important Englishman, James Fillis, was to break away from the by now established English sporting seat and return to the old principles of the classical school.

---

[7] He attended the manège at Angers as a young man.

Just at a time when it seemed as though the different prerequisites of equestrianism would finally settle themselves down into two distinct categories – that of manège riding or dressage according to classical principles and that of sporting riding across country, along came the Italian Caprilli who caused yet another revolution, this time in the twentieth century. The Caprilli Revolution was to render enormous good to sporting riding. Today's hunting men and women have all benefitted by being balanced and at one with their horses as they take their weight off the horse's back and stream over the still remarkably beautiful hunting country of the Shires in England or Virginia and Kentucky in the United States. Yet vicariously, the Caprilli Revolution hit at the very heart of schooling and training for dressage in much the same way as hunting had done two centuries earlier. It therefore cannot be disregarded in this our story of classical riding.

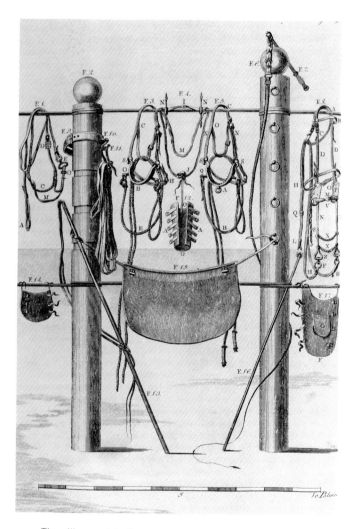

The pillars and the horseman's tools from the work in hand from the eighteenth century.

TEN

French Brilliance at Saumur and the Contribution of Baucher

The famous French cavalry school of Saumur had been founded in 1771 by the Duc de Choiseul, the French Minister of War, on a site once used by Roman mounted legions. Severely disrupted by the French Revolution, work was not seriously re-established until 1814 under the royal edict of Louis XVIII. Its revival brought many talented figures to the fore, pupils either of the *ançien régime* or of the military d'Auvergne. One of the latter was the Marquis de Chabannes and his protegé M. Rousselet who became renowned commandants, but there was a continual power struggle between adherents faithful in every detail to Versailles and those who looked towards the future. One of the most influential chief instructors (from 1847–1855) who represented the new breed of French *écuyer* was the Count d'Aure.

The Count D'Aure (1799–1863)

In the history of dressage d'Aure, who was promoting the relatively new idea of extended gaits more suited to outdoor schooling, is often best remembered for his vehement quarrels with a rival, François Baucher (1796–1873), who was only interested in collected work. When a coveted instructional position at Saumur was almost within Baucher's grasp under the patronage of the Duc d'Orleans[1] and the support of Commandant de Novital, the progressive d'Aure ensured its denial. Thus Baucher was left out in the cold, whilst d'Aure reigned supreme until his resignation in 1857.

It is curious that d'Aure the aristocrat should seek to free French equitation from the restrictions of court etiquette whilst Baucher, who came from humble origins, nostalgically yearned after virtuosity and ceremony. D'Aure was a realist however and surprised everyone at Saumur by being the first to recognise and broadcast unashamedly that riding as practised at Versailles could never be the same again. Freed of traditional values, he wanted the horse to be ridden 'as Nature had made him'. This was summed up as: 'Breaking a horse to obedience, appropriating his means to our necessities, and conserving and developing the qualities inherent in him.'

In his *Traite d'Equitation* (1834) d'Aure explained the new attitude to riding: 'When the revolution came, equitation suffered cruelly; of all the arts it was the one to suffer the most. Its sanctuary at Versailles, supported by royal munificence, disappeared with royalty. The other schools fell away also and our horsemen became exiles or found refuge in military camps.' Recognising that there was no longer the time to educate new riders and that very few possessed the mental application or sensitivity to be taught in the old manner, he continued: 'Riding at this period, consisted with few exceptions in permitting horses to go freely . . . the reins floating . . . since those riders had neither the time nor the ability to supple their horses or to put them on their haunches, horses were left to themselves to a considerable extent, and remained in balance as well as they could.'

---

[1] Who died in an accident at the very time Baucher needed him most, i.e., after a number of successful experiments with officers' horses had established Baucher's credibility as a trainer at Saumur.

Since he neither wanted nor felt able to put the clock back, d'Aure set out to provide cavalrymen with a new method which would allow the horse to go freely forward, but with a rudimentary set of principles to eliminate stiffness, crookedness and irregularity of gait. He concentrated on achieving rhythm, allowing the horse to move *d'une seule piece* (like a ship) and his pupils were taught how to shorten or lengthen the stride to balance the horse over difficult terrain. Conducted outside, these lessons incorporated jumping natural obstacles, and this led to a complete departure from collected work. D'Aure's contribution to modern dressage was the definition of the working trot (unofficially practised as the *trot anglaise* although never on full military exercise) His introduction of the extended trot (probably more of a medium trot at that time) led to the extravagant gait which now tends to dominate the competition world. He pointed out however that true rhythm in the full trot can only be developed on straight lines and where 'one is certain of continuing on the same track for a given length of time' (as seen in test riding today).

In his own personal riding, he was a talented High School rider. A great admirer of the English Thoroughbred, he insisted that this breed could be made as 'supple and easygoing as any Spanish horse.' It was merely a matter of 'lifting the head, instead of letting him stretch his neck forward, bringing it to the position in hand, and engaging the haunches . . . You will then see that horse, which looked so ungainly, take on the most elegant lines, and he will also gain the lightest and most collected paces . . .' Easy words for a genius, incomprehensible for a novice, and in content, not so different from those of his great rival Baucher.

Arguments on Balance

Like d'Aure, Baucher also sought the classical ideal of natural movement in the horse. Since the weight of the rider destroyed any natural balance, he insisted that equilibrium could only be restored through the necessary interplay of *imparted forces*. With the Baucher method, the

effect of the rider suppressed any inherent resistances in the horse at source, so that the usual time-consuming remedies became superfluous. Cause and effect was the name of the game but too many subsequent writers have criticised Baucher for attempting to theorise on this. With hindsight, Baucher, who became more moderate as time went by would probably

Monsieur le Comte d'Aure, *écuyer en chef* at the Manège of Saumur (1847–1855), who was generally accepted as the figurehead under whom the extended gaits of equitation were developed (although the Earl of Pembroke had written about these almost a century earlier – see previous chapter). (*Courtesy L'Ecole National d'Equitation, Saumur*)

have retorted that any person who attempts to rebalance the horse for whatever purpose is relying upon *imparted forces* and the above description from d'Aure is surely no exception.

In a sense, both Baucher and d'Aure could have come to terms in their teaching since both were bound by an appreciation of beauty, harmony and balance. From the time of Xenophon, classical equitation was considered the only true one since it asked nothing of the horse which was not natural to him in freedom – even the more extravagant airs above the ground. At the same time however, it had always been recognised that in order to allow the horse to carry out these natural movements with a rider on his back, it was necessay to bring the horse's weight a little rearward. This would merely help the horse regain his equilibrium and was brought about by lowering the quarters and engaging the hocks further underneath the horse's body mass.

Over the centuries, various programmes of suppling exercises to strengthen the muscles and mobilise the joints in order to bring about the necessary collection were developed. Once the horse was strong enough to flex his legs further underneath himself, his neck would automatically arch and be carried higher, with the head in the perpendicular (the *ramener*). This would give a convexity and roundness to the entire frame which was as effective in its stretching capacity, as the lengthening and lowering effect on a horse being ridden freely forward in a more horizontal frame. Where the first achieved a shorter, more elastic gait and suspension, the second found economy of movement, increased length of stride and smoothness. Both had their place in the natural order of things and both should have been possible for the same horse working under the same trainer.

Unfortunately Baucher and d'Aure chose to polarize their approach. Baucher saw no virtue in hacking or hunting; to d'Aure it was the key to the future of riding. Where Baucher with his continual quest for supreme lightness made more of an impact on conoisseurs of the High School and on French equitation during his lifetime, the freer work of d'Aure has left a greater mark on competitive dressage. Yet there are many purists of the Versailles School, who deeply regret the d'Aure influence on French equitation.

Commandant Jean Saint-Fort Paillard, formerly of Saumur, wrote in 1975 of the gross misunderstanding that took place after the Count d'Aure redefined one sentence from La Guérinière on the subject of contact, or *appui*. Unfortunately, this redefinition was included in the Count d'Aure's book, and was passed on to generations of riders, with the result that there now exists in modern dressage a dogma about the amount of weight which riders should feel in their hands. This is pursued by some instructors to the extent that so many pounds or kilos of weight are defined.

Yet, La Guérinière's original principle did not involve weight. It is only misinterpretation which has led to such an idea. 'Because this theory was difficult to prove, and because nobody bothered anyway,' wrote Paillard, 'it was accorded the status of a *principle*, of a sort of article of faith, a *dogma* . . . Are riders to be considered backward or mentally retarded? If not, why should they continue to accept ideas that no logical explanation can make believable?'

This digression is important since d'Aure would appear to have a far greater influence today than at first supposed. As though to sum up, Henriquet, an *aficionado* of the Versailles school wrote with some bitterness of d'Aure: 'not one of his many admirers or pupils ever attained the slightest renown and with him the precious thread linking old classical equitation and contemporary equitation was definitively broken.'

Perhaps this is unfair. But there is no doubt that he was an innovator in the world of classical riding, certainly far more so than our next master, who nevertheless has always attracted

Francois Baucher mounted on one of his favourite horse, Partisan (after a lithograph of 1840 by A. Giroux), showing a highly collected passage. Note the lightness of the reins, so typical of the French School until the mid twentieth century. (*Courtesy L'Ecole National d'Equitation, Saumur*)

far more emotional reactions. Whilst many of these are based on admiration, there is also intense dislike. Perhaps the ghost of the Count d'Aure lives on.

François Baucher

In love with the noble tradition of court riding, having been brought up in the shadow of Versailles, Baucher was determined to return to the rounded collected outlines of the Baroque riding hall. Working with all breeds of horses, and like d'Aure, particularly admiring the English Thoroughbred, he achieved this by putting the rider in a foolproof position which gave him total command over the horse's natural forces, by practising flexions which would supple the jaw, the muscles of the neck and back and ease the joints.

Collection was defined thus: 'The true collection consists in gathering into the centre of the horse his whole energy, in order to lighten the two extremities and to place them completely under the control of the rider.'

Rejected by Saumur, Baucher was able to find a platform for his extraordinary talent and showmanship in the circus. This was a very different affair in the late eighteenth and nineteenth centuries from the circus of today, and names like the English Philip Astley (who died in 1814) were synonymous with brilliance and romance. Often operating from a permanent site, the great glamorous circuses of Europe (the Russian was the most famous) attracted the influential and wealthy in the same way as the theatre and ballet do today. Elegantly attired figures from high society had their own boxes, and there, by the light of a thousand candles, watched their feted favourites of the ring. A discerning public, they knew and understood the work being enacted; High School riding was top of the list of entertainments. Riders were of a very high calibre and names like Pellier, the Franconis and others could command enormous fees. Atmosphere was everything! Glittering chandeliers swung over small, intimate arenas, and there was a sharp intake of breath as a pair of magnificently festooned horses swished through the red curtain and passaged slowly round to a dramatic roll of drums from the orchestra, eager for their prestigious act.

Baucher, who had been classically trained under two fine *écuyers*, Mazzuchelli, the Neapolitan, and d'Abzac in France, soon became admired by all society as a genius when he entered the Cirque des Champs-Elysées. In those days, the standard of the High School riders whether in Moscow, Paris or Turin had to be impeccable. Baucher chose to exhibit mainly English horses; he loved the fire and the sensitivity of the Thoroughbred, and as a perfectionist no doubt enjoyed the challenge. Movements (nowadays dubbed tricks) demanded by the expectant spectators included canter on the spot and to the rear, the Spanish walk and trot and other spectacular gaits, but these had to be executed as correctly as the piaffes and levades to gain applause. One of his most brilliant horses, Partisan,[2] was a Yorkshire coach horse which

[2] According to Dwyer, Partisan was sold for a song because no-one could manage him and Baucher converted him into 'a first-rate and most docile school-horse'.

he produced for the Russian Pauline, and several of his horses noted for their suspension in passage and piaffe were bought by the Russian State Circus.

Like so many great horsemen, Baucher was a workaholic. Tempting social invitations from his adoring public were rejected and he lived only for the riding school. Devoted to his art, he schooled scores of horses, and whatever time remained was occupied with writing and teaching. His first book *Dictionnaire raisonne d'equitation* (1833) was followed by *Methode d'équitation basée sur de nouveaux principes* (1842) which went into four editions within only a year.

Despite the rebuff by the military authorities, many young French officers from Saumur studied under Baucher. Perhaps the best known was Alexis l'Hotte who was able to combine the best of d'Aure and of Baucher and would eventually achieve the coveted place of Commander at Saumur – the position denied his mentor. Many of l'Hotte's sayings are still used at Saumur today. The most famous, '*Calme, en avant, droit!*', calm, forward, straight, is legendary. He also insisted, 'From head to haunches, the horse must be straight when travelling on straight lines, and curved when he follows a curved line'. The Baucher-inspired sensitivity led to his writing that the whole horse should be obedient to the 'breath of a boot', and as a proof of lightness, he wrote that the seat will give the feeling of riding on 'the gentle waves of a lake.'

Another disciple, General Faverot de Kerbrech (1837–1905), was a brilliant teacher and his book published in 1891, *Dressage methodique du cheval de selle d'apres les derniers enseignements de Baucher*, is still widely quoted today. Two others who reached high posts in the army and were able to combine outdoor training with High School work were Captain Raabe (1811–1891) and Colonel Guerin (1817–1841). The work of all these men devoted to the Baucher method was to encourage and effectively help others such as Dutilh and later Captain Beudant (died 1949) who was described by General Decarpentry as 'the most dazzling horseman I have ever known'. Baucher therefore exerted an enormous influence on the French School which continued well into our own century. The criticism levied from certain opponents that he was 'the gravedigger of French equitation' verges on the absurd and stems from the vehement resentment borne by the pamphlet-writing German Seeger against Baucher's disciple Seidler.

It was Baucher who invented the flying change at each stride, changes *à tempo* which was adopted by every serious dressage establishment in the world. It was Baucher who wrote 'The walk is the mother of the gaits . . .' and 'The mouth of the horse is the barometer of his body'. And it was Baucher who, on one of his frequent and successful visits to Prussia replied quietly to the young officer who told him that they liked their horses in front of the hand: 'I like my horse behind the hand and in front of the legs,[3] so that the centre of gravity is placed between these two aids, as it is only on this condition that the horse is absolutely under the control of the rider, so that his movements will be graceful and regular, and that he will change easily from a fast pace to a slow one whilst preserving his balance.'

An honest enough man to change and soften his approach later in life, so that students of equitation usually now refer to his second method rather than his first, he finally rejected the curb bit, having the brilliance to obtain collection and produce extraordinary displays of High School virtuosity in a snaffle.

To Baucher, there was no such thing as a horse with a bad mouth. He was able to achieve lightness with any horse, often in a matter of minutes, simply by readjusting the balance through a scientific use of the seat and simple weight aids and using his suppling methods. Carried

---

[3] A sentiment still widely used at Saumur today.

out first in hand, later mounted, these were based on flexions of the head and neck to eradicate the resistances which usually prevent the horse yielding himself to the rider and offering the *ramener* or true collection. Later he softened his approach, eliminating the lateral flexions after realising that few possessed his marvellous equestrian tact, and were trying to obtain flexibility[4] through force, the very antithesis of what he wanted. In later life he wrote of 'equitation in bedroom slippers', but his 'hands without legs and legs without hands' is still often largely misinterpreted.

The master of suspension, Baucher's passage, piaffes and levades, were second to none. All of this he put down to the rider's sense of timing and feeling in the seat, knowing exactly when to apply or displace the weight and how it will act on the horse's equilibrium. He put much importance on the pressing power of the knees and thighs,[5] a weight aid all too often overlooked by today's riders. The importance of a correct classical seat was paramount.

The Seat

'In order to press back the shoulders, he [the instructor] should tell his pupil to hollow his back and press his waist forward; and in the case of a man with slack loins keep in this position for some time without considering the stiffness which it will cause at first. It is by acting energetically that the pupil will become supple and not by taking the easy position so often and so wrongly recommended.' Another useful passage commences: 'The rider should sit as upright as possible so that each part of his body rests on that which is immediatley below it, and produces direct vertical pressure through the seat . . . through their force of adduction, the hips and legs should seek to discover the maximum number of possible points of contact between the saddle and the horse's flanks . . .' Like Xenophon, Newcastle, La Guérinière, Beringer and so on, he abhorred the back of the buttocks seat. There was only one way to make a 'lazy' rider use himself correctly; that was to make him practise suppling exercises, teach him to separate and co-ordinate at will different parts of the body, and finally, when mounted, to encourage an initial hollowing in the lower back whilst sitting very upright.

Lightness in Hand

In his book, *Methode d'Equitation Baser sur de Nouveaux Principes*, at the beginning of his chapter on how to achieve the suppling of the horse's lower jaw and neck, he writes: 'The head and neck of the horse are at the same time the rider's helm and compass . . . the balance of the whole body is perfect, and the lightness in hand complete when the neck and head themselves are supple and in an easy graceful position.' For Baucher, the required flexion was the foundation upon which everything else was built, and 'which instantly gives the rider a sense of coordinated effects and provides the horse with the necessary means to execute them.'

For those modern trainers who spend over-long periods on stretching the horse horizontally, he gives these encouraging but at the same time warning words. 'The lowering of the neck which I recommend especially in the case of horses whose withers are considerably higher than the quarters or who have narrow quarters or feeble loins is not a position which they should permanently maintain, but it is a means which will help in establishing the balance, which will assist the weak parts, and give then, in consequence, an energy and level movement which they would never have had but for the low position of the neck.' At the same time

---

[4] The idea of Flexibility by Force was, according to a twentieth century Portuguese writer, de Souza, in his *Advanced Equitation*, unfairly seized upon and misinterpreted by D'Aure in his vendetta against Baucher.

[5] Similar to the Duke of Newcastle.

The Duc d'Orleans by Lami (1842). Under his patronage Baucher made several officially approved experiments with troop horses at Saumur. These took place with great success before the admiring eyes of Commandant de Novital, and many officers were converted to Baucherism. Unfortunately for Baucher, Orleans died before he was finally accepted into Saumur as a civilian instructor (*Courtesy L'Ecole National d'Equitation, Saumur*)

he urged that unless the horse's head continued in the correct angle given by the neck, the work was rendered useless.

Because of his spectacular results, some of Baucher's opponents insinuated that he resorted to unkind[6] or unclassical methods. There is simply no evidence of this, and his regard for the horse as a noble living creature shines out of his book. He exhorts the rider not to be angry or resentful in handling and always to have 'a kindly expression in the eyes'. He also rejected the severe bits of the past, referring to them as 'instruments of torture'. He continually looked for the grace and elegance of the horse, describing the transformation of feeling in a schooled horse as to being 'on springs . . .'

In the spirit of Xenophon and again of La Guérinière, he wrote of the importance of releasing the contact, or the *descente de main*. 'This liberty gives such confidence to the horse that he unconsciously yields himself to the rider and becomes his slave whilst thinking that he preserves his absolute independence.'

As well as his French pupils, Baucher left one devoted English pupil, James Fillis, who made a great impact abroad, but who is still insufficiently known in England despite the fact that his book, first written in French, has been translated into English. It is noteworthy perhaps that one of our greatest modern classical horsemen, Nuno Oliveira of Portugal was a devotee of Baucher.

Ironically, Baucher's riding career came to an abrupt end amongst the people that loved him most. During one of his spectacular acts at the newly established Cirque Napoleon, one of the beautiful but excruciatingly heavy circus chandeliers broke away from its chain and crashed to the ground as Baucher rode underneath. His horse escaped, but Baucher was pinned down in the sawdust on his stomach. Despite enormous pain in the back, he was able politely to turn his head and ask to be freed. Even in crisis, his incredible sense of discipline prevailed to the last.

Baucher's work, despite the fact that he never achieved his dream of becoming a national instructor to the military, nevertheless made a greater impact on Saumur than perhaps he ever dreamed. His pupil General l'Hotte, who was with him at his deathbed, successfully combined Baucher's methods with the sporting requirements of the modern cavalry horse and his *Regulations* remained in force up until the second World War.

After the First World War, academic equitation was reinforced again at Saumur under Generals Wattel and Decarpentry and Colonel Danloux (famed for the softest of reins whilst his horses moved through spectacular collection). Commandants Liçart, Susanna, de Cosilla and others all reflect much of Baucher.

Certain sectors of the Prussian and Swedish Army also followed Baucher. However, it was within the Russian cavalry that Baucherism really made its mark through the teachings of James Fillis, and there are still some today who believe that the gentle feel and artistry of the Russians for the very refined work of the High School can be traced back to teaching that came directly from this remarkable man.

[6] An American writer, Colonel T.A. Dodge, wrote of Baucher in 1894: 'The first man who showed the world that intelligent kindness was the real secret of horse training was the Frenchman Baucher.'

ELEVEN

Fillis – The Forgotten English Genius

James Fillis, although born in England (1834), was always acclaimed as the epitome of the artistic French School. He left British shores at the age of eight and it is significant perhaps that having lost his heart to the art of High School riding, he never returned to live in England. Yet even from the British hunting fraternity came enthusiastic admiration. Horace Hayes, the distinguished veterinarian and knowledgeable hunting man who translated his book, wrote: 'Mr Fillis . . . acting on his motto *en avant* has succeeded in showing how a horse can be made clever in his movements, without in any way diminishing his usefulness on the road or over country. I therefore trust that all English-speaking horsemen, and especially cavalrymen and polo players, will profit by his valuable instruction.' Colonel McTaggart (of whom more later) quotes Fillis at least seven or eight times in his own book which deplored the general standard of equitation at home in the mid twentieth century.

Fillis and Saumur

Fillis' one burning ambition was to become Chief Instructor at Saumur which through the influence of good friends would have taken place but for the opposition of General l'Hotte. Thus like François Baucher, he had to resort to the platform of the circus to explore and display his art, which he achieved with great success becoming the undoubted High School star of the world at that time. He never swerved in his devotion to Saumur however and his philosophy can best be described by his own hand:

> 'There is but one School in Europe[1] where the real school horse is to be found; that is Saumur. Its horses are schooled in a manner to be ready for any kind of work because they are well-balanced, light and obedient to the hands and legs . . . the riders are quiet in their movement. They are united with their horses by a suppleness and ease which they owe to their seat and their attitude . . . and it is only there that one finds the school horse as I understand it, that is schooled so that it will be able at a moment's notice, without further preparation, to hunt, race, or go to war . . .'

Baucher did not live long enough to influence Fillis to the extent often understood. Rather he learned what he wanted from Baucher through the latter's writing, but his practical instruction came from François Caron, one of Baucher's pupils, to whom he later dedicated his book *Principes de Dressage et d'Equitation*.[2] Fillis' early career was versatile; after his apprenticeship to Caron, he supervised the private manèges of a number of prominent people including that of the Rothschild family and of Queen Maria of Naples. An insatiable worker, he was quite capable of riding up to sixteen or seventeen horses a day, and began to school horses for the cavalry and enjoyed much unofficial recognition by the officers at Saumur.

---

[1] Fillis was opposed to the School of Vienna since he disliked the use of pillars, feeling them to be artificial and even harmful. In turn, Vienna never forgave him for these remarks.

[2] Now available in English under the title of *Breaking and Riding*. The first edition appeared in 1902. The most recent edition is J.A. Allen's version of 1977 from which these quotations are taken.

The Circus

After turning to the circus, he began to give private exhibitions to illustrious international socialites, and was soon to be acclaimed as the most brilliant school rider of all time.

Of his audiences he wrote: 'In Paris I have worked for 25 years in front of the élite of society, artistic and literary, who are most observant and not prepared to applaud you tomorrow if you do not do even better than today; and whose lucid and pitiless, though constructive criticism meant at the same time redemption and stimulation to he who endeavours to develop a science or art.'

His great moment for lasting recognition came when with the famous Circus Ciniselli, he went to Russia. The Grand Duke Nicholas was so impressed with his riding, that he asked Fillis to give a trial clinic to the officers of the Imperial Household. The results were so spectacular that Fillis was offered a commission as Colonel and took up his new authoritative position to re-organise and instruct the Russian cavalry.[3] Fillis made a lasting mark in this vast country. A new breed of cavalry instructor emerged who for the first time in Russia's history enjoyed a profound and educated knowledge of High School riding. As a result of this enlightenment within the military, there are those who still remember the Russians' remarkable success in the Olympic Games of the sixties (see Chapter 19) and directly attribute it to the Fillis influence.

Faithful to Versailles

Although Fillis brings us up to the twentieth century in our pursuit of equitation, there was absolutely no divergence by him away from the old classical principles of collection and lightness. At the beginning of his book, he sums up his method in the simplest terms. 'My method of equitation consists in distribution of weight by the height of the neck bent at the poll and not at the withers; propulsion by means of the hocks being brought under the body; and lightness by the loosening of the lower jaw. When we know this, we know everything, and we know nothing. We know everything, because these principles are of universal application; and we know nothing, because they have to be applied practically.'

Today the principles to which Fillis referred are no longer of 'universal application'. Few riders are now instructed in the suppling of the lower jaw or the practice of valuable flexions, such an important prerequisite for classical riding.

Flexions

Always looking for pure forward movement, Fillis criticises Baucher for having set down in writing theories which could lead to the horse being behind the bit. 'I consider

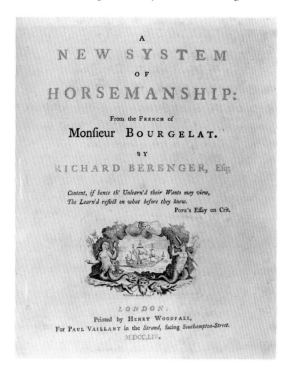

A NEW SYSTEM OF HORSEMANSHIP:

From the French of Monsieur BOURGELAT.

BY RICHARD BERENGER, Esq;

Content, if hence th' Unlearn'd their Wants may view,
The Learn'd reflect on what before they knew.
POPE's Essay on Crit.

LONDON:
Printed by HENRY WOODFALL,
For PAUL VAILLANT in the Strand, facing Southampton-Street.
MDCCLIV.

During the eighteenth and nineteenth centuries the most important French treatises had been translated into English by scholars of classical riding. This influenced many thinking riders such as Fillis, but only in France could they find a real platform for their academic studies. Here we see the frontispiece of Richard Berenger's translation of Claude Bourgelat's book.

[3] Vladimir Littauer's book *Horseman's Progress* provides a clear and concise background into the state of the Russian cavalry during this period.

that by criticising him and by showing where he has failed,' he writes, 'I shall render increased homage to the great horseman.' Fillis' strength therefore lay in his ability to improve and perfect the work started by Baucher. Direct flexions were only to be undertaken during forward work; indirect or lateral flexions could be started on the ground, but when mounted, again only in forward work.

The purpose of flexions was to achieve a supple, balanced horse which, unable to resist, did not block the impulsion (produced by the hindlegs) from streaming through an unrestricted back to a controllable, light forehand. Fillis warned against allowing the power to diverge sideways onto the shoulders. Too much bend in the neck to one side or another would overload the opposite shoulder. 'Lateral flexion, by strengthening and bringing all the parts together, places them in a state of reciprocal dependence, which enables the rider to act on the entire forehand. Without flexion, the fishing-rod . . . will be held by the thin end; that is to say there will be a heavy head . . . at the end of a slack neck.' Only through flexion of the jaw could lightness be preserved in all changes of direction and gait.

Flexions, straightening, suppling of shoulders and hindquarters, lightness, and above all collection were the cornerstones of his schoolwork. There is a fashionable theory in some modern schools that a horse cannot go forward with true impulsion unless his head is low and the frame horizontal rather than rounded. A footnote in Fillis' book dispels such ideas. 'I have already said that a high position of the neck can be obtained only during forward progression, and that the reason I keep the necks of my horses very high is because I continue to drive them forward during all the work I give them. In fact, the greater the forward impulsion the more do the hindquarters get under the centre, and the more is the forehand lightened.'

A Practical Man

Yet Fillis recognised, unlike Baucher, that *rassembler*, the supreme collection, could not be achieved with every horse. 'It is possible that we can succeed in making all horses light in hand, but I deny that we can give them the same lightness and sensitivity.' If some antagonists find the movements of the classically trained horse too slow and stately for their liking, they could scarcely have been disappointed by Fillis. A former pupil reports that Fillis' horses 'moved as if the devil was inside them', and although the High School was his real love, he produced horses for every type of work and purpose. Like Newcastle, Guérinière, Marialva and Steinbrecht before him, Fillis recognised the outline of the sporting horse must differ from that of the collected school horse. He stressed that it is the prerogative of the rider either to collect, or to allow the horse to become 'straight or in horizontal equilibrium' for 'we must not think that the horse should be always kept in hand. I certainly do not advise that this should be done the whole time one is hacking, hunting, foraging or charging.'[4] On the other hand, the good rider 'should know how to be able to get the horse in hand' at any time and in any pace. 'Getting him into hand restores his balance and is of great use in every respect.'

Not every writer, past or present, has defined collection in clear simple terms. There is little to fault in Fillis's definition: 'The *rassembler,* which is the act of getting a horse into hand to a maximum extent, is the complete equilibrium of the animal in all his movements. It is the perfect form of collecting the well-suppled horse. In it the loins, hindquarters and hocks are flexible; the hocks stoutly press the mass forward; the shoulders are free and movable; the neck is high and the jaw readily obeys the feeling of the rider's hands on the reins, and

[4] How different this attitude of Fillis was from that of his contemporaries Caprilli, Santini and Chamberlin will be seen in the next chapter.

Fig. 2.—Jaw contracted.　　　　　　　　　　　Fig. 3.—Jaw and bit free.

Flexions of the jaw, a practice which had formed part of the education of the manège horse since the early seventeenth century, is put into effect by James Fillis in his *Principes de Dressage et d'Equitation*. The illustration on the left shows the horse restricted in the jaws, and on the right the jaw now relaxing.

all the parts of the horse being in action and equally enterprising, combine to form an energetic, harmonious and light whole. The equilibrium is so perfect and so unstable [fine], that the rider feels that he can make his horse do whatever he desires by the slightest indication of his wishes. Both of them so to speak, are in the air. They are ready to fly!' Inspirational words! and how true of the supremely collected horse! All this could only be achieved of course with 'equestrian tact' and Fillis wote of 'the delicate and constant play of the fingers, which may be compared to the fingering of a piano as regards delicacy and speed.'[5] Further on, he confirmed that the give and take of the legs must be as discerning as that of the hands (*descente de jambes*).

Establishment Prejudice

The tragedy of Fillis is that prejudice prevented his book becoming one of the great classics of all time. His connections with the circus and his introduction of some innovatory work, such as canter to the rear, which appealed to the audiences of that time have clouded the image of this genius. Whilst he still remains appreciated and revered throughout the United States,[6] Russia, France, Portugal and Spain, scarcely one quotation or explanation from his work appears in any modern official British or German manual of horsemanship despite his initial popoularity and success in Germany. In fact today's German Official Handbook criticises him for leading riders 'astray'. Attitudes such as this go a long way to explaining the poverty of information which exists concerning our understanding of the collection and lightening of the horse in modern literature.

One of the most attractive features of Fillis's writing, again so often missing from modern

[5] Similar to Decarpentry's description of the fingers on the rein 'rather like the vibrato of the violinist on the strings of his instrument'. (From *Academic Equitation*; see Chapter 15.)

[6] Fillis's book *Breaking and Riding* was the official text book at the American Cavalry School of Fort Riley at its outset.

works, was his obvious patience and understanding of the horse's sensitive nature. There is a particularly telling passage in relation to breaking the young horse, which echoes Xenophon's theories of punishment and reward. 'It is most important always to let a horse be free and quiet after he has obeyed. A horse will accept this as a reward, which we should not be chary in giving him. Stoppage of work and pats on the neck are the only means to make him understand that he has done well. We are so often obliged to have recourse to punishment during breaking, that we ought eagerly to seize the opportunity of patting him on the the neck, when he shows the slightest sign of obedience. The more we pat him on the neck, the less will we be forced to punish him.'

An Appraisal of German and French Riding

A much travelled man, Fillis was unstinting in his praise of the German crosscountry and cavalry schools of riding, but he held considerable reservations about their dressage. He described their outdoor riding as quite superior to that of other European countries, and wrote: 'In Germany, everyone knows enough about equitation to school his horse without the help of a teacher. In every city in Germany there is a quantity of excellent schools . . . In a word, civilian riding is as widespread in Germany as it is neglected in other parts of Europe. When it comes to military riding it is absolutely first class; the horses are as obedient as the men. I consider it one of the most perfected of Europe.'

What he disliked in German dressage is summed up as follows: 'They [the horses] lack delicacy and particularly suppleness. What is particularly noticeable is the complete lack of those co-ordinated movements by which the rider collects his horse and makes him very light. The reason for the inferiority of the German riding, as far as the High School goes, is the result of the lack of an outstanding rider. There was one, named Steinbrecht, whose example has not been followed . . .

'French equitation requires the horse to be schooled by the mouth, German by the neck. This is why German equitation seems so stiff and hard next to the French. The mouth is a piano, the neck is an organ. A horse schooled by the mouth can be kept in hand by a mere thread at the end of the fingers, but one schooled by the head and neck requires taut reins and ever taut arms. That is why the first type of equitation is all delicacy, the second all force. The schools of Dresden and Munich are quite inferior to Hanover; in these places the iron glove has replaced the velvet glove.'

In this illuminating piece of text written at the threshold of our own century, lies much of the true definition between the ideas of the old classical school and the modern competition (or neo-classical) school at which the Germans excelled long before the rest of Europe produced its own Olympic celebrities. General Decarpentry (1878–1956), that great *écuyer* of Saumur who made his mark on the international dressage world several decades after Fillis, and whose own book *Academic Equitation* is a must for all modern students of dressage, drew similar comparisons between the Romanic and the Germanic Schools. In 1949, he wrote:

'. . .although the Germanic school preserved the method or rather progression of this master [La Guérinière] who was not of its blood, it did not put his theories into practice without some modifications . . .

'. . . without resorting to as much as harshness, the masters of the Germanic school persisted too often in their direct opposition to forces of resistance, instead of having recourse to a skilful disassocation from them.

Canter on the spot and backwards were favourite movements of the Baucher School so admired by Fillis. Here the *galop en arrière* is demonstrated by Lt Colonel Wattel, *Ecuyer en chef* at the Manège of Saumur (1919–1929) on his Thoroughbred horse, Rempart. Note the relaxed reins and jaw of the horse and the roundness of the movement.

'They demanded not just submission, but unconditional surrender of the horse, instead of seeking the latter's general co-operation towards perfection of the common task.

'They attached greater value to strict exactitude of execution than to the joyous ease of their mount in his attitudes and movements.'

These thoughts will be explored further in Chapter 20 but before we close our chapter on James Fillis, the Englishman forgotten by today's Englishmen, let us hear what he has to say about riding in Great Britain. Honest to his art to the end, he wrote: 'There is no artistic riding in England; there is only sporting riding'.

Let us not forget the year was 1905.[7] Fortunately, much has changed since then. We must not overlook the fact however that Fillis was perfectly accurate in his summation. His viewpoint was neither singular, eccentric or unpatriotic for it was the British themselves who encouraged just such a Corinthian image. We fool ourselves if we do not admit that it has only been in the last thirty years or so, that there have existed a fair complement of horses adequately schooled beyond elementary dressage level in Great Britain. Prior to 1960, apart from the circus, the number of British horses schooled to perform credible pirouette, passage, piaffe and tempi changes, could be counted on two (sometimes one) hand(s). This dearth of artistic talent covered a span of over two hundred years. That is why, in the words of a British International dressage judge, '. . . we are now running to catch up'.[8]

---

[7] Year of publication for original French edition.
[8] Mrs J. Gold, personal interview. Article in *Horse & Rider* magazine, November 1988.

TWELVE

Caprilli and the Forward Seat

In Chapter 9, we remarked how sporting riding affected attitudes to work in the manège. We noted how in particular the British moved away from classical dressage because of hunting, and how eventually in France and Germany military riding transformed dressage itself, despite adherents to the old school such as Baucher and Fillis and their followers.

If we are fully to appreciate the difficulties and conflicting ideas with which modern dressage has been, and will continue to be, faced, it is important now to understand the Federico Caprilli revolution which came about with the advent of showjumping at the turn of the twentieth century.

Freedom for the Jumping Horse

The Caprilli seat originated to give the horse more freedom in the back as he extended himself across country or over jumps. More than that however, it gave the sporting rider a proper technique or method which would complement the Thoroughbred, or thoroughbred type of horse both physically and mentally, allowing him to work with freedom and confidence.

It was Italy which again opened the equestrian way, this time into a sphere which was the complete antithesis of manège riding. Crosscountry riding had led to showjumping, and the Italians developed this new sport with tremendous enthusiasm. People who had never previously been interested in horses, were captivated by the excitement of the sport, and since they could now watch jumping from the comfort of a stadium, instead of a rainswept, windy field, this form of equestrianism began to appeal to more people than ever before.

From the beginning, Italian army officers shone in this new discipline. Their style was distinctive and radical compared to all that had gone previously. Instead of leaning back as the horse landed over a jump (the normal practice up until then) they folded forward, over the horse's withers, from the waist, using the closed angles of their bodies and the pressure in the stirrups to balance themselves. Worldwide, this method became known as the Forward Seat. Riders all over Europe began to examine the teachings of its innovator, an army officer Federico Caprilli (born 1868) who commanded the Italian Cavalry School at Pinerolo, and later became established at Tor de Quinto, a newly created training centre just outside Rome.

Equine Locomotion

Caprilli had been studying the mechanics of the horse at liberty, on a free rein, over jumps and on the flat for several years. His research was facilitated by the invention of the camera, and the subsequent findings of an American, Eadweard Muybridge. In 1887, Muybridge published *Animal Locomotion* which fully explained the sequence of footfalls in each gait as well as the balance of the horse in slow and fast gaits and over jumps. Other books which dealt with locomotion, bones, muscles and tendons followed, including the important *The Exterior of the Horse* by two veterinary surgeons from France, Goubaux and Barrier.

In the context of dressage, Caprilli is important in that he abolished all forms of collected

H. Grant on Horseback, an engraving by Henry Alken (1785–1851). It was riding such as this which prompted the Italian Caprilli to invent the forward seat for riding across country. Nevertheless, Englishmen such as Adams and Dwyer had been criticising the backward seat long before the Italians.

work in the manège, and eschewed the classical seat. This was done not for the future of dressage, but in the interests of the jumping and sporting horse. For too long horses moving at speed had been hampered by riders clinging to the theory but not the practice of the classical seat. Since most recruits seemed incapable of accepting that there were two essential styles of riding, one for collected work, and one over jumps and at the gallop, Caprilli decided that the first would have to go.

Abolishing Classical Dressage

Caprilli's first act was completely to reject the slow cadenced collected gaits. Collection in inexperienced hands could impair the horse's natural locomotion, therefore it must be discouraged. To remove any temptation to ask for collection or flexion, his next step was to remove the curb bit. Arguably, it was felt that no one would attempt to fix the horse into a collected outline from the snaffle, a bit originally designed for the racehorse. From now on equestrian recruits must use a light elastic contact and follow each movement made by the horse with their hands. This would allow the horse to stretch his head and neck, using them to balance the whole extended frame.

Caprilli's next move was to end the practice of drilling recruits without stirrups since unlike the classical school, he had no desire to create a solid base of support in the saddle. Neither did he wish his pupils to be upright 'as though standing on the ground' as Xenophon required. On the contrary, the new position relied on a different balance achieved through the angles of the body being closed. As exemplified by the downhill skier or the human hurdler, these angles would give spring and lift to the body over jumps and bumps and could only be obtained with the support of the stirrup. 'The balance of a rider without stirrups is completely different from that which he must have with stirrups,' wrote Caprilli.[1]

Revolutionary Methods

Out of concern therefore for the sporting horse and to make life easier for the cavalry instructor, Caprilli revolutionised the work of the riding school. It is unlikely that he had any idea that his method would influence riding all over the world to the extent it did. Primarily, he was concerned with simplifying riding for the Italian army, and his reasoning is realistic:

[1] Caprilli did not live long enough to write the book he intended. Dying from a riding accident in 1907, he only left a number of articles which were published first in Italy and much later translated into English by Santini.

(*left*) The piaffe, executed in front of Queluz Palace, near Lisbon by a rider of the Portuguese School of Equestrian Art, on a Lusitano stallion from the royal Alter stud. These horses have changed little since the days of hand to hand combat when the Romans came to the Peninsula and founded stud farms and remount depots for their cavalry around the River Tagus and Guadalquivir. The piaffe, correctly performed, with the horse round and springy, bouncing like a ball on the spot, prepared horse and rider for the sudden surge forward into a *sorte*, or attack. It was important that the croup was lowered in order to create sufficient engagement of the hind legs for these highly collected battle movements. (*From 'Cavalo Lusitano – O filho do vento' by Arsenio Raposo Cordeiro*)

PLATE 9

(*below*) The Art of Marialva is kept alive by these gentlemen riders of the Portuguese School of Equestrian Art in Lisbon, dressed in traditional eighteenth-century court costume. (*From 'Cavalo Lusitano – O filho do vento' by Arsenio Raposo Cordeiro*)

Nuno Oliveira, known worldwide as the Master. A man who could bring magical steps out of the most ordinary horse, a man who rode like a king, so that his horses carried him like a king. (*From 'Cavalo Lusitano – O filho do vento' by Arsenio Raposo Cordeiro*)

PLATE 10

Author and master of equitation, Don Diogo Bragança (Lafões) enjoying himself at home in a soft passage with his Lusitano stallion from the Infante da Câmara stud. (*From 'Cavalo Lusitano – O filho do vento' by Arsenio Raposo Cordeiro*)

First, like d'Aure, he had recognised that there was insufficient time for the modern recruit to adopt a sufficiently good classical position which could serve as a basis.

Second, he had recognised there was little place or time in the twentieth century for the refined techniques of the manège when dealing with a quantity of ill-assorted men.

Third, the day of the Spanish and Neapolitan chargers with their aptitude for manège work was clearly over. The Thoroughbreds and troop horses which replaced them had a pronounced forward balance of their own which was not difficult to maintain provided they could extend their necks. Physically and mentally they were more suited to speed and extension rather than collection and elevation.

These were some of the contributary factors which led to the Caprilli revolution. 'Things cannot go on in this manner,' he wrote, '. . . Manège riding presents such difficulties and so many demands, such fine tact in practice that is impossible that a soldier, considering the brevity of his enlistment and the variety of his other instruction should succeed in learning its principles and applying them properly.'

Non-Intervention

This method of riding struck a visceral blow to the heart of the High School worldwide. By abolishing the influence of the rider's seat and back, the rider could no longer collect his horse. Whereas the Count d'Aure had encouraged outdoor riding with more liberty for the galloping horse, he had still retained the classical ideals of disciplining, suppling and lightening the horse for work in the ring. Caprilli on the other hand would have none of this. All from the past was to be rejected. Collection, flexion, rounding and bending – none of these had any place in the Caprilli school which came to be known as the non-intervention school. For him, the horse should be allowed to take the predominance of its weight on the forehand; by scrapping the collected exercises, there was no need to put him on his hocks.

The public appeal of the Caprilli approach was obvious. Here was a general purpose way of riding which required no literary study, certainly no social standing or traditional background, no special premises in which to practise, not even – necessarily – an expensive horse. Instead, talent could be developed solely from natural balance, boldness across country, the confidence and desire to achieve, and initially, some luck.

British Resistance

Whilst Italy virtually forsook dressage from then onwards, France, Germany,[2] the Nether-

Caprilli's forward seat over obstacles as epitomised in *Riding Relections* by Piero Santini. Note the closed angles of arms, legs and trunk, and the light 'following' hands.

[2] In *Riding Reflections*, Santini grudgingly admired the Germans for beating the Italians 'at their own game' in many international events.

lands and Scandinavia gradually allowed Caprilli's methods from around 1910 onwards to infiltrate showjumping and crosscountry riding, although they still clung firmly to the traditional classical seat for dressage which formed too great a part of their continued heritage to be abandoned. Thus these countries, happily adapted to two styles of riding – one for flatwork; one over jumps.

It is interesting that the two countries with the greatest tradition of crosscountry riding and the finest horses, namely England and Ireland, should have been the last to be converted. An American writer W. S. Felton wrote in *Masters of Equitation* that when the British foxhunters discarded classical riding 'they developed nothing to take its place. As a result we find the English . . . mounted on the finest horses in the world and riding with superb courage, great boldness and often with great athletic ability but with a complete absence of sound technique. Often their horses carried them extremely well, but this was in spite of and not because of their methods of schooling and riding.' An honest, if melancholy comment.

Until Caprilli however, there had been little practical advice on jumping technique even from the military schools. The general rule at the turn of the century had been to sit well back into the horse for the approach, to lean forward slightly as the horse left the ground, and to lean backwards and raise[3] the hand as the horse landed. Even Fillis, a schooler of Thoroughbreds and with a great fondness for outdoor riding as well as for the manège had little to offer on jumping technique, and the only person who had come remarkably close to Caprilli's forward style, John Adams (see Chapter 9) had been largely ignored.

The attitude in England therefore amongst those sporting gentlemen with their elegant but determined sidesaddle ladies at their sides was one of measured disinterest in yet another foreign concept of riding. The works of La Guérinière, Baucher and even their own Fillis had passed them by. It was going to take many decades for matters to change and technique to be taken seriously. The British attitude to jumping was probably best summed up by J. G. Whyte-Melville, 'When there is no fear, there is no danger . . . if the man's heart is in the right place, his horse will seldom fail him.' Or even more by R. S. Surtees' fictional hunting character, Lucy Glitters, who declared 'Throw your heart over . . . then follow as quickly as you can!' Perhaps such sporting verdicts would have been revised, if the authors had caught a glimpse of just one of the jumps at Badminton Horse Trials in the 1980s.

Gradually however, the British, particularly the military came round to the Forward Seat as showjumping became the sport of the future. Whilst the old guard of the English hunting field were slower to convert, there was a swifter response in the United States. Caprilli's ideas were promoted in the West by three influential horsemen, Major Piero Santini (1881–1960), Sergei Kournakoff and Vladimir Littauer, both born just after the turn of the century, and the last of whom still lives in the United States. Their understanding and enthusiasm for the new seat ensured that it continued to be correctly taught outside Italy the mother country and they paved the way for America's own great jumping instructor, Colonel Harry Chamberlin who died in 1944.

American Enthusiasm for Caprillism

America was ready for just such a revolution as we shall see in the next chapter. Whilst hunting folk were arguably as entrenched in the 'English' way of riding as their counterparts in Ireland and the Shires, there were many people who lived in and around the cities of the East Coast who avidly embraced a concept of riding which seemed less stilted and more natural than

---

[3] Known as 'calling a cab'.

The forward seat as practised in the drop by Italian cavalry cadets at Tor de Quinto's famous double bank was still a revolutionary sight for many, prior to the 1920s.

much of what had gone before. In fact, the Caprillists referred to this as 'natural schooling', emphasizing that the Forward Seat was not merely intended for jumping, but provided an alternative method for the all-round horseman.

Santini who had trained in Italy under the Caprilli system, and who later translated and published a number of articles written by Caprilli through the British *Light Horse* magazine,[4] was the first Caprillist to influence America through three highly popular books published by Derrydale Press in New York. The most important of these, *Riding Reflections*, published in 1932 showed his absolute devotion to the Italian formula and an almost obsessive demand to convert the whole world to it at the expense of every other school of riding. Patronisingly, he wrote of 'little Austria, obstinately clinging to the florid manège schooling inherited from the Habsburgs' as though by some peculiar phenomenon.

Since Caprilli had been diametrically opposed to dressage – 'Manège and cross-country equitation are, in my opinion, antagonistic; one excludes and destroys the other' – Santini succeeded in discouraging many people from any form of collected work, continually stating that it was harmful to the free-moving hunter or hack. A strong advocate of the snaffle '. . . any tune can be played on a horse's mouth with a snaffle', he nevertheless allowed that a self-respecting horseman could have up to three varieties of bridle in his stable, the snaffle, plain double bridle and the pelham. It is interesting that his own personal opposition to the curb did not preclude the use of the running martingale.

Somewhat surprisingly, he was also opposed to competition work, declaring 'Horse show riding is a game which has strayed far indeed from nature and natural conditions . . . The centuries-old association between man and horse had its origin in the chase; the more we keep this basic idea in mind the purer our diversions will be.' Later he commented, 'If the ribbons and flower pots of Olympia and Madison Square offend, we in Italy are by no means blameless . . . If the public knew what sometimes goes on behind the scenes, their unreasoning admiration for the sleek animals that go back to their boxes adorned with all the colours of the rainbow would receive a rude shock.'

Chamberlin

Colonel Harry D. Chamberlin who had received some grounding in classical work at Saumur,

[4] Still owned by D.J. Murphy Press, it became *Horse & Rider* in 1981.

was also able to write firsthand of the Italian method. As a young American cavalry officer, he and Major West were sent to Tor di Quinto in 1923 and on return to the United States convinced many of their countrymen of the value of forward riding. A brilliant jumper and trainer, Chamberlin proved the efficacy of the Forward Seat by winning a silver medal for his country in the Showjumping at the Los Angeles Olympic Games in 1932.

More relevant to our story was his absolute bias against all forms of collection for all but the expert few. '. . . high collection should be undertaken only by finished horsemen . . .' he wrote in *Training Hunters, Jumpers and Hacks* in 1946. Of course Chamberlin's fears about collection ('a razor in the hands of a monkey' was how he described it)[5] has probably haunted instructors for generations. Countless books, essays, articles have been written in an attempt to instill in the less experienced that collection can only be brought about correctly with disciplined and progressive work whereby the horse begins to strengthen in the back and haunches, until eventually he is able to bring his hocks further underneath him and gather himself. Judging by the level of dressage that existed at this time in both the United States and England, it seems however, that Chamberlin and his colleagues carried this message rather too far, to the extent that it either became distorted, taken out of context, or developed into an excuse for loose and sloppy horses and riders.

In Germany, as we have seen, the *campagne* school had successfully combined collected work in the manège with fast outdoor work across country, but Chamberlin was not convinced. Taking the view that once the horse had reached a high level of dressage training, he was useless as a hunter or hack, he wrote: 'All the airs of *haute école* have great value in developing in the horseman tact and artistic finesse. For the outdoor horse they are of little, if any, value. The High School horse habitually works with an abnormal amount of weight on his hindquarters and this is neither possible nor desirable at fast gaits.'

Chamberlin also disliked any form of flexing, bending and rounding in the crosscountry horse. This was also debatable. The day was not far off when horses, even in the showjumping arena, would require to be supple longitudinally, as well as able to half-halt and collect in order to deal with the tight turns, the tricky combinations and the obvious jumping traps of modern competition.

Even Littauer, an ardent exponent of the Forward Seat, found Chamberlin's views initially hard to accept. In *Horseman's Progress*[6] he wrote, 'I must confess that it was hard for me to relinquish the belief once taught me that the horse should be bent to correspond to the curve of the line along which he moves. I had preserved this tenet of dressage longer than any other.' Yet, along with countless others, Littauer followed the new doctrine virtually to the letter, apparently convinced by Chamberlin's words that bending the horse on a small circle was a 'ruinous practice'.

High School movements such as the Spanish Walk, demonstrated here by an American sidesaddle rider in the late 1800s, soon disappeared with the Caprilli revolution which was received with enormous enthusiasm in the United States.

---

[5] An expression borrowed from Baucher who first used it to describe the action of the spur when applied by the unskilled rider.

[6] Now published under the title *The Development of Modern Riding*.

Such was the power of his personality and his success in the world of international jumping, Chamberlin's ideas influenced equestrianism in all its branches at home and abroad. Yet in defence of Chamberlin who had the horse's best interests at heart, he never intended his advice to permeate dressage itself. The whole point of his writing was to separate the two disciplines of crosscountry riding and dressage and to insist that the techniques for one were not applicable for the other.

Sadly for posterity, many of his ideas became misinterpreted. There are dressage instructors today who will not encourage their pupils to rebalance their horses, yet expect them to perform exercises such as voltes and the shoulder-in with ease and gymnasticity. There are dressage judges who interpret Chamberlin's definition for the trot ('The Trot, though springy, should be low with feet moving close to the ground as a result of minimum flexion of knees and hocks . . .') as the correct one for dressage, oblivious to the fact that Chamberlin was here discussing the locomotion of the crosscountry horse and not for the horse required to carry out any collected work.

To this day, many competition horses are penalised by inexperienced judges for showing a rounded, deeply flexed action of knee and hock. Yet Chamberlin himself clearly pointed out that in 'High School collection, the hocks are flexed, the croup lowered, the neck raised and the face brought into an almost vertical plane . . .'

Another practice, so valuable to the schooling of dressage horses, has virtually been lost from modern practice because of the warnings of Chamberlin. In the following quotation, Chamberlin was objecting to Baucher's dismounted flexions of the horse's lower jaw. Yet flexions dated back to the time of La Guérinière and earlier, who had recommended that the horse's jaw must be as yielding and as soft as the rest of his anatomy. Baucher, as we have seen, developed a series of logical exercises to teach the horse the *mise en main*, yielding to the hand, and Chamberlin wrote: 'These flexions were perhaps essential when few horsemen owned thoroughbred horses . . . For the most part, riding horses of those days were coarse, thick-necked and poorly bred.' How little this otherwise highly educated American understood the horses of the eighteenth and nineteenth century French manège and how sad that so few of today's dressage riders have ever heard of flexions of the lower jaw!

To sum up this very brief discussion on Chamberlin; clearly he had the comfort and happiness of the horse at heart in his concept of how riding should be, preferably fairly fast and over jumps. The pity of it is that many of the people who read his books have not counterbalanced these with others putting across the case for classical dressage. If they had, they would find that instead of seeking to ride the horse forward on a fixed rein contact, thus subjecting this noble animal to a slavelike existence as increasingly happens in many modern dressage schools, the true aim of the enlightened High School masters was something quite different. This was to produce a horse so light on the hand, so supple and strong in the back and the haunches that 'it is then, for the spectator, the horse would seem to move with the lightness of a bird.'[7]

Littauer

Vladimir Littauer truly loved the horse. This shines throughout his writing. Convinced how-ever of the frailty of man, or rather the frailty of the average pupil, he developed a method along Caprilli and Chamberlin lines which would give the average rider some degree of control and technique whilst allowing the horse to work *naturally*. This involved discontinuing the

[7] From General l'Hotte's *Questions Equestres*.

'dressage seat', as Littauer refers to the classical seat since it was too difficult to acquire; he promoted in its place the Forward Seat, with preferably no sitting trot. The rider was to use a 'soft contact' most of the time, loose reins part of the time, and always a freely going horse.[8]

Littauer's methods were extremely successful in all aspects of basic school work as well as jumping. In his own words the forward method worked both for the experienced and for the Sunday rider and they have to be admired for the lack of distress caused to the horse. If all this sounds too easy, we have to remember that the whole essence of the Caprilli doctrine was to make riding easy and natural. Nevertheless, Littauer was a stickler for position, and provided many illustrations in his book of how not to ride. He was well aware that there were many misinterpretations of the Forward Seat, and was more than a little scathing about what he saw across the Atlantic (see Chapter 14). In *Commonsense Horsemanship* a pupil of Littauer describes his main directives in simplified terms. These were 'Weight in stirrups, squeeze with legs, hollow loins, light feel on reins'. Littauer also placed great importance on the pelvis being tipped forward, and the torso in a 'normal, alert position with chest open and head up.'

A prolific writer, Littauer's books including *The Forward Seat, The Defence of the Forward Seat, More About Riding Forward, Schooling Your Horse,* and others are full of commonsense. He makes no claim other than to be new and progressive, his theories in keeping with the modern age when people no longer have time for study and dedicated commitment. An honest remark made about himself at the beginning of one of his books reads: 'What I have just said about collection would be anaethema to any nineteenth century rider, but today I am far from being alone in my estimate of it.'

For schooling at the levels now known as Preliminary and Novice Dressage level, the Littauer method is one which could well be adopted, but which would nowadays find little admiration from the dressage judge. Loose reins at novice level seem currently as unpopular as reins of silk at advanced level in the eyes of most judges, but if the horses themselves could speak, the verdict might be very different.

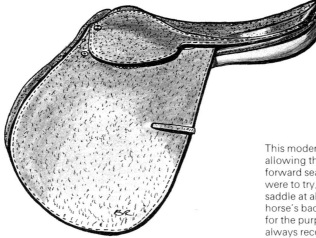

This modern version of a Caprilli saddle is perfect for allowing the rider to balance in his stirrups and adopt the forward seat for crosscountry riding and jumping. If the rider were to try, however, to maintain a sitting position in this saddle at all gaits, he would bump unmercifully on the horse's back close to his weakest point. An excellent saddle for the purpose for which it was designed, although sadly not always recognised as such.

[8] Vladimir S. Littauer, *Commonsense Horsemanship*.

THIRTEEN

The Natural Dressage of the United States of America

The history of riding in the United States is very interesting since it was not something which evolved gradually over hundreds of years, dictated to by socio-economic influences as well as the more obvious historical events as we have seen in Europe. Instead the boundaries of American equitation are far more clearcut and defined. Fashion has played a lesser part on American equitation in general whereas function has remained paramount.

Although this chapter is not specifically concerned with academic riding as we have discussed to date through the annals of European history from the time of the Greeks to the halls of Vienna and Saumur, it nevertheless deserves an important place in our international story of dressage. Let us therefore start at the point when the horse as we know him today first set foot on American soil.

The Conquistadores

Most people realise that there were no horses in existence in America when the Spanish Conquistadores landed on the Mexican mainland in the early 1500s;[1] neither of course were there any indigenous white races. Both horse and the white man therefore came suddenly and bloodily to North and South America. Columbus and later Cortes, Pizarro, de Soto and Coronado all relied for their vanquishing success against the American Indians on their Spanish chargers who filled the enemy with such fear that many refused to fight, believing them to be gods. Tough, honest horses, they had somehow survived the long sea journey often enduring intense cold, searing heat, foul storms and desperate calm in their cramped stalls on the scantiest of rations.

Early Stud Farms

Conquering and colonising as they went, the Spanish first set up flourishing stud farms on the Caribbean islands of Jamaica, Santo Domingo (now the Dominican Republic and Haiti), Cuba and Nicaragua. From this early foundation stock they bred enough horses to supply Mexico, Panama, and Peru. Later it was the turn of the Portuguese who brought the Lusitano horse to Brazil.

The famous wild mustang (*mustunego*) of the pampas was also derived from this stock. As colonial-bred horses escaped into the wild and thrived in their new environment, the first truly American progeny emerged, soon to multiply and multiply. Within a generation, a plethora of feral horses provided the pedestrian Indians with the opportunity for mobility, swiftly changing their whole mode of existence.

With obvious environmental changes and the passage of years, peculiarly American/Hispanic-based breeds evolved. These included the native Peruvian Paso, the Criolla, Costeñõ, Appaloosa, the Paints, Pintos and others. Even the famous cutting horses and American Quarter Horse owes some of its genetic makeup to those early colonial horses.

[1] There had been a very early prehistoric dog-sized horse with four toes, *equus eohippus*, before the Ice Age but this became extinct many milleniums ago.

Statue to Simon Bolivar (born in Caracas 1783), soldier, statesman and liberator. Although stylised, this portrayal is faithful to the natural classical riding style of the Americas as introduced by the Spanish, 'riding down to the crotch', with a proud upright bearing. The horse is also typical of the Spanish-derived American breeds.

Riding *à la Gineta*

Not only did the Spanish bring their horses; they also introduced a style of riding which dominated South America, Mexico, round the Panama Canal and the Western United States. The conquistadores brought their great deep-seated, high pommelled saddles to the Americas, as well as their long-cheeked curbs, sharp spurs and highly ornate, tooled leatherwork. There was only one way to ride with such accoutrements and that was in the *gineta* style (see Chapter 4).

Gradually, over the centuries, the cowboys of North America transformed this saddle to include a horn in front for the roping of steer, and various additions behind for the carrying of supplies, rope and camping gear, but the base of this comfortable campaigning saddle remained essentially the same.

The Stock Saddle

Although heavy, the stock saddle was designed first and foremost to fit any horse. Complemented by a long skirt, the weight was spread comfortably from front to back over as wide an area as possible, and allowed a channel of air to pass under the pommel, over the horse's spine and under the cantle. Secondly, it was constructed in such a way that the man's seat was also evenly spread to relieve the horse of pressure points – so important for long distance riding. Thirdly, the knee guard, later replaced by a roll, encouraged the leg to hang down, long and unconstricted, in a style remarkably similar to the long-leathered classical style of the early European manège.

One feature which still today sets the untrained Western cowboy, Mexican gaucho, Spanish *vaquero* or Portuguese *campino* apart from the rest of the world is a quiet seat and a proud upright bearing. This has not been perfected in any riding hall, under the eagle eye of a pernicious instructor. It is simply the result of riding in this saddle using a functional and natural position.

Today's Western saddle has changed relatively little in purpose or design from that of the early Mexican *charros*. Deep, but flattish

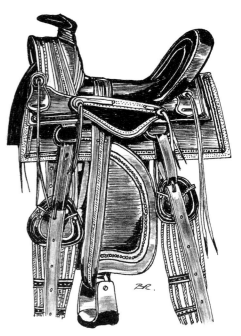

Working cowboy's saddle from the nineteenth century, similar to that used on the great plains of the United States. The flatness of the seat encouraged depth of position and a proud upright posture, although the sloping cantle encouraged riders to straighten the leg on long leathers and push against the stirrup. Many Mexican stock saddles of the same period had a completely flat cantle which allowed a slightly bent leg, with the seat more redolent of the *gineta* style of riding.

in the seat, it provided even the most humble cowpuncher with a natural classical seat from which to collect his horse. There was no need for these people to adapt to the Forward Seat as they drove the long-horned cattle which flourished so well on the Western plains over hundreds of miles to the slaughter-houses of the big cities. The wide open spaces of the cattle states, liberally interspersed with cactus and boulder, necessitated no jumping, rather a sustained balanced handcanter with the rider always able to turn or sidestep at a given moment. (Flat out galloping into the sunset in a a whirl of dust belongs more to the film industry than to the sober reality of practical Western riding).

Indian Horse Culture

The story of horsemanship amongst the native Indians was also governed by practicality. Under the domination of the white man, many had worked as grooms for the Spanish settlers, and later, stolen Spanish tack became much prized. Whilst some tribes eventually abandoned the whole idea of saddlery and learned to ride bareback, with little more than a leather thong tied around the horse's lower jaw, others such as the Sioux and the Comanche rode their horses fully accoutred. Despite their many tribal differences, they all adapted brilliantly to a versatile style of riding.

In his definitive book *A History of Horsemanship* Charles Chenevix Trench quotes contemporary sources to describe the Indian riding posture: 'At a walk or trot he sat bolt upright, riding down to the crotch, not quite straight-legged, but with a forward slant to his thighs which rested on the pony's barrel, his lower leg vertical [gineta style]. At a gallop, he leaned forward, his long thighs gripping like a vice, his lower legs slightly behind the vertical [forward style].'

It is remarkable that the American Indian, with no formal teaching or hereditary practices or tradition to follow, should have discovered for himself the perfect balance for every equestrian requirement. Within a few generations, he had cleverly combined a natural classical seat with the forward seat of Caprilli – a feat which had taken European riders centuries to discover. It is telling also perhaps that it took an American, in the form of Tod Sloan, to develop the forward crouch of the modern race jockey (see Chapter 12) long before his contemporaries at Newmarket on the other side of the Atlantic.

Mexican and Western Riding

By the nineteenth century, the horse culture of the Wild West, the great cattle breeding states of California, Texas, Arizona and Utah was well established. Even now, many of the old Spanish ways are largely retained, particularly in California where the Mexican *charros* had played such an important part in the early days of cattle ranching. In Mexico itself, there was nothing so colourful as a Mexican swell on high days and holidays, sitting on a saddle 'worth a fortune . . . loaded with silver trimmings, and hanging over it . . . an expensive *xerapa*, or Spanish blanket, which adds to the magnificence of the whole.' As Colonel Dodge, a nineteenth century writer goes on to illustrate: 'The canter of the Mexican is the old park canter, with a superabundant use of the curb to make the horse prance and play and show his action. The horse is as fond and proud of this as his rider. Because his horse is prancing is no reason to look down on him. He is doing nothing more than the men who used to go titupping down Rotten Row every fine afternoon of fifty years ago.'[2]

This Spanish style has permeated all aspects of riding on the range to a greater or lesser degree, but when talking of the style of the early Spanish settlers, let us remember that theirs

[2] From *Riders of Many Lands*, New York 1894.

was not the sophisticated style of the Baroque manège. The Conquistadores were expert but not particuarly educated horsemen. Few if any of them would have had any academic training at Madrid or Cordoba. Mostly they were a motley but incredibly courageous band of mercenaries and adventurers, burning with the conviction that they had a divine right to claim the Americas for God and the Spanish throne. Much of their riding would have been cut and thrust, but from all accounts they rode as centaurs, life in the saddle comprising their life and their destiny.

For the North American cowboy, the seriousness of riding was much the same. Less colourful perhaps than his *vaquero* cousin, he nevertheless stayed on his horse for 'an almost unheard of period, often forty-eight hours at a time, when holding big bunches of cattle' and knew how to conserve energy both for himself and his partner. Nowadays, the proud, upright Western style is beginning to draw the admiration it deserves. Of course, standards vary enormously. Some of it, particularly amongst the bronco-busters, may be a little rough and ready yet this is universal in all disciplines, and few see fit to criticise the lack of finesse reguarly displayed in polo or other exciting equestrian sports, so why look down on cow herding?

Rein Control

More often than not, the genuine cowboy or *vaquero* handles his rein with dexterity. In order to herd and separate out these steers he requires at least his roping hand free, and his horse must find his own balance and be controlled with minimum fuss. It would be ridiculous for the Western rider to have to organise two sets of reins from the standard double bridle, so a simple, often mild curb is used, with a generally very light contact of the rein. Neck reining and a refined use of weight or seat aids are used to control the horse, and the typical cowboy's mount has all the agility and impulsion that we have come to associated with the polo pony or showjumper.

The ideal mount is a horse which can start, turn, half-halt, gather himself and thrust forward with impulsion all at a split-second's notice. 'If the trainer is able and has suceeded in his work,' writes W. Sidney Felton, the American (whom we have encountered in an earlier chapter), 'we find the trained horse nicely collected, well flexed at the poll, laterally mobile and flexible, highly responsive to the leg aids and ready to move out with great speed or to come to an equally fast stop at the slightest indication of the rider's wishes . . .'

Happily today this heritage of the West is no longer relegated in the eyes of fellow Americans to the backyard of the cowhand. With an enlightenment of ideas and the gradual realisation by so many Americans going to Europe that here is a living if modified remnant from the days of classical riding,

'The canter of the Mexican is the old park canter, with a super-abundant use of the curb to make the horse prance and play and show his action . . .' Note the superb trappings, the bucket stirrups and the ornate saddle.

attitudes have changed. Western riding now exerts considerable appeal to riders from all social backgrounds. Felton sums up the situation today very fairly: 'With this change, has come a definite tendency to modify the rough and ready methods of an earlier generation, and to adapt to western conditions some of the methods of schooling and riding of the Classical School.'

Another admirer from across the Atlantic, this time a former cavalry officer, John Paget, wrote a letter to *Riding* magazine[3] which rued the '"heavy handed and two fisted" riding of Mittel Europa which is both neo-classical and an inexcusable breach of cavalry tradition' and applauded the light rein technique of the American Western School and in particular that of Mr Lougher who has given demonstrations in England. This work, he wrote, was based 'on exercises of Iberian horse-lore which have been practised successfully from the Pyrenees to the Andes and from Tierra del Fuego to Alaska.'

One cannot help feel Xenophon would have heartily approved of the true expert in Western riding . . . balance, being at one with the horse, instant obedience, light happy horses, co-operation . . . ideals as ageless as the Rocky Mountains themselves.

The East Coast

What was happening to horsemanship on the eastern side of the United States was rather more complicated. Apart from the developing Quarter Horse, it was the workhorses, cobs and ponies of English, Irish, Dutch, Flemish and German descent which first provided the early settlers with their useful farm animals. Later came the European gentry: refugee Cavaliers from the English Civil War, Scottish nobles who had lost their land in the aftermath of Culloden, Huguenots from France and Holland, and later French royalists fleeing from the guillotine. All brought horses of quality, in latter times the horses of Thoroughbred descent, pure or crossbred, far outweighed any other breed. Hacks, hunters and trotting horses came in abundance. The Cleveland Bay, Yorkshire Coach Horse and Norfolk Roadster introduced special qualities to an amalgam of bloods which would provide America with some spectacular breeds of her own in years to come.

In states like Virginia where the English colonists felt so much at home, the Anglo influence produced enormous enthusiasm for racing. Initially it was the Colonial Quarter Pather which was used to race between the homesteads down one makeshift central dusty track; later it was the Quarter Horse which could 'start like a jack-rabbit and stop on a dime', finally it was the Thoroughbred and with it came the desire for proper racetracks.

As the great New England forests were felled, the prosperous farmers and plantation owners began to take up hunting with hounds, and an anglicised form of riding separated those on the East Coast of the United States from those of the Wild West. Not unexpectedly, the Western stocksaddle had no place in this society; neither did the Western form of riding. As stirrups shortened, natural obstacles were jumped in the hunting field and posting to the trot became popular and fashionable. Soon, the English saddle had become the norm, and no one would have dreamed of riding in a Western one.

Pleasure Riding

In the mid nineteenth century, wealthy Americans took up pleasure and park riding. Horses with easy gaits, the *slow gait* and *rack* being distinctive of the American Saddle horse for example, became popular and according to Dodge, 'no one who has learned the Southern gaits can

[3] 1968.

deny their superior ease' to carry the road-rider from homestead to homestead. Initally, park riding was developed from a semi-classical, upright seat, the nineteenth century park saddle being close to a modern straight-cut dressage saddle. Dodge describes this Southern seat as being easy on horse and rider.

Gradually however, we read that Anglomania took over and as breeders selectively bred for more extravagant pacing action and developed four and five gaited horses, a seat which was based on what was now being referred to as 'English style' took over at the big shows of Kentucky or New York. This was a bastardised seat since all that was bad in the old English hunting seat was converted for the riding of gaited horses. Riders, unable to maintain a proper balance began to slip behind the horse's centre of balance, pressing uncomfortably close to the loins. Dodge warned against this departure from true American riding, commenting, 'We may love our British cousin and yet not adopt his style.' To complement this latest style, lengthened flat-seated, low-cantled show saddles were designed with cut-away heads. It was thought that by sitting further back, the front of the horse would be more exposed and impressive. Riders compensated for this unatural balance by pushing their legs forward against the stirrup, and holding the hands unnecessarily high, a style still in vogue today in certain showing classes.

Originally designed for English Pleasure classes, this seat was 'developed first for the American saddle horse to accommodate his regally high head carriage' wrote Jeanne Mellin in her definitive book on the Morgan horse in 1986. Later on she describes this saddle as a 'logical choice' since it 'allows for greater freedom of motion in the forehand.' This may be so: it also has the disadvantage of restricting the rounding of the horse's back, and with a heavy unbalanced rider could seriously hamper the action of the hindlegs. Nevertheless because this flattening effect often causes a more exaggerated use of the horse's frontlegs to compensate for the problems behind and under saddle, the park saddle seat has remained immensely popular.

Those Americans who had ridden in Britain in the early part of the twentieth century were somewhat scathing about standards in their own country. In 1921, Lida L. Fleitmann remarked in a book entitled *Comments on Hacks and Hunters*, 'To be a horseman over here stamps you as rather a freak . . . The average American is not a horseman . . .'

This comment in a country where riding on the range was the daily work of thousands of expert people, and where fox hunting had now been in existence for generations after generation in Virginia and Kentucky, seems surprising. One concludes that if more riders had listened to writers like Dodge, such a state of affairs would never have been reached. A final word from his book rued the fact that 'A horse nowadays is not even permitted to guide by the neck, whilst as for suppling his croup, or giving him a light forehand, no one ever dreams of it at all. All this is, to say the least, a distinct loss . . . Taking him as the type of a class, the Central Park rider has his good points and he has his bad ones. When he is new to his

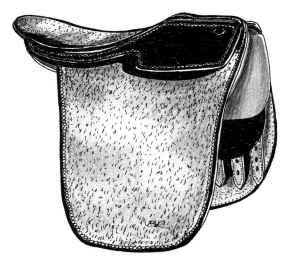

This flat-seated gaited saddle with its long cut-back head is designed to place the rider well back on the horse's back, from which position the thigh would inevitably lie behind the flap in a normal saddle. This is circumvented by the extremely wide cut of the gaited saddle flap, thus protecting the rider's smart attire from the hair and sweat of the horse's flanks. This seat is the antithesis of the traditional classical seat of the dressage masters.

work and over-imitates the English style, he is at his worst . . .'

If the civilian population had lost the art of riding, there were many distinguished US cavalry riders who had not. These included the great Captain Guy Henry, who competed in the 1912 Olympics, as well as the famous Captain Harry Chamberlin (see Chapter 12), who together with team compatriots Majors Doak and Barry went to Antwerp for the 1920 Olympics. Unfortunately, not everyone had recourse to teaching from the military which was confirmed by the writings of Captain Vladimir Littauer (see Chapter 12) of the Russian Imperial Army who, fleeing from the Bolsheviks, arrived in the United States in the early 1920s with little money and even less English.

Vladimir Littauer

Working as a labourer initially, he opened in New York City in 1927 his well known academy, The Boots and Saddles Riding School. Together with two other talented Russian cavalry officers, Captain Sergei Kournakoff and Colonel Prince Kader Guirey, this dedicated man was to play a vital role in the progress of horsemanship in the United States.

Strongly of the opinion that it was not sufficient to be a born rider and stressing the importance of study and work, Littauer determined to enlighten American riders by leading them away from the riding of the hunting field and other so-called English influences and introduce a proper technique developed from Caprilli and the Italian School. 'Prior to about 1930 the United States had made no contribution to educated riding . . .' he wrote, '. . . when other than English influences made their appearance here and cities grew large, park riding and musical rides in the covered rings of riding clubs were common under the influence of dressage riding. The latter however, was usually much simplified and often considerably corrupted in a provincial manner.'

While this was fair comment of riders in general, the US military was was well served by the great cavalry schools of Fort Riley in Kansas and Fort Sill founded at the end of the last century. The emphasis (as in England at the same time) was largely on jumping and cross-country riding and the Americans were notably quicker to embrace the teaching of Caprilli than their counterparts in Britain, and the transition from backward to forward seat amongst those who rode 'English style' was quick and relatively painless.

Twentieth Century Instructors

It was at this point that the Caprilliists got to grips with the mammoth task of educating the civilian riding fraternity of East Coast America, but there was one semi-classical instructor of the old school at the turn of the twentieth century who deserves a mention.

The Portuguese Count Baretto de Souza was a very average riding master in his own homeland, but coming from a background where equestrian classicism was *de rigeur* he made an enormous impression on a young country which lacked all form of academic riding tradition. De Souza's methods, so vastly different from that of the proverbial family groom turned instructor, were based on a mixture of Marialva, Baucher and Fillis.

Largely concerned with collection and flexion in the horse, de Souza believed it was possible to teach novice pupils the basis of classical riding by concentrating first and foremost on a balanced, still seat and introducing the lightest of aids initially, which would later become as second nature to the horse. The rider must apply himself '. . . to begin all leg actions with the lightest possible, touch, albeit holding himself ready to a firmer, more energetic, rapid or intense touches *that the horse may show to him*. He must . . . *allow the initiative of the horse*

Count Baretto de Souza, a fashionable East Coast instructor at the turn of the century. He believed that with tact, gentle hands and progressive training, the English Thoroughbred was as fine a manège horse as any.

to indicate the amount of softness, vigour, energy, vivacity or any other qualities of the aids.'

In order to obtain a good seat, he was one of the few of this generation in America to insist that riding be undertaken without stirrups, sitting and not posting to the trot. This was something of a phenomena to his American students who, brought up to ride 'English', had vigorously resisted a form of riding which echoed the cowboy's seat. He also remarked that horsemen who enjoyed a good seat, i.e. with torso erect and expanded, were never known to complain of any 'digestive-organ trouble'. As for 'the young female rider, whose bust when not properly carried – even apart from riding – does not properly develop . . .', good carriage was even more important.

Although somewhat quaint in both text and illustrations, De Souza was both articulate and persuasive and soon enjoyed an enormous following. Such was the demand for his ideas, that whilst in America he wrote two books – *Elementary Equitation* (1922) and *Advanced Equitation* (1927). Very much of the old school, de Souza's concern for preserving the courtesies of the manège sometimes leads to prolixity, but this does not preclude some sensible and sound advice. Work in hand is thoroughly discussed and a progressive series of school figures are illustrated with useful comments. Amongst the more interesting observations is his belief that students would much better understand lateral work if the classical shoulder-in (discussed in Chapter 7), for example, was described more literally, i.e. as work on four tracks instead of the usual modern term 'two track work.'

In place of the shoulder-in, he suggests an exercise he terms 'flexion of the shoulder' which is in reality the equivalent of today's three-track shoulder-in. This exercise would, he wrote, 'flex the horse more, precisely on account of the remainder of his body being meanwhile compelled to move forward on the straight line.' Another original idea is his 'balancer' exercise, based on a sequence of half-passes at walk or trot to alternate sides, until by reducing the number of steps, the movement is executed on the spot taking up a waltzing effect on the haunches. In this de Souza looks for 'the general airiness of the animal who seems not to touch the ground.'

Stressing always the need for correct preparation, he writes of the 'poised walk' when the horse must conform to the 'slightest possible leg and hand touches . . . before even *thinking* of trying to execute them [any exercise] at trot.' At every new stage of the horse's training, the rider is urged to reward the horse whilst he is *in the movement* by both caresses and compliments. The horse likes the human voice, especially when its owner knows how to modulate it according to requirements, and render it sympathetic; as much can be obtained . . . by its use, there is no valid reason for not employing this God-given means . . .'

It was not until the appearance of Mestre Nuno Oliveira in the early 1960s in America, that a classical rider of the old Portuguese school was to have such an effect on so many pupils. But de Souza was soon to be forgotten and eclipsed by the jumping revolution which took the United States by storm.

The Forward Seat was to change so much of what had gone before; it literally paved the way for a tremendous interest in international competition. Although the first resurgence was obviously for jumping, it was not long before Americans were determined to catch up with Europe on the previously unexplored discipline of dressage. Initially, it was the army who provided America with a state of excellence in competition. The army cavalry school at Fort Riley exchanged ideas and instructors with the better-known military schools of Europe, such as Saumur, and in 1932 at the Los Angeles Olympic Games an American army team comprised of Colonel Isaac Kitts, Captain (later Colonel) Hiram Tuttle and Alvin Moore took the Bronze Medal for dressage, with Tuttle winning the individual Bronze.

Colonel Kitts' horse American Lady was something of a legend in her lifetime. Unbelievable as it sounds, Kitts had trained her to Grand Prix level within the space of a year. His son, Alfred, known as Bud, who also became a full colonel in the American army, became interested in High School work at an early age and gave demonstrations first with American Lady and later with a Lipizzaner stallion, Conversano Deja which had been given to the US army by the Austrians in recognition of the debt owed to General Patton in rescuing the noble white stallions at the end of the last war (see Chapter 14).

Today, Colonel Kitts Jr, is one of America's most experienced dressage judges. In a recent article in *Dressage and CT* the author, Glencairn Bowlby describes how Kitts would like to see dressage tests made shorter, easier on the horse, and that movements like counter change of hand, do not necessarily have to be duplicated each time. He would also like to see a more obvious award of marks to how the rider has ridden rather than who he or she is.

Only with the disbandment of the US army teams after the 1948 Olympics did civilians begin to shine in the three disciplines of competition. Today, with a wealth of international instructors visiting or settling in America and Canada, every opportunity exists for sophisticated schooling. The US coaches Jack Le Goff and his fellow team trainer, Bertalan de Nemethy (further discussed in Chapter 19), have made an outstanding contribution to general riding standards in America, together with many lesser known but nonetheless dedicated immigrants.

With continuing help from Europe and through their own now well-established talented, though somewhat widespread instructors, competitive dressage for these enthusiastic sportsmen and women, is as advanced today in the United States and Canada as it is elsewhere in the world.

FOURTEEN

General Purpose Riding – A Dilution of Dressage Principles?

With the advent of showjumping and the inevitable changes in approach to riding which resulted, dressage in the early decades of the twentieth century was in a continual state of uncertainty, and more often, confusion. Whilst the major classical schools of Saumur, Vienna and Hanover continued in the disciplined classical mould of earlier times (albeit with certain national modifications), the English speaking countries and those countries which had a large civilian riding population struggled to bring cohesion out of the chaos of new and outmoded ideas and develop a general purpose style of riding. This, however, did not happen overnight.

In retrospect, it is clear that where jumping took hold amongst a riding public who had never enjoyed the benefits of a thorough grounding in classical riding, the principles of the various disciplines became increasingly blurred. Many riders were unsure of the reasons for pursuing certain practices in the schooling of their horses. Imperceptibly, the latest doctrine for riding horses over jumps became incorporated into the schooling methods of *all* horses. Where there was no classical establishment to define and lead the way ahead for dressage, every area of riding suffered.

Dressage at the Olympics

Even the dressage phase of the first Olympic Games to include equestrian events was affected by the universal passion for jumping. Due to the efforts of the Swedish Count Clarence von Rosen who had persistently lobbied for their inclusion since 1906, the three disciplines of Horse Trials, Showjumping and Grand Prix Dressage were introduced for the first time at Stockholm in 1912, with jumping in each phase. This may seem strange to us today, but we must appreciate this was a time when the teachings of Caprilli were just being grasped; in addition, only cavalry officers were to participate, in order to prove the suitability and versatility of their various cavalry mounts. The creators of the early Olympic tests thus positively removed dressage from the sphere of artistic equitation and gave it the sporting mould, from which some regret it has not yet recovered. They are surely mistaken.

The First Tests

Let us look at the content of that first important Olympic dressage test. The use of the name Grand Prix is quite misleading in today's terms since none of the advanced movements of today's Grand Prix were required. Instead, the rider was to enter at the gallop, show collection and extension in all gaits, rein-back, turn on the hocks, perform four flying changes on a straight line, and finally jump five small obstacles which included a barrel being rolled towards the horse. The object was to test courage, calmness and obedience in the cavalry horse. It encouraged general purpose riding on a general purpose horse.

Remember this was just before the First World War, so the idea behind this test of obedience was extremely sound at a time when countries still relied greatly on the efficiency of their cavalries. In 1912, it was the Swedes who dominated the dressage, and six years later at Antwerp,

Riders of the Spanish Riding School of Vienna enter the lofty portals of Fischer von Erlach's Winter Riding School. Somehow the white austerity of this classical building complements the discipline of the noble white stallions as they take their place for the stately carousel. (*Courtesy of the Spanish Riding School*)

PLATE 11

(*below*) *Bereiter* Johann Riegler greets his Lipizzaner which has just arrived at the specially prepared stables at Wembley Arena for the 1989 London performance of the Spanish Riding School. Genuine joy showed in the faces of riders and stallions as they were reunited after the four-day journey from Vienna to London. (*Photo by the author*)

Granat ridden by Christine Stückelberger in an extravagant extended trot at Goodwood in 1978, the year she became World Champion. The power and thrust of this movement, so prevalent in modern dressage, contrasts sharply with the suspended collected movements of the Baroque and Classical Schools of a byegone age. Note the firm contact with the bit, and the driving position of the rider, an interpretation which found favour with the majority of international dressage judges, but again differs from that of dressage at the beginning of the century. (*Photo: Kit Houghton*)

PLATE 12

The half-pass of world champion Christine Stückelberger's Granat was considered unbeatable by the dressage world of the late seventies. This was marked by a surge of forward power, with the lateral bend well emphasised by the degree of contact with the rider's inside hand. (*Photo: Kit Houghton*)

Young cavalry officers such as (*left*) Jousseaume for France and (*right*) Podhajsky for Austria, who excelled in competitive international dressage, including the Olympics, just prior to the Second World War, illustrate the changing face of dressage from freestyle virtuosity on slack reins to test riding where a stronger contact was more acceptable to military judges.

they proved themselves again by winning the gold, silver and bronze in the Dressage phase.

The Olympic Games were interrupted from their initally six, later four year cycle by the War to end all wars, and only much later in 1932 when the venue was Los Angeles were the piaffe and passage introduced into Grand Prix Dressage. With the change to more artistic requirements, it is not surprising perhaps that two officers from Saumur[1] took the gold and silver in that year for France. By the time of the 1936 Olympics, staged in prewar Germany, all the movements with which we are familiar today, including the pirouette, were included. For the dressage, this Games drew a very illustrious field of competitors including Colonel Podhajsky of the Spanish Riding School (see next chapter) and the composition of the test had now gone far beyond the capabilities of the general purpose rider.

It is important to understand the difficulties faced by the civilian population after Caprilli. Without doubt, Caprilli's Forward Seat had allowed great progress to be made in the field of jumping. For those who practised it, the benefit to the horse was enormous since now he was able to work forward in a more natural balance, unrestricted by the backward posture of his rider. Second, he no longer had to sustain intermittent banging on the back from a seat which attempted to remain in the saddle, but which was unable to absorb all the bumps and jerks of riding across country and over obstacles.

The Cost of the Benefit

Unfortunately, not everyone who practised the Forward Seat possessed the fine tact and sense of balance of people like Chamberlin and Littauer. As discussed in Chapter 12, the whole concept of the Forward Seat was to be finely balanced on the stirrups, allowing the horse harmonious, fluid, forward movement with total mobility of back, head and neck from an

[1] Lesage and Marion with their famous horses, Taine and Linon.

Many riders, unable to master the balance of riding in the stirrups using closed angles of body and legs, etc., actually straightened the leg and stood up in the stirrups using the bit as a means of support.

elastic, unrestricted contact. History often repeats itself, and not surprisingly perhaps bad horsemanship produced in many quarters a bastardised version of the new style. This not only damaged jumping, it hit hard at the schooling or dressing of all horses. In England, this was particularly noticeable.

One major problem had arisen over bitting. In keeping with the Italians, many riders abandoned the curb, often replacing it with a thin jointed snaffle. With less control over the mouth, and seats which left much to be desired, many riders became heavy-handed. Where once riders had asked their horses to flex or bridle – the English expression at the turn of the century – by restraining mildly on the curb rein – it became necessary to resort to pulling. Many, unable to master the balance of riding in the stirrups, using closed angles of body and legs, actually straightened the leg and virtually stood up in the stirrup, unwittingly using the bit as a means of support. Hard hands led to hard mouths, and where horses had suffered through their backs, they now suffered through their mouths.

'Snaffle Mouths'

The double bridle, or gentleman's bridle, became the brunt of a new prejudice.[2] Some regarded its use almost as a form of cheating; and regardless of a horse's conformation, age or mouth, and the use to which it might be put, you were all at once no good as a rider unless you used the snaffle. Thus the bit designed for the racetrack or steeplechase became the everyday bit of the twentieth century.

This led to complacency. In the old days, riders of every nationality had respected the use of the curb. Hunting and manège riders alike prided themselves on their ability to handle the reins with finesse. 'He has good hands,' was the accolade every horseman aspired to, and the constant exhortation to lighter hands not only echoed from the walls of the riding school, but were passed on from father to son, mother to daughter in every riding family. With the coming of the snaffle, much of this natural respect for the horse's mouth disappeared completely.

In Britain, riding was at a very low ebb. By the mid twenties, even showjumping and eventing had produced no Olympic medals whatsoever for a country which acknowledgedly had the best horses in the world. Altogether, the situation looked extremely gloomy. Frustrated by what they saw, a group of retired cavalry officers founded in 1929 the Institute of the Horse. This was the pre-runner to today's British Horse Society and the idea was to lend some form of cohesion to all forms of equestrianism which was now within the purse and reach of thousands. Determined to instill some form of method or technique, the Institute inaugurated the passing of examinations for certificates in instruction at various levels. Although the army had produced some good dressage instructors, the country was only interested in jumping.

[2] This has continued to the present day.

This passion was echoed within the junior equivalent of the Institute, the Pony Club. The majority of Pony Clubs were affiliated to the bigger Hunts in the country, therefore not unnaturally, the emphasis was almost totally on riding across country and over obstacles and dressage was regarded with reluctance and suspicion.

Weedon, a Last Bastion

The British cavalry school of Weedon (founded in 1919 by Lord Baden-Powell) whilst anxious to promote a modern, all-round approach to riding, nevertheless tried to preserve some of the old classical tenets of the High School for the schooling of horses. Various enlightened officers had returned from the Continent determined to help the English discover balance, suppleness and lightness in their horses. Keen to improve national success in all-round competition, some instructors tried to produce at Weedon, what the Count d'Aure had achieved at Saumur (see Chapter 13). On the whole, this worked reasonably well between the two wars but not enough took advantage of these dedicated instructors.

The purists of the Caprilli School were of little encouragement. In the United States, Vladimir Littauer wrote: 'All the English writers of the time took the Forward Seat out of the context of the method, often partially corrupting it, combining it with a few old military dressage principles, and adding a dash of traditional foxhunting practices.'

This was unfair, since Weedon[3] produced some remarkable all round horsemen, including Colonels V.D.S. 'Pudding' Williams,[4] Arthur Brooke, Michael Ansell (also Saumur), Nat Kindersley, 'Handy' Hurrell, Bill Froud and Brigadier Dick Friedberger, who contributed so much to the early Manuals of Horsemanship. Intervening cruel war however left insufficient instructors to reach the hearts of the vast civilian riding population and it was gradually left to the Institute and the Pony Club run by dedicated amateurs to promote national riding. As the military influence faded, within a generation names like Fillis and Baucher were forgotten. Between the wars, travel abroad for pleasure or study became more difficult, the days of the Grand Tour were over and even classical academies such as the Spanish Riding School and Saumur began to seem remote and removed. In Britain, many people, whilst essentially horse-mad, were quite happy to remain selftaught. As a result dressage had no chance to develop and was simply not considered except by the fortunate few who had ridden abroad. It would be another thirty-six years after the founding of Weedon that Britain would send her first dressage representatives to the Olympics.[5]

Prior to this however, the work of two exceptional cavalry instructors, McTaggart and Hance, was read by thousands at home and abroad. Perhaps one of the reasons their books did not have a greater effect on the riding population may be blamed on the saddle of that time. As McTaggart pointed out, the average English saddle did little to help the rider sit in balance with his horse and he expressed the hope that one day, a saddle would be designed which would allow the rider to sit closer to the horse's centre of gravity, instead of sliding the seat towards the horse's loins. If riders read these words, it is obvious saddlers did not. The new spring tree jumping saddle would soon come into vogue and for normal schooling purposes this was worse by far than the established hunting saddles. Even the later general purpose saddle would be designed around the jumping saddle which promoted riding in the

---

[3] Weedon's equivalent at Sangor, the British Cavalry School in India, also produced some competent instructors including Colonel Jamie Crawford.

[4] Father of the late Dorian Williams, a man devoted to dressage whose wife Brenda competed internationally for Britain.

[5] In 1956 Mrs Brenda Williams with Pilgrim, Mrs Lorna Johnstone with Rosie Dream.

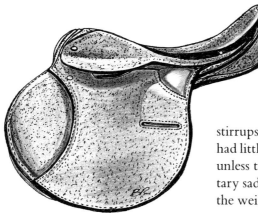

This type of twentieth-century English jumping saddle is too often employed for other disciplines such as the schooling of young horses, novice dressage etc. Since the cut is specifically for the forward seat it does not lend itself for other purposes.

stirrups, and not into the horse. Dressage riders therefore had little chance of finding the correct balance at that time, unless they sat in one of the heavy and rather crude military saddles which at least had the advantage of spreading the weight on the horse's back.

McTaggart

Fortunately, not everyone was so blinded by jumping that they blotted out all the academic principles of the past four hundred years. Lieutenant Colonel M. F. McTaggart was an exponent of the Forward Seat over jumps, but he was convinced that all schoolwork would benefit if more attention were paid to the principles of the classical school. In his Preface to the third edition of a highly popular book *Mount and Man* published in London in 1935, he wrote: 'The more we study the art of riding the more we understand how all the different parts fit together. The steeplechase jockey would be all the better if he studied *haute école*, the High School rider would be improved with steeeplechasing, and the hunting man with a course of show jumping. We can all learn from each other.'

To pursue his point, McTaggart aimed his criticisms at the very heart of the British horse establishment. 'In public estimation,' he wrote, 'any rider who rides in the National must be a good horseman, and everyone who wins it must be superb. But from photographs and slow moving pictures we are now able to see that there is often much to be desired . . .'

In other words, he felt everyone in England required some self-examination and that riding would never improve until people began to use an established technique. Appalled by the pulling horses and pulling hands he saw all around him, he departed from the teachings of Caprilli to write that for general riding a horse correctly flexed or bent from the poll with his head in the vertical was infinitely safer, more obedient and pleasurable for all riding, whatever his specific role in life. With typical dry humour, he made an amusing but oh so true allusion to this: 'The natural position of a horse at the standstill or in motion is with his nose protruded and his neck straight. The natural position of a yokel on parade for the first time is also with his head thrown forward and his chin out. Both require drilling.'

In McTaggart's school, pupils were to learn how to handle their reins correctly with a proper double bride on a properly schooled horse. 'The horse that flexes properly gives himself body and soul to the commands of his master . . .' Later he regretted the new craze for the snaffle, most particularly for hunting. 'The practice of hunting in snaffles is hardly to be recommended and it is very mysterious why so many people do so, as it is much more tiring and unsatisfactory. The snaffle is useful for grooms at exercise or for jockeys when at work, but those would seem to be the only occasions when it should be used, except of course with novices and children.'

Similarly he was against all gadgetry, or harsh pelhams. 'Let us stick to the simple double bridle, and we shall find we shall achieve by comfort and knowledge what we have never been able to effect by severity.'

As well as expressing concern over the horse's mouth, McTaggart had strong ideas about preventing abuse of the horse's back. Apart from the ever continuing arguments about the jumping position and showing his disapproval of what he called 'the backseat brigade', McTaggart commended the position of the High School rider with a quote from Fillis. 'The High School seat is forward in the dip of the saddle. Personally I prefer this seat for all purposes, for the horse carries the weight on the strongest part of his back, just behind the withers, where there is also the least amount of movement if he "plays up".'

Simple diagrams are shown to explain the relative gravity line through rider and horse, and McTaggart expresses the hope that one day saddles will be vastly improved to complement a more balanced seat.

Captain Hance

Captain Hance, a product of Weedon and a brilliant teacher was also disappointed by much of what he saw in England in the late twenties and early thirties. 'Confusion of Thought' is one of the subtitles of his book *School for Horse and Rider* (1932) and later, he commented drily: 'During the years in which I have taught riding since I left the Army, one fact has become increasingly obvious to me. It is this: that very great confusion abounds in civilian life as to the meaning of the phrase "to ride" and the expression "horseman". If we define the former as "to move about by means of sitting on a horse", then no doubt there is a great deal of riding done and this country abounds in horsemen. But if we allow to creep into our definition the suggestion that any but the most elementary form of skill is required "to ride" or is possessed by the "horseman", then I must definitely state that the percentage of those people who habitually sit upon horses and may properly be described as able to ride *is very small indeed*.'

Hands

Pupils who have worked and studied under Captain Hance remember his gentleness with the horse and his absolute fury if any roughness was demonstrated with the hands. In relation to this sensitive subject, he wrote: 'To every branch of art or sport there are some who devote themselves entirely, but the pupil, however elementary the degree of proficiency which he wishes to attain, must be prepared to study . . . In order that the hands may be able to execute their intricate functions smoothly, it is absolutely essential that the seat be entirely independent of any support from the reins. *It is for this reason that*

The eighteenth-century engraving of the Capriole by John Vanderbank may look European but it is actually British. It exemplifies the old High School seat so favoured by McTaggart where the rider sits into his horse 'in the dip of the saddle . . . and the horse carries the weight on the strongest part of his back'.

Members of the 'backseat brigade' were heartily condemned by early twentieth-century writers McTaggart and Hance, whose ideas were influenced by Saumur and Weedon. Not every hunting man rode with such a lack of consideration for his horse, but it says much for the courage of the hunter that so many performed generously for this type of rider well into the century.

riding without reins is so strongly recommended.'

Like McTaggart, he saw no virtue in abandoning the double bridle. Many students, 'through ignorance of the real functions of a double bridle . . . never know half that pleasure in riding which is derived by a good horseman from the *correct* use of one.'

At some length, he pointed out how the most severe bit could be comfortable for a horse, if the rider had discerning hands and a knowledge of flexions. 'It is this knowledge which enables the expert to use the severest bit; he will, by the lightest use of his fingers, first of all produce a flexion, and through flexions complete subjection.'

Whilst the snaffle had its uses, particularly for novices, both horse and rider, he found little sympathy for those '. . . who will not ride their horses in anything but a snaffle. They "like their mounts to take a nice hold" all the time, which, of course, hides a lot of things! We are also invariably informed by these folk that "a snaffle is much less severe than a curb-bit" – this despite the fact that the animals they ride lean on their hands all day long.'

Like McTaggart, Hance's book contains a wealth of information from basic schooling to jumping. For the dressage student there is a noteworthy section on long-reining and advanced mounted training, which includes simple explanations on the theory of flexions.

Sensible advice from both books were included in the early publications of the British Horse Society and Pony Club, but this advice is less popular today and rarely pursued.

In Conclusion

Throughout the thirties, forties and even fifties, only a few dedicated people throughout the English-speaking world appeared in international dressage events but showjumping and the three day event blossomed. In 1936, Great Britain won her first equestrian Olympic medal, the team bronze for eventing, and in the following Olympics held in London, she achieved another team bronze this time for showjumping.

Whilst the Continentals, who continued to pursue all three of the Olympic disciplines, dominating dressage at every turn, the British seemed at last to have found their forte in the world of jumping and the time was not far off where they would provide the most formidable teams in the world.

Until very recently, few horses in Italy, Britain, the United States, Australia, Canada and New Zealand were schooled primarily with dressage in mind. The average horse was and often still is expected to cope in every sphere of riding, often through a mixture of training ideas and objectives. Where the non-intervention philosophy of Caprilli and his supporters had worked in the days of straightforward jumping, even this began to suffer from its limitations as the years rolled on and more showjumpers returned to old methods of control and collection.

Long after the Second World War, the practice of dressage tests was regarded by many as a necessary evil towards gaining admittance to the more exciting demands of jumping compeitions. Work on the flat – as it came to be known – having dropped the ideals as well as many of the methods of the High School – held little appeal to either the riding or general public, indeed often it was flat, lifeless and onerous to both horse and rider.

It would be quite wrong to blame the innovators of the Forward Seat who were brilliant in their field for the subsequent practice of non-intervention in dressage. Nevertheless, by preaching the disadvantages of collection, of the double bridle and flexion, academic study became unfashionable and enormous damage was done.

Brought up to let their horse find its own balance (usually permanently on the forehand), allowing it to move round the ring like a ship, seek neither flexion, bend nor rounding in back or limb, many riders had no conception that dressage made demands of their horses which were quite impossible to execute. It was only when the West Germans, the Swedes, Dutch, Swiss, Danish and the Russians continued to collect the gold, silver and bronze in every success-ive Olympics after the war, that Britain, America and the other jumping nations realised that if they wanted their up-and-coming riders to succed at dressage, everyone must first go back to school.

Dorothy Morkis, one of the first US women riders to achieve a high place in the Olympics. Here she took fifth place in the individual dressage on Monaco at Montreal in 1976. (*Photo: Leslie Lane*)

FIFTEEN

Three Great Men

WYNMALEN AND DECARPENTRY

Just prior to the Second World War, a minority of remarkable riders were demonstrating the most beautiful and talented advanced dressage at home, in the academies and in the competition arenas of Europe. Those who competed were still largely drawn from the cavalry or classical establishments and included such notables as Major (later Colonel) Podhajsky of the Spanish Riding School of Vienna, Major Lesage and Major Marion and Lt (later Colonel) Jousseaume of the *Cadre Noir*, Baron von Langen, Lieutenant Pollay and Major Gerhard of the German cavalry and Lieutenant-Colonel B. Sandstrom, Linder and Olson of Sweden and others.

Henry Wynmalen

In Great Britain, a Dutch civilian born in 1889 reintroduced the riding population to higher equitation. Henry Wynmalen, a record-breaking aviator[1] and dedicated horseman from a distinguished cavalry background settled in England in 1927 where later he was to meet and marry Julia Ward, another great horselover, and today a senior dressage judge. Despite a degree in engineering and enormous success in flying and business for one so young, Wynmalen had already suffered three huge setbacks in his life.

The first of these was that he never knew his father, a young lieutenant in the Dutch Hussars who had been killed at Java, before Henry was born. The second, when he failed an eye test, precluded him from entering the proud Dutch cavalry, a lifelong dream for the horseloving Henry. The third was the tragic death of his first wife, mother of his two daughters, from the long, wasting disease of multiple sclerosis.

Perhaps it was these sadnesses, together with his gratitude for newfound happiness in England, that made Wynmalen the sensitive, enlightened person that he was, particularly with his horses. Despite pressures of business life, he was able through his teaching, demonstrations, articles and books, to free English dressage from the military influence and introduce a greater sense of refinement, artistry and genuine enjoyment of the horse working at higher levels. This was to prove an inspiration to many people at a time when, as we have seen, dressage in England was at its nadir.

Wynmalen's early dressage training had been undertaken at the Utrecht Manège, often under the eagle eye of a celebrated *écuyer* of the day, August Diemont, who had been in service with the Jurgens family. 'Diemont,' wrote Wynmalen, 'was a rider of great finesse . . . a lovely horseman to watch . . . a classical seat, beautiful hands and, above all, understanding of the horse, so quiet, so patient, that every horse in turn understood him.' As his wife, Julia, has since confirmed, those words were applicable to Wynmalen himself for the rest of his life.

Some have criticised this tall, bespectacled emigré for a self-admitted, unimposing seat

---

[1] In 1910 Wynmalen was an international hero, breaking the altitude record of the time and receiving the French Grand Prix d'Aviation for being the first man to fly Paris-Brussels-Paris in a set time.

Henry Wynmalen, the classical dressage writer and rider, advocate of the *descente de main* as shown here on Bascar. (*Photo courtesy of Mrs Julia Wynmalen*)

without realising that as a brave pioneer pilot in the early days of solo flying, Wynmalen had sustained over thirty crashes, some of which had ended in long periods in a hospital bed under traction. These permanent injuries took their toll so that Wynmalen never enjoyed a flexible spine, so precious to the classical horseman.

There, however, any divergence from the classical ideal most certainly ends. Despite often riding in great pain, Wynmalen's first concern was that the horse should enjoy his work and that gentleness should prevail at all times. This sets him apart from many, then or since, and the real achievement of his work was that he applied this maxim to every aspect of riding and training. Like McTaggart, Wynmalen saw no earthly reason why a horse which was required to jump and gallop across country could not also be schooled on to learn the fine airs of the High School. He proved this in 1949 when he gave a full dressage display at the Horse of the Year Show on Bascar, his hunter. This led to an invitation to ride before the Queen at the Royal Windsor Show in 1951. As he and the elegant grey moved effortlessly through their movements in floodlight, to the music of the band of the Royal Life Guards, thousands of excited spectators rose in enthusiasm.

Where it could be said that Caprilli, Santini, Littauer and Chamberlin had found a system best suited for the average rider, Wynmalen sought to teach dressage to those who were naturally sensitive to their horses, and who had the application and desire to explore riding as an art.

Wynmalen the Author

Wynmalen's first book, *Equitation*, was published by Country Life Ltd in 1938 and such was its success that it went into reprint in 1943 and 1946. It covered every aspect of riding from lungework and preliminary schooling, to handling difficult horses, bitting and saddlery to general jumping and showjumping. The end of the book deals with advanced equitation. 'It remains true . . .' wrote Wynmalen, 'that the more finely and highly a horse be schooled, the better and more delightful he will become as a ride for the man or woman who understands this work.' He warned however that advanced schooling is 'a very specialised work, which requires a great deal of tact, infinite patience and considerably more than average love of the horse.'

The refreshing aspect of Wynmalen's book as well as his flowing style was his frank and unprejudiced approach. Dismissive of what he believed to be absolutely wrong, i.e. the 'backward' seat of the hunting field (a dislike shared with McTaggart and Hance) he was constructive and philosophical about the schooling practices of earlier times and of other countries. Too many writers of our century have tended to regard these as mistaken or out of date, but Wynmalen was far too wise and familiar with the classical principles of the past to seek discord. On the contrary, his depth of academic study together with knowledgeable practical experience takes his writing into a higher realm than we had come to expect from British riding literature at that time.

Even as late as 1950 however when he published his masterwork *Dressage: A Study of the Finer Points of Riding*, he was the subject of some prejudiced criticism within his adopted country. Lively debates appeared in magazines particularly after his third book, *The Horse in Action*, was published in 1954, but he handled them all with elegance and dry humour. One argument which simply would not go away was 'the ever delightful squabble about the forward seat! I admit that it amazes me how this matter of the forward seat, which since a quarter of a century or longer has ceased to be a subject of controversy in every country of the world but England, still manages here to produce its regular opponents.'

The Seat

Evidently conversant with Caprilli's methods, Wynmalen is one of the few writers from Britain who have defined accurately both the Forward Seat and the Classical Seat in the same book.

Of the latter, he wrote in a similar vein to Baucher, but with considerable more sympathy, '. . . it is always difficult to mend one's ways, the rider too intent on mending his seat, will meet with initial difficulties. Some of these are apt to appear disconcerting . . . In actual fact he will begin by finding what seems to him a distinct loss of balance and a distinct feeling of stiffness. And some stiffness there undoubtedly will be, due, not to assuming an erect position with open shoulders above hollow loins, but due to counteracting the previously existing habitual, and therefore not realized, stiffness of a curved back and high knees.' All this would improve with practice and riding without stirrups 'just so long as is necessary to learn that art so thoroughly that one can do it with real, complete and absolute comfort for hours on end – in fact, without noticing any effort.'

An Open Mind

Wynmalen was fascinated by every aspect of the High School. Photographs of favourite horses such as Molly Malone and Bascar show him over fences, out hacking and (with the latter) demonstrating all the 'artificial airs' of passage and piaffe as well as the Spanish Walk and Trot. Of the latter two movements so loved by Baucher and those masters of the Iberian Peninsula, he wrote: 'A good many modern High School riders content themselves with the passage and the piaffe and do not practise the Spanish walk or the Spanish trot . . . It is sometimes held that these airs are injurious to the horse's collection because of the high head-carriage which is necessary for their performance. I do not believe that there is anything in this objection, for it might then as well be said to be injurious if a horse were galloped out from time to time!

Henry Wynmalen, a bold crosscountry rider and dedicated follower of hounds, here mounted on Whitsun. Note the use of the double bridle and the absence of any form of martingale, a gadget which became very popular after many adopted the snaffle bridle in the 1930s, '40s and '50s. (*Photo courtesy of Mrs Julia Wynmalen*)

And it is obvious that the whole of this elaborate schooling would be a mere waste of time if we could not, in the end, produce both collection and extension as we wish and as circumstances demand.'

Lightness

The first thing he taught Julia his wife when she decided to become a dressage judge was to look at a rider's hands. Never, ever give high marks to a horse unhappy in the mouth! was his maxim. Not a writer to swing with the tide of fashionable opinion, Wynmalen put into practice all that he preached. His piaffes show marked suspension and elevation with the horse light and soft on the hand. One cannot help but wonder if his definition of *la descente de main* (see Chapter 7) had been better understood and taken more seriously by the people for whom he was writing, England today could have led the world in matters of collection and the High School airs. The light approach which included teaching flexions of the lower jaw, obviously suited Wynmalen's mainly Thoroughbred and Anglo-Arab horses and would not have necessitated the recent fashion for the heavier Warmbloods. In direct contrast to Chamberlin, Wynmalen insisted that a high degree of collection in the manège would have no deleterious effect on normal outdoor work. Throughout his career he proved this by hunting and jumping with the best of them.

In the Foreword to *Equitation*, Colonel V.D.S. Williams wrote, 'No book written in English deals so clearly and exhaustively with the Art of Advanced and High-School Riding . . . This book, I believe, will have a great future and occupy a position among the classics.' This has been achieved amongst the specialist few; perhaps now with the great dressage boom, it may enjoy a revival amongst increasingly wider circles.

Whilst the minority in Britain who were interested in dressage began to enjoy the effect of Wynmalen's teaching, France, a country which had always enjoyed a veritable wealth of specialist instructors, was moving through yet another brilliant epoch bound together by the academic idealism of Saumur. Inspirational teachers such as Baron Faverot de Kerbrech, Lenoble du Teil, Charles Raabe and others had come and gone. The teachings of L'Hotte and Guérin, influenced by Baucher, may have differed slightly from those of the Count de Montigny, scholar and former instructor at the Spanish Riding School, but both retained the classical principles. Thus, the tenuous thread which linked the new generation to the idealistic past struggled to survive.

In a wonderful way, Saumur, although firmly re-established as a cavalry school which concentrated on an all-round form of horsemanship, with excellent cross-country and showjumping facilities, still provided a living stage for those who were drawn to the classical art.

The Talent of the *Cadre Noir*

Individual members of the élite *Cadre Noir* were free therefore to explore whichever aspect of dressage most motivated them, provided that it did not interfere with their normal work. This liberality brought forth a new generation of thinking horsemen from the ranks of those who wore the distinctive black cloth trimmed with gold.[2] On the impressive role board of honour which hangs in the main lobby of the Academie at Saumur, and which dates back to 1825, certain names such as the celebrated Wattel (1919–1929), Danloux (1929–1933), Lesage (1935–1939) and Margot (1946–1959) stand out from the list of *écuyers en chef* of our own century. These together with a number of further distinguished satellites of Saumur, such as

[2] M. Cordier, who was appointed Chief *Ecuyer* at Saumur in 1825, created this famous uniform.

Beudant (1863–1949),[3] Saint-Phalle (1867–1908), Decarpentry (1878–1956), Jousseaume (1894–1960), Liçart, Saint-Fort Paillard and a host of others have all combined to bring classical dressage into the modern age. Whether through their teachings, articles and books or active participation in the competition arenas of the world, they have carried the torch for France and ensured that Saumur today still preserves many of the equestrian principles of a bygone age of splendour.

General Decarpentry

One of the best remembered of France's classical horsemen of modern times is General Decarpentry. Brought up in an enthusiastic riding family, the father and grandfather having been pupils of Baucher, he served at Saumur from 1904, and later returned after fighting a brave war, to become second in command from 1925 until 1931.

As cavalry rider, teacher, international dressage judge and later President of the FEI Dressage Committee, he enjoyed a spectrum of dressage life than most people only dream of. He was also able to take a broad view of the way in which dressage competition was shaping as opposed to the everyday empirical work of the riding hall. When he died in 1956, Decarpentry left four exceptional books two of which have now been translated into English. Both are faithful to the spirit of Versailles, the smaller, *Piaffer and Passage*[4] explains these airs mainly with photographs and captions. The second, *Academic Equitation*,[5] a thick and handsome volume is written with detailed eloquence. Since few people these days have the time or the opportunity to delve into the past and study La Guérinière, Baucher, Fillis, Faverot de Kerbrech, Steinbrecht and so on, they will find all the age-old ideals of lightness and harmony in horse and rider included here with stunning clarity and succinct explanation.

In addition to a general discourse on the aids, the gaits, bitting, etc., such elusive and misunderstood subjects as the *Mise en Main*, placing the horse in hand, the *Ramener*, the raising of the neck and poll, the *Descente de Main* (already discussed), the effect of the rounding and bringing together of the horse in the *Rassembler* (collection) and so on are elegantly defined. Thereafter, the book deals generally and specifically with the various movements on two or three tracks, rein-back, passage and piaffe, pirouette and tempi changes in canter, etc., followed by an Appendix concerning work in hand, between the pillars, on the lunge and so on.

There are some outstanding thoughts in this all-embracing work. As already indicated, none of these are new or revolutionary, but General Decarpentry had the knack of providing clearcut remedies or counter-effects for every difficulty or problem. Telling of his style which always looks forward to a state of perfection is the following quote: 'The pursuit of collection is not limited . . . to a special stage of dressage, but from the very first lesson must be the object of each day's work, so that the rider can master eventually all his horse's forces and control their output as he wishes.'

Lightness in the Horse

Decarpentry finds much to commend in Baucher to whom he refers again and again with high respect. He advances Baucher's contribution on flexions and the suppling of the horse's lower jaw. The following tribute is indeed generous from one who some regard as the superior

---

[3] Noted for his brilliant mastery of the High School, Etienne Beudant wrote *Exterieur et Haute Ecole* in 1923 and *Dressage du Cheval de Selle* in 1848.

[4] Translated by Patricia Galvin, 1961.

[5] Translated by Nicole Bartle, 1971.

General Decarpentry (at this time a colonel) demonstrating the passage on his French Thoroughbred horse, just outside the manège at Saumur. Note the snaffle rein has been dropped and the horse is ridden on the curb alone.

teacher: 'Finally, and it is in this that Baucher has enriched equestrian art with a truly capital discovery; when the horse does not offer a spontaneous *Mise en Main* sufficiently frequently, or refuses a requested *Mise en Main*, he is manifesting a deterioration of his physical or mental balance. Once the *Mise en Main* is eventually obtained, it restores this balance because of its particular effect on the whole body of the horse, and does so far more rapidly and with greater precision than does any other effect of the aids.'

Straightness

Time and again, Decarpentry stressed the importance of suppleness to achieve straightness and balance. 'There is no better procedure than bending work on the circle, as described at length and in great detail by La Guérinière, to obtain and to develop the lateral suppleness of the back – which determines suppleness in the vertical plane.' Riders of today are not sufficiently aware that only a horse which is able to flex and bend will successfuly swing through the back and achieve straightness. Decarpentry also pointed out another prerequisite. Alluding to canterwork he wrote '. . . we should remember that absolute straightness is only obtainable if a marked *Ramener* already exists, requiring a much slower pace than the canter used out of doors . . .'

He admitted that 'Absolute straightness in the whole length of the body is never natural to the horse at any pace, because of congenital asymmetry,[6] but it is at the canter that the bend is most pronounced, and the task of straightening him at this gait is especially difficult.

The modern requirement for flying changes in the canter made straightness even more important than in the past. 'It is especially with these in view that it is absolutely necessary to make the horse familiar with a straight position in the canter on both leads.' Changes *à tempo* are dealt with in considerable depth, the importance of establishing a horizontal balance of the horse particularly stressed, even a slight overloading of the forehand, and a certain freedom to the neck. In this context Decarpentry is at pains to point out that the old masters placed little importance on the changes. Since it was Baucher who developed the one-time changes, one wonders how consistent his critics are by not calling these a circus trick.

As well as dealing with the more advanced movements, always rich in sources from the past, Decarpentry provides the reader with many useful elementary tips which, for lack of space, have been simplified as follows:

[6] Which is as prevalent in the human being as in the horse.

Shoulder-in should not be asked for until the horse is absolutely supple and correct on the circle. When schooling, always if possible work from the circle into shoulder-in.

Half-pass: too much bend will make the movement inferior. Quote from General l'Hotte, 'the flexions must be very slight so that the action of the rein producing the flexion does not react on the haunches'.

Pirouette/Turn on the Haunches: this action shortens and 'swells' the horse's loin muscle, encouraging rounding of the back.

(Pirouette/Turn on the Forehand: this action (not recommended) stretches the loin muscles, tending to lower or hollow the horse behind saddle).

Canter: when teaching counter canter or changes, great care must be taken never to punish – or even to scold – the horse if he changes the lead or becomes disunited. He must be brought ' back to the original lead with unflagging perseverence . . .'

General Decarpentry was only too aware of the demands Grand Prix competition placed on the horse. For this reason, he continually exhorts patience and forbearance in training. There is the feeling throughout his book however that he regrets the degree of submission necesssary to achieve accuracy in the modern dressage test. Frequent allusions are made to the days when great riders could present their horses as the finished proof of progressive training in a spontaneous display of fine High School. Albeit a thoroughly modern participant in the competitive world, the General quite obviously had a very strong affinity with France's great equestrian past.

COLONEL PODHAJSKY

A man who understood the pressure of competition riding only too well was Colonel Alois Podhajsky, Director of the Spanish Riding School from 1939–1965. Born in Mostar (now part of Yugoslavia) but then part of the swiftly fading Austrian Empire,[7] Podhajsky started his cavalry training in Stockerau, and after the First World War, was selected for the *Militär-Reit- und Fahrlehrer Institut* at Schlosshof. Later, he was transferred to the Spanish Riding School in Vienna and derived enormous benefit from *Oberbereiter* Polak. A perfectionist who adored a challenge he represented Austria in international dressage from 1933 to 1953. In the beginning, he competed alongside fellow Austrian General Pongracz, later he appeared more often alone.

What was remarkable about his success (he won almost every Grand Prix event prior to the War) was the fact that his mounts were not the glamorous Lipizzaner, but often the most unlikely troop horses which other officers had rejected for being highly strung or difficult. Always schooling his competition horses himself, he recounts in his moving autobiography *My Dancing White Horses*[8] how other riders openly jeered at one brilliant horse, Nero, when he first commenced work. Where, they wanted to know, had he come by 'that sausage'?! His response was to grit his teeth, work like a maniac, thereafter to prove his Nero almost unbeatable at every turn.

The young Podhajsky also enjoyed enormous success with a very common mare, Nora, from the Burgenland. He wrote of his great sadness when she fell foul of the military authorities and had to be sold because of persistant lameness. Although he tried to buy her back privately,

[7] Austria became a Republic in 1919.
[8] English translation published by George G. Harrap, London, 1964.

Colonel Podhajsky exemplifying a perfect classical seat as he and the Lipizzaner, Maestoso Alea execute a highly elevated passage in the Winter Riding School. (*Photo courtesy of Madame Eva Podhajsky*)

this was forbidden and great was his grief when he learned she had gone as a riding horse to a Viennese butcher who showed off her beautiful passage in the Josefplatz. Sadly, he wrote 'I can still recall how the news of Nora's fate, which I had learned during a lively party at Aachen, took all the pleasure out of this happy occasion, and I felt sick at heart and went sadly away.'

Setting aside his determination, obvious ability and disciplined sense of technique, it is clear from these personal glimpses, that Podhajsky's real success lay in his love for and psychological understanding of horses.

'In dressage the rider sets himself a fascinating task,' he wrote, 'for to learn the character of his horse thoroughly he must study it in detail and turn himself into an animal psychologist. Success will only come to the dressage rider who wins the friendship of his four-legged partner and turn him into an ally.[9] But even then there is still much more to be done than with a jumper.'

The Olympics

With Nero, Podhajsky was a close contender for the gold medal at the 1936 Berlin Olympic Games which was attended by Hitler and his elite within the National Socialist Party. No one was very surprised when Germany took the gold and silver, except for Podhajsky for whom winning only the bronze medal was a bitter blow. Up until that point, his partnership with Nero had been without equal and they had been the pride of Austria.

After the war, Podhajsky again represented Austria in the Games. this time staged in London

[9] This expression is used frequently by the American horseman, Monty Roberts, who exhibits his special methods (known as join-up) of breaking horses all over the world. The last one, in the United Kingdom, took place in 1990.

in 1948. By now, he had been Director of the Spanish Riding School for over nine years and was the acknowledged favourite for the gold with his Hungarian troop horse Teja. Here again however, he was doomed to disappointment. One bone of contention was that the piaffe and passage was dropped from the test, and since for him the happy execution of these movements was the proof of a well collected horse and a sure indication of the correctness of his training, the event was a disappointment.

After this, Podhajsky always maintained that mistakes in judging were less likely to be made at the highest levels, since it was the advanced High School movements which most clearly illustrated training discrepancies. One wonders what he would have thought of the standard of piaffe and passage as carried out in world Grand Prix today and what conclusions he might have drawn.

The visit to London was not without other success. Podhasjky gave an outstanding exhibition organised by the Institute of the Horse on his Lipizzaner, Neapolitano Africa. If he had failed to capture the hearts of the dressage judges, he certainly won the hearts and minds of ordinary British riders in the packed stadium at Aldershot, and the British press praised unreservedly his performance. Despite his love of *haute école*, Podhajsky always gave the impression that he did not altogether approve of the inclusion of one tempo changes in the Grand Prix test. In his definitive book *The Complete Training of Horse and Rider*[10] he wrote: 'Changes at every stride are one of the most controversial exercises as a number of experts consider them circus movements and disapprove of them for this reason. Many arguments took place at the Spanish Riding School, without ever coming to a satisfactory conclusion. But the Federation Equestre Internationale, as the ruling body on international equitation, declares that they belong to the classical exercises and demands them in the dressage tests at the Olympic Games. It is therefore superfluous to discuss the matter in this book.'

The State of the Art
Podhajsky was one of the few authors of our age who was able to comment with first hand knowledge on the standard of dressage between 1936 and 1972 when he either rode or attended each Olympics and took careful notes.

In his last book, *The Art of Dressage – Basic Principles of Riding and Judging*,[11] Podhajsky examined the whole concept of dressage competition from two essential viewpoints, that of the competititor and that of the judge. Taking the reader through the dressage tests of the Olympic Games from 1912 to 1972, some controversial remarks were made about the general system of marking and in particular how co-efficients could be used to favour a particular participant, thus making a mockery of sworn impartiality. Podhajsky preferred by far a system which would range the contestants by way of their individual placings. This method, he wrote would limit '. . . the judge's chance to manipulate the decisions of his colleagues by biased evaluation with disproportionate scores for those contestants whom he wants to see in the top places. All this can happen if the results of the score sheets alone decide the test.'

Podhajsky also claimed that from the purely classical point of view, dressage reached its peak in 1936. Freed at last of the sporting emphasis of earlier Olympics, he believed that this particular Grand Prix 'did justice to the principles of classical riding in every respect, allowing sufficient space for the basic requirements expected from a dressage horse such as the purity of the paces, impulsion, suppleness and so on.' Perhaps even more importantly, he pointed

[10] Translated by Eva Podhajsky and Colonel V.D.S. Williams, 1967.
[11] Translated by Eva Podhajsky, 1976.

out 'It was clear that this test was not designed by a rider in theory but by men who themselves were capable of practically demonstrating on horseback what they expected from other riders. This fact became obvious in the structure of the test.'

Considering his own disappointment at Berlin, these words have to be taken seriously. After that date, although actual numbers of contestants increased out of all recognition and the sport seemed really to have taken off, Podhajsky displayed his growing unease about the design of tests, with their propensity to cause tension in the horse from a lack of harmonious sequence in the movements.

The Problem with Judging

His other concern was the discrepency in the viewpoints of the various judges as to what constituted the ideal performance. In 1972 he wrote of the modern judge '. . . quite a few of them were never dressage riders and cannot boast of any acclaim in this sphere, such as winning trophies or being outstanding in their teaching.'

To put things in perspective, I conversed at length with his widow, Eva Podhajsky, in her elegant apartment at the Hofburg. This still beautiful woman, many years younger than the Colonel, smiled wistfully at my questions, and began to explain how much had changed. 'You must remember that when my husband was competing, Europe was full of the most distinguished and educated riders. After the collapse of our Empire, in Austria and Hungary alone there were literally hundreds of cavalry officers with time on their hands to help, teach, judge and advise. Not only did the majority ride at Grand Prix level, they had schooled horses and riders to that level. The story was the same in Germany of course, so we were all rich in the culture of topclass dressage.

'Judges were therefore drawn from this background, and this explains why standards were maintained, and generally judges were in agreement one with the other since all had enjoyed a classical background as well as the practical experience necessary to make an educated and allround judgement.

'Sadly today, there are very few of these people left. It must be frustrating for competitors to have to ride before people who seem often quite unqualified for the job. To compete today, you must have to be not only accomplished, but extraordinarily enduring in spirit.'

An Imposing Figure

Podhajsky was not only a great competitor, he was also the epitome of the classical rider who had successfully brought all the old principles together and harnessed them for the modern world. To enter competition and not to sacrifice some of your ideals has never been easy. Too many modern competitors even at Olympic level appear anything but elegant and classical on their horses as they make violent movements

Colonel Podhajsky wearing the bowler hat, traditional headwear of the Director of the Spanish Riding School, sharing a private moment with one of his beloved Lipizzan, Maestoso Mercurio. (*Photo courtesy of Madame Eva Podhajsky*)

with hands, legs and bodies to achieve precise transitions from one difficult movement to another. This spoils the whole concept of classical dressage and indeed has alienated many purists from entering the competition arena. Not so with Colonel Podhajsky; his superbly straight, proud and still figure in the saddle was unmistakeable whether he was between the white boards of a foreign arena, or at home in Vienna under the shining chandeliers of the Winter Riding School.

The Complete Training of the Horse and Rider

Podhajsky's training book is probably the most fundamental definitive dressage book that exists in English. It contains less technical detail and less reference to the methods of past masters than Decarpentry's book, but for the modern dressage rider is probably more serviceable and concise. If it lacks the French subtlety of Decarpentry, it probably appeals more to English and American readers because of the directness.

From a discourse on the ideals of classical equitation, which includes a particularly note-worthy section on reward, an emphasis too often forgotten by modern instructors but not thankfully at Vienna, Podhajsky takes the rider through the training of the young horse to the work of the High School. Forward and straight, is the absolute priority at all times. Podhajsky is at pains to explain the correctly swinging back which produces Xenophon's 'divine sensation' as opposed to the artificially suspended tense back of the horse not working correctly through from behind. Down to earth similes are used to get these important prerequisites of correct training across to the reader such as the following: 'In terms of mechanics the hindquarters are the motor which produces the movement and the place where the energy is stored. Just as with a mechanical vehicle, steering is only possible when the motor produces the power, so with the horse the aids with the reins will only produce the required effects when the impulsion is developed from the hindquarters.'

The importance of suppleness and longitudinal bending on the circle is stressed, particular attention being paid to the increased flexion in the three joints of the horse's hindquarters, the thigh, hock and fetlock. This leads into clearcut definitions of collection and the half-halt, and gradually the more advanced work. Useful is his recommendation to teach the horse pirouette from the renvers 'as recommended by Guérinière. That is why the renvers plays such an important part at the School.' He also offers an alternative method of teaching the pirouette on the large circle which would avoid any tendency to crookedness from the renvers. 'Even if the rider cannot control the hindquarters as well on the large circle as he can in the renvers, he will have better command than he would have on a straight line, as preparatory voltes can be ridden within the circle.'

Much importance is put on the degree of contact and the calmness of the horse's mouth. In contrast to the majority of French masters who encouraged an active chewing of the bit, Podhajsky preferred a quiet closed mouth, omitting from his book any exercises for flexing the lower jaw although he stressed that the horse must learn to yield the jaw to the rider's hand.

A Man of Many Parts

Whilst Podhajsky's name will live on through the pages of his ten books, a splendid contribution to equestrian literature from such a busy man, through military records, and the dusty pages of competition files, and the work of his protégés, now themselves *Bereiters* and *Oberbereiters*,[12]

---

[12] Podhajsky's original trainees included Tschautscher, Kottas, Eichinger and Steinriegler.

he will always be remembered most for his role in saving the Lipizzaner horses from the very real threat of destruction during the last world war. With his faithful Chief Riders Lindenbauer and Neumayer at his side, he initally placed the School under the command of the German cavalry. Later, by moving them out of Vienna, and finally as the Allies moved in, securing the American General Patton's interest and goodwill, the horses were saved. Yet, so often the School hovered on the verge of dispersal or even death: first from highhanded members of Hitler's SS, later from horrendous bombing over the city of Vienna, and finally from being swallowed up into the communist bloc. Years of agonising decisions, worry and the constant search for fodder, care and stabling for the magical Lippizan are beautifully recounted in *My Dancing White Horses*. To Colonel Podhajsky and his aides, Vienna and the world will always be grateful.

Pluto Theodorosta, one of Colonel Podhajsky's favourite Lipizzan which he brought to England in 1949 for a display at the Horse of the Year Show.

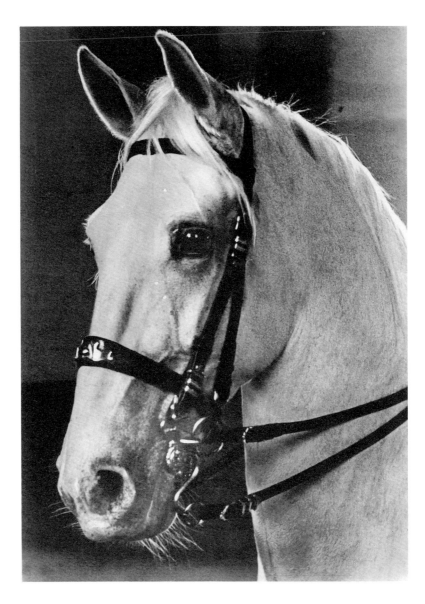

SIXTEEN

The Competitive Success of the Germans

A STORY OF PROGRESSIVE ENDEAVOUR

Up until the reforms of Prince Otto von Bismarck (1815–98), the architect of modern Germany, there were no German people as such, but rather an imperial collection of states and nationalities. Each of these states, some large, some small had their own aristocracy. Not unnaturally therefore, at the beginning of the twentieth century, dressage in Germany was dominated by a number of impressive figures drawn either from the old aristocratic families or the cavalry or most likely both. Paul Plinzner (1852–1921) was typical of the time, a pupil of Steinbrecht's and later, through his remarkable work and writing, the royal equerry to William II. Another devotee of Steinbrecht's, Hans von Heydebreck (1866–1935) made many footnotes and additions to the master's work which brought it within the sphere of military riding.

Others followed their national equestrian studies with a spell at one of the academies within the Austro-Hungarian Empire. It was a great honour to attend the Spanish Riding School of Vienna as a German serving officer. Those who did so, like Gebhardt (1842–1918), a chief instructor at the Hanover Cavalry School and Julius Walzer, who took over its command just prior to World War I were able to pass on the best traditions of both academic and practical military training.

Further distinguished names such as Burchard von Oettingen[1] and Count Siegfried Lehndorff[2] prevailed in the world of stud management, and with others like Oskar Stensbeck in the sphere of civilian teaching, the German equestrian system was then without doubt one of the most established, well-balanced and prestigious in the equestrian world.

Setting the Objectives for Dresssage Competition
Even before the first World War however, the political wind of change began to affect the traditional world of the riding instructor. Whilst many of the old school remained, particularly amongst the hierarchy of German cavalry, a new sect of bureaucrats was emerging within the military. The attitude of these often politically

---

Gustav Steinbrecht (1808–1885), a classical master of the old German school, exerted a considerable influence on early twentieth-century riders. His motto 'forward and straight' is still used at Vienna, but his use of the *descente de main* has largely been eclipsed by the stronger contact of the neo-classical school.

---

[1] *Landstallmeister* and director of the Royal Stud of Trakehnen and author of an important book *Horse Breeding in Theory and Practice*, first published in Germany in 1907.

[2] Who succeeded his father Georg. Both had superb Trakehnen horses.

Morning Exercise in the Winter Riding School (1900), an oil painting by Julius von Blaas. Many German cavalry officers attended the Spanish Riding School of Vienna in the tradition of their forefathers. Note the soft reins on the bridoon whilst the horse remains poised and balanced in full collection – another reminder that the stronger contact and weight into the hand of the schooled horse is a very modern idea. (*Photo courtesy of the Spanish Riding School of Vienna*)

motivated newcomers did not altogether favour the slow, steady approach to schooling and training, neither was artistic virtuosity viewed with much sympathy. Instead, they concentrated on creating a system which would regiment proceedings. The previously rather loose format which had left room for a variety of interpretations (to suit horse and rider) in the old dressage tests, would now be replaced with rigid rules and conditions.

At a meeting in 1914 in Paris, the German Committee for Equestrian Games put forward a set of objectives to go before the International Congress for the Olympic Games. The authors of the new proposals were Germany's Inspector General of Cavalry, von der Marwitz together with Secretary General Gustav Rau. Their wish was to abolish the old freestyle test with its list of specified movements, and replace it with a memorised test, the movements to be performed in a particular order, in a particular way and within a set space of time. The degree of difficulty of the new test was that deemed suitable to prove the 'well-schooled horse that is an accomplished campaign mount' rather than that suitable for the *haute école* horse. For this reason the arena, traditionally 20 × 40 metres was now to be increased to 20 × 50/60 metres to add an element of space for more extended work.

To Win at all Costs

As it happened the Games for which these proposals were intended, the 1916 Olympics, never materialised because of war. Nevertheless national competitions run on these lines were now taking place, and one of the only civilian riders to appear (and uniquely to compete) at this time was Richard Wätjen (1891–1966) who had studied under Meixner and Polak at the Spanish Riding School.[3] Competing however was still the prerogative of the military and great was

[3] One place where civilian riders could train under visiting instructors was at Tattersalls in Berlin. 'Here the amateur spirit prevailed as well as a little old world chivalry' . . . the words of Daphne Machin Goodall, companion to the Princess Friedrich Sigismund von Preuszen.

the pressure on individual officers to prove the supremacy of the German cavalry horse, generally an East Prussian or Trakehner.[4] Thus, officers whose ability and sense of endeavour had never been in question, found their old methods often under attack by those who sought only quick results.

Since nearly all the top German competitors during this period were riding state-owned horses, it was hard if one wanted to keep one's ride, to avoid outside demands for power and success. This pressure was often at the expense of lightness and harmony in training, since officers were no longer given the time necessary to produce their horses in the old, slow, painstaking way. To combat this, it became acceptable under the new system for state-employed professionals to school horses for amateurs to ride in competition.

Professionally trained Horses

Because of the war to end all wars, Germany was not allowed to participate in the 1920 Olympics in Antwerp which was won by the Swedes. Nevertheless, nationalistic pride in their horses and horsemanship was undaunted, and throughout the years that followed a formidable array of professional instructors including Felix Bürkner,[5] August Staeck, Otto Lörke and Wätjen dedicated themselves to the cause. By now the dressage arena had been fixed at 20 × 60 metres which suited the horses, and by the 1928 Olympic Games held in Amsterdam, Germany was well prepared to dominate the the international competition scene.

In an article entitled 'Equestrian Olympic Games' published in *Dressage and CT*, in March 1984, Ivan Bezugloff wrote of this period: '. . . Germany took no chances, and used its best trainers to prepare the Olympic mounts. Draufgaenger, von Langen's horse, was trained by *Stallmeister* Staeck, Linkenbach's Gimpel by Stensbeck and von Lotzbeck's Caracally by Bürkner. This combination of the most talented horses, the best available trainers, and highly knowledgeable and talented riders set the scene for the German dominance in dressage which we experience now.'

Although he admired many of these riders, Podhajsky expressed his utter distaste for this amount of professionalism to enter into what was essentially amateur sport, and his sentiments were shared by many older members of the German cavalry. By 1940 it was somewhat late to remedy the situation, however he remarked '. . . how harmful it could be for officers to get the credit for riding horses schooled by professional trainers.'

The Competitive Thirties

Throughout the 1930s, there was plenty of opportunity for enthusiastic dressage riders to enter advanced competition around Germany, Austria, and Switzerland. Dressage riders from the United States or Britain, however, had little facility at home and those few who were prepared to make the journey based themselves in Germany for both the training and the opportunity to compete. The first official non-Olympic FEI Grand Prix was held in Lucerne in 1930. In 1932, letters around the arena as used today were introduced and this suited the German fondness for discipline and accuracy. Other important venues for dressage competition at this time included Vienna, Budapest, Thun in Switzerland, and of course Berlin, Cologne, Dusseldorf, Verden[6] and Aachen where the only outsider who could challenge German superiority at the

---

[4] The Hanoverian was in the early days of the century still considered a carriage horse and not a cavalry officer's horse.

[5] Bürkner competed for Germany at the 1912 Stockholm Olympic Games when a lieutenant in the cavalry.

[6] Administrative heartland of the Hanoverian horse.

time was Alois Podhajsky. In *My Dancing White Horses* he recalled the thrill he enjoyed when his horses Nero and Otto beat the famous German Olympic champions Kronos and Absinth.

The Anschluss

In 1938, Austria was absorbed into the German Reich through the Anschluss. This inevitably brought the Spanish Riding School under the command of the German Wehrmacht and much needed funds were now allocated which allowed the School to renovate its surroundings and improve many of its ailing material conditions and traditions which had badly suffered during the break up of the Austrian Empire in 1918. Whilst commanders of the old German school such as Colonel von Langermann and General von Fritsch, openly welcomed the Spanish Riding School into the arms of the Reich, other important figures seemed less enthusiastic now that competition had replaced the age of the imperial academies.

Rumblings about a change of emphasis and the role of the white stallions were heard in high places. Podhajsky had long recognised the difficulty in fairly judging the Baroque horse against the modern German troop horse or Thoroughbred, but he was shocked to the core when the powerful Dr Gustav Rau, from the Quartermaster's department, suggested that Hanoverians be used at the Spanish Riding School.[7] For the next five years, Podhajsky fought a lone but finally successful battle against wartime bureaucracy to save the bloodlines of his precious Austrian Lippizans.

The German Cavalry Horse

Rau and others before him were great reformers. If misguided in some areas, their intentions were entirely honourable and as far as Germany was concerned, their achievements were great. Diligently, they ensured that breeding methods were constantly improving. The handsome equine material which was being produced by the state studs for the mighty German cavalry certainly towered head and shoulders above that of the rest of the world. This naturally stood many competitors in good stead. It also fulfilled Germany's dream expressed so well by her old Master of the Horse, Seidler, who had written 'Our goal is the utility horse, we are followers of the hunt riding.'

To understand further the success of German riders both just before and after the war, it is important to weigh up first the national character, and secondly the evolution of the modern German horse.

Otto Lörke, one of the most highly respected German professional dressage trainers between the wars. Here the extended trot is demonstrated on 'reins of silk'. A heavy man, those who remember him say his horses always looked light and happy. (*Photo courtesy of Madame Eva Podhajsky*)

[7] After many disagreements with Rau over the future of the Lipizzaner, Podhajsky wrote after the Second World War, 'He has done so much for German Riding that his name deserves to be inscribed in letters of gold.'

The German people have enjoyed a tremendous sense of discipline and organisation since time immemorial. They have also been swift to accept change when it has become necessary, and in equestrian history, the transition from the High School to a bolder, more forward style of general purpose riding under Seydlitz and later Seeger, was accomplished easily and with expediency. Method has always preceded whatever they have undertaken. Of prime import- ance therefore to the success of twentieth century German cavalry and consequently to national dressage was the very organised system of breeding which had developed in Germany over two or more centuries before that. First under royalty, later under the state, no effort had been spared in producing the Ideal Cavalry Horse.

Several distinct breeds served to produce the Ideal Cavalry and artillery horse. Initially the Trakehner, or Trakehner cross, later the Hanoverian and Holstein,[8] they would all play their part, leading eventually to a superb competition horse. The Westphalian and Oldenburg pro- vided a secondary force of powerful blood and in many cases were used for cross breeding with the forerunning strains or the Thoroughbred.

The German Warmblood

Let us for a moment take a step back into history and look a little more closely at how these breeds evolved. German horses had always been renowned for their weight-carrying ability and their power, the old troop horses having had more than a fair complement of cold, draught blood. Then came the Spanish influence which produced lighter, longer limbs and convex faces, but it was when the Hanoverian kings came to England that horsebreeding in Germany received a frequent and generous impetus of hotblood from the streamlined Thoroughbreds across the Channel. Indeed, it was George II of England who founded the renowned stud of Hanoverian horses at Celle, just north of Hanover, in 1735.

Careful breeding here was to produce a most superior artillery horse for the German army in the First World War. From the old, convex-headed, rather high-stepping carriage horse, the Hanoverian became considerably lightened with regular infusions of Throughbred, and some Arab blood. By the mid-twentieth century it had evolved into a tall, elegant all-round riding horse, although it still retained much of the pulling and weight-carrying power of its earlier ancestor. In the last twenty years or so, performance testing with the strictest controls imposed by the state on studwork, has led to the Hanoverian Society becoming probably the most efficient and prolific Warmblood breeders association in all Europe.

Well suited to all three disciplines of competition riding is the Trakehner. The state stud flourished under Frederick the Great, having been set up by his father in 1732, but in modern times it was Kaiser Wilhelm II (1888–1918) who determined that this breed should be regularised through careful selection and breeding programmes into a uniform type suitable for the perfect troop horse. Again, as with the Hanoverian, rigorous performance testing methods ensured that only the best horses went forward to stud, and the breed has enjoyed the utmost success in the competitive field, particularly in jumping and horse trials.

Both the Holstein and the Oldenburg are heavier horses, retaining a mixture of large coach- horse characteristics and lightened in latter years by English blood to give speed and an extrava- gant extended action full of characteristic power and thrust.

Taking all these improvements into consideration, together with the indomitable spirit of her people, it is not altogether surprising that despite the outcome of the Second World War, Germany was soon on course to dominate the competitive world. Yet everything had seemed

[8] One of the most successful competition dressage horses of our time was the Holstein, Granat. See Chapter 19.

against her. The old German cavalry was in tatters, the illustrious Hanover Cavalry School[9] had been destroyed, even the Spanish Riding School was in exile. Yet thanks to the efforts of a few dedicated men like Gustav Rau, who still believed the German horse to be supreme, German equestrianism was resurrected. By 1949 dressage competitions were once again being organised often on sites which had been reduced to rubble, and in the years that followed, it is perhaps ironic that the occupying British and Americans should have turned to their so-called German charges to learn the principles of equitation.

Where the old classical school had always looked towards a final picture of beauty and perfection in the dressage horse, the new objective was to become more and more concerned with stage by stage testing. Thus, dressage tests became useful at every level and once this became acceptable amongst the professionals, the imagination of the civilian rider was firmly caught. No longer did you have to be amongst the educated elite to ride a horse in a dressage competition, here at last was a chance for everyone, however elementary.

German Riding Club Life
Another factor probably contributed to this interest and dedication. Unlike the English, German horses are rarely kept in one's own backyard. There is less opportunity to ride freely out across country, although there is draghunting which has been much promoted by the Rhine Army. Hacking out or leisure riding where the fancy takes you is discouraged in most areas, the average horse and rider being restricted to a scheduled number of tracks, or bridlepaths paid by annual subscription. Consequently, most Germans prefer to ride in an arena or school provided by the local livery yard. These livery yards comprise far more than the word denotes in England. They are generally modern, fully-fledged clubs providing excellent indoor stabling, exercising facilities, changing rooms, social and eating facilities, in fact every convenience that any rider could want.

Most clubs also provide highly trained schoolmaster horses as a matter of course. Voltige and lunge lessons are given to establish a really sound seat, and lessons are available to advanced levels. Many clubs run their own private competitions to test the progress of pupils thus creating further interest. During the fifties, the minority of English and American dressage enthusiasts who wished to compete at higher levels, were still quite unable to find sufficient opportunities at home. By 1952, non-commissioned officers and women were allowed to participate in the Olympics, so dressage hopefuls went to Sweden, Belgium, Switzerland, France and above all Germany to try their luck. By the time of the 1956 Olympic Games held in Stockholm, most people recognised that the Federal Republic of Germany, covering 248,000 square km was the centre of dressage competition.

This was yet another transitional period for dressage. As the demand for good competition horses grew amongst the civilian population, Podhajsky's *bête noire* of professionally trained horses for amateur contestants became commonplace. Idealistic ideas were replaced by idealism of another nature, competing not to show and prove a finished work of art, but competing for its own sake. In this way, dressage itself joined ranks with those other equestrian activities in the competitive field, racing, cross-country, polo, showjumping and so on . . . in short it had become an important civilian sport.

An extra impetus was provided by the German Olympic Committee, the DOKR, originally formed by the Kaiser in 1913 with the sole purpose of winning more medals for the fatherland.

---

[9] The Hanover School transferred to Potsdam-Kramprintz (Berlin) in the autumn of 1939 before being dissolved at the end of the war.

Today, the DOKR is concerned with providing proper training for Germany's most talented young riders. With the closure of the proud Hanover cavalry school, backbone of the old empire, the DOKR set up training facilities after the war close to today's other great civilian centre, the *Deutsche Reitschule* at Warendorf near Munster. All the great riders of modern Germany have at some time set foot in the disciplined atmosphere of one or both these establishments. The Federal German state has always been generous to the horse industry, so while no expense is spared to provide riders of the future with the very best in facilities, instruction and horses at the young instructors' school (the *Reitschule*), the DOKR provides the extra impetus in all three equestrian disciplines by using the Centre at Warendorf as a permanent training site for all Olympic contenders. Not only has this support at government level provided Germany with a stunning equestrian success internationally, it has also given the most talented trainers a base from which to work either permanently or on a visiting basis. Many of today's top competitors, such as Nicole Uphoff, are able to keep their horses there.

The German attitude has brought its rewards. Since the late fifties, early sixties, the West Germans have risen to new heights in the competitive field. Names like Lisenhoff, Neckerman, Boldt and Klimke have shone like the Olympic gold that draws them, and at every Olympic Games since 1956, and every World Championship since they commenced in 1966, the Germans have brought home the treasured medals.

Support has come from every angle. At the state studs, new methods and scientific research is constantly applied to bring horses out into the public eye at the earliest opportunity. Horses are brought on to early maturity[10] so that breaking and early schooling takes place at three and four, rather than four and five. Some horses are even working at Prix St George level by five years of age, something simply not contemplated in the days of the Wehrmacht. At the huge stallion sales of Verden and Munster, magnificent horses of seventeen hands or more belie their babyhood. More and more they are judged by their performance at an early age, the essential ingredient being big, free, extravagant movements from an unconstricted, supple back.

Whereas in the past, dressage judges in Germany were drawn from their own superior cavalry or from neighbouring Austria with its great tradition of High School, civilians began to take over the task of judging. Many of these were closely involved with breeding and became more concerned with an exposition of sheer strength than of delicacy and lightness in performance. Those riders of the old school regret many of the changes, but with each passing year their voices grow less in a dressage world which like it or not, is nowadays dominated by high finance.

A luxury German dressage saddle. Note the straight flap to bring the thigh and knee down and under the rider. The lowest point of the seat is central to the saddle but the high cantle sometimes tends to fix the rider's position. For comfort and freedom to apply weight aids, the ideal would be a slight softening in design all round, with particular attention paid to the width of the twist, which should be as broad and comfortable as possible to ensure all-round contact and adhesion of the rider's seat, thus spreading the weight on the horse's back at his strongest point.

---

[10] A practice of which many disapprove and which brings its own problems later on in the life of many horses (see Chapter 17).

WRITERS AND TRAINERS OF MODERN GERMANY

Waldemar Seunig (1887–1976)

A writer who was deeply against any form of rushed training, thus denying the horse physical and psychological time to absorb the work was Waldemar Seunig. He grew up against a background of imperialistic horse culture enjoying some of the best cavalry training in the world. Generally thought of today as German, he only took German nationality after the final breakup of the Austro-Hungarian Empire, and in fact competed for Yugoslavia in the 1924 Olympic Games. As a young cavalry officer, he completed three years military training in Vienna under the renowned instructor Sigmund von Jospovitch, then after fighting bravely on the Russian front, returned to his home which had now become part of Yugoslavia and was offered the post of Master of the Horse to King Alexander. A further time of study followed when he went first to Saumur, then to England to study ceremony and protocol at the Royal Mews, and finally to the Spanish Riding School of Vienna. By the time the Second World War was under way, he had settled in Germany and actually served in German uniform, having lost his ancestral home in Yugoslavia.

Seunig's major book *Horsemanship* (first published in German in 1943) illustrates his complete dedication to the horse, and for the more experienced reader is a fount of practical good sense. To ride good dressage, the author insists, the mental attitude of the rider must be correct. 'Most important is his *love of the horse*. It is this *leitmotif* [byword] that should underlie all our intercourse with this most lovable of creatures. A horse will overcome its inborn shyness and gain confidence, the fundamental condition for mutual understanding with a man whose love it feels . . .'

The Seat

Seunig's second stipulation, this time of a physical nature, was that the rider must acquire a strong, discerning and deep seat. Like Müseler, another popular German writer whom we shall come to shortly, Seunig believed in the driving aids of the seat. His understanding of the weight aids is far superior however, and he is at pains throughout the book to explain when also to take the weight a little forward to 'ease the load and facilitate the activity of the back'.

This book was much criticised by the Russian Littauer for being 'cumbersome' and over scholastic in style, and he accuses Seunig of saying nothing new. In fact Seunig's interpretation of the driving aids of the seat and constant referral to 'driving legs' were in direct contrast to much of what had gone before and were somewhat revolutionary when compared to La Guérinière, Baucher, Steinbrecht etc. It does much to explain the more modern German seat, although could perhaps be open to misinterpretation particularly with the somewhat complicated detail about the use of the back and how to distribute the weight on the seatbones.

Finesse

In *Horsemanship* Seunig approaches the more advanced work in a thoughtful empirical style. There are some particularly attractive passages such as the following: 'In a truly well-schooled horse it is no longer the rider who has to seek harmony with his horse. The contrary is true. The lightest weight controls cause the responsive horse to bring its centre of gravity into harmony with that of the rider. The harmony between the two is so far-reaching that it is sought and found by the horse, so to speak.' In the same chapter, he explains the importance of lighter leg aids, in contrast to the impression given elsewhere of rather strong aids:

'A piaffe or a passage squeezed out of a horse by laborious leg and weight controls will always be faulty. The rider's domination is most complete and the school figures are purest when the observer obtains the impression that the movement costs neither horse nor rider any appreciable effort. In such a pair fused into one, the most difficult exercise will look like free play.'

After the writers of the Romanic and even the English school of Newcastle and much later McTaggart and Hance, it is noticeable by their absence that Seunig does not believe in practising the flexions of the jaw and poll as discussed hitherto. His interpretation of relaxing or yielding the hand is also incompatible with that of the French. In keeping with competitive dressage today, the relaxing of the rein is only to be employed when the horse is tired and the rider wishes him to stretch forward; in this book it is not a proof of lightness when the horse continues in the same carriage and cadence.

Seunig's interpretation of 'on the bit' is therefore the modern one which stops one stage short of what the Romanic riders called the ultimate proof of correct training, *descente de main et des jambes*. 'Then the action of the reins can traverse the entire spinal column through the pelvis down to the hind pastern joints under the most favourable conditions, i.e., directly, without being stopped or deflected at any point by stiffness or bends. This requires that the horse 'come to the bit' by itself, with a supple poll and extended neck and positive contact with the bit due to driving action.'

Between the writing of his major tome, and a second one which was not published in English until 1983 under the title *The Essence of Horsemanship*, Seunig travelled the world instructing and judging but sadly a stroke put an end to his career and he died in 1976, one of the most highly respected writers and teachers of our time.

Richard Wätjen (1891–1966)

Wätjen, of whom we have already spoken, was German by birth and born into a middle class shipping family from Bremen who were understanding and wealthy enough to encourage him with his own horses from an early age. Later he went on to study agriculture and stud management first at the state stud of Trakehnen, and then at Graditz and Hoppegarten in Berlin which led to a love affair with the Thoroughbred racehorse. Finally after taking instruction from Stensbeck and discovering the need for a more academic approach in order to ride good dressage, he secured a place at the Spanish Riding School. This involved a huge transition from good campaign riding to that of the High School. Wätjen gradually began to accept the need for a psychological approach which was bound into the tradition of Vienna, and through application and dedication developed as a model pupil under, first, Chief Rider Meixner and then Maritz Herold and *Oberbereiter* Polak, who later made such an impression on Podhajsky.

With the interruption of war, many of the instructors of the Spanish Riding School were called to the front, and Wätjen who had been excused active service was finally given the job of guest instructor at the School which gave him the opportunity to work with the young stallions and participate in public performances. Finally, after twelve years at Vienna, political change forced him to leave the city, but back in postwar Germany he was able to run his own riding school in Berlin and later join the successful instructor Felix Bürkner. During the

Richard Wätjen (1891–1966), a successful competition rider in the 1930s, represents that transitional period for dressage when Germany and other nations moved towards a more rigid, more demanding style of riding (sometimes referred to as neo-classical), largely necessitated by a degree of difficulty of the various tests.

late 1920s and 30s, he successfully competed in dressage and was responsible for bringing on many of today's top instructors, who like him, were successful in competition. One of his greatest successes was in the 1935 Grand Prix at Aachen where he tied for first place on a horse named Burgsdorff. Particularly noted for a beautifully erect, still, quiet seat, Wätjen was highly acclaimed by many international riders of his generation. In 1952, he became instructor to the British Team for the Helsinki Olympics, and is credited with having made a vital contribution to the winning gold medal of the British Three Day Event team at Stockholm in 1956.

There is no doubt that Wätjen's influence is still felt to this day. His translated book *Dressage Riding – A Guide for the Training of Horse and Rider*, first published in England by J.A.Allen in 1958, has gone through several reprints. Although it lacks the inspirational quality of Seunig, Wynmalen or Decarpentry, in the German fashion it provides an accurate summation of movements correctly made, together with the basic aids.

Wätjen advocated the two point seat and appeared from photographs to ride with a shorter stirrup than many of his contemporaries at Vienna. He warned against overbracing of the back or exaggerated seat aids, and in this context his writing contrasts sharply with another popular writer of the period, a hunting man, Wilhem Müseler. There is no doubt that Wätjen is important as a dedicated forerunner of today's German competition riders.

Wilhelm Müseler

Another writer who has made his mark on modern dressage, though lacking the classical background of Seunig or Wätjen, was the German born Wilhelm Müseler. Müseler served as a major in the first World War, and when peace came he founded the Berliner Parforce Riding Club, later becoming a director of the Beermann Riding Institut in Berlin. Formerly Master of the Berlin Hunt, he was a brilliant all-round rider and teacher, and his book *Riding Logic*, first published in Hamburg in 1937, is seen by many as the epitome of the German equestrian method.

Müseler was probably the first writer to attempt an illustrated explanation of the *aids* of the seat. As we have seen throughout this book, the posture of the rider, and the position of the seat in the saddle had been well explored by the great masters of the past. It had always been assumed that by maintaining that correct position, the rider would then become united to the motion of the horse which in turn would be able to execute the various movements required of him with the general aids of weight, hand and leg. This is undoubtedly so for the more collected work of the High School, but Müseler was not interested in High School, and was obviously influenced by cross-country riding and the modern emphasis for brilliant extension in all gaits.

He therefore described in great detail the driving aids of the seat and back which have led to many readers believing his theories to epitomise the modern German method. Not everyone agreed with this however, particularly since unlike Seunig or Wätjen, Müseler had no real classical background although was obviously highly articulate and well read. There is the argument that Müseler has no place in a book on the development of Classical Equitation, but such an influential figure deserves an important place in the development of dressage and an insight into Müseler will answer many questions about modern dressage methods.

The Conventional Side

In many ways, Müseler was totally conventional. His basic dressage position was merely that of the old masters. As Littauer pointed out in his *The Development of Modern Riding* it had all been said before, all over the world and particularly in Germany. Compare the following:

> *Müseler*: 'The very first thing the rider must acquire is balance. By balance alone he must keep in the saddle and not by means of his arms and legs. The body should rest vertically upon the two pelvic bones and the crotch, i.e. on three points of support, exactly at the lowest point of the saddle. It is important that this lowest point should be right in the middle of the saddle.'

> *Bobinsky (a Russian colonel writing in 1836 under the German influence of the time)*: 'Lean back with the upper part of the torso and push the belt and the stomach forward . . . sit resting on . . . the two seat bones and the crotch. These points . . . form the base of the rider's position at the lowest point of the saddle.'

> *The German Official Dressage Handbook Advanced Techniques of Riding today*: 'This saddle [La Guérinière's *selle à la francaise*] enabled the development of the modern seat, based on both seat bones and the crotch . . .'

The Braced Back

Where Müseler was innovatory was in his description of a backwardly braced back and a pelvis rotated towards the rear in order both to drive the horse forward and to collect or half-halt him. According to Müseler the action of the back is the same for both requirements, a theory which disregards the subtle use of weight aids forward as well as back. Where previous writers only advocated an upright position of the rider at all times, with the spine retaining its natural S shape and bracing occurring forward by pushing the waist towards the hands, Müseler produced diagrams to indicate a totally new idea at that time. These indicate a flattening of the lower spine, the pelvis rotated clockwise so that only the rear point of the seatbones are in contact with the saddle, and the rider sitting well behind the vertical. This is in total contradiction to his original description of a full contact of the seat.

There is the argument that Müseler only used this position for remedial schooling on very strong horses. Unfortunately the text does not make this clear, and too many *aficionados* have adopted it as 'the German competitive seat'. Yet by no means all Germans employ this harsh driving position, and other nations are equally responsible for this non-classical position.

Theoretically, the effect of such pronounced driving extends the frame of the horse horizontally, possibly producing the sought-after *Schwung* or swing to the back. This may be achieved with a very powerful Warmblood horse for example, but generally with the more sensitive lighter types, hollowing is caused and impulsion lost through resistance.

Yet Müseler was only too mindful of the need to take care. In his section on 'Influences of the Back', he wrote 'Nervous and timid horses, highly-strung Thoroughbreds and also most English-bred horses, very strongly resent crude aids and often strike if the rider does not use tact and discretion in his influences.' From this and the photographs employed to illustrate his point (all of which demonstrate riders bracing more conventionally through an upright classical posture) it seems he may have been mistaken in his understanding of the mechanism of the spine and pelvis. Many excellent riders are renowned for their sense of feel, but it is well known that some of the most brilliant ones are quite unable to explain how they achieve what they do.

A former student of the Spanish Riding School and of the late Nuno Oliveira, Daniel Pevsner now working in England, wrote a thoughtful article on the subject of Müseler which pointed out the harmful effects of his prescribed driving seat. 'In leaning back the rider interferes with and distorts the horse's balance. The horse is pushed not only forwards but also downwards and thus. . .onto the forehand. The croup at the time rises whilst the hind legs stiffen . . . although there is an apparent surge of extra energy, the horse's engagement is actually impaired and diminished.' Pevsner also comments on the apparent disparity between the photographs in *Riding Logic* which show a more classical position and Müseler's own exaggerated drawings.

Despite these discrepancies *Riding Logic* has proved the dressage best seller of the century. The first English translation appeared in 1937 and it is still an international bible to many riders. Without the drawings, Müseler's book is full of excellent advice for the average dressage rider, and is certainly easier to assimilate than that of Seunig. In simple language Müseler offers assistance in understanding collection, flexion and showing the horse the way to the ground as well as excellent advice on the leg and hand aids. All in all therefore, he deserves a place in this history of dressage, since his writing has helped thousands of ordinary riders develop a taste for a more sensitive approach to their horses.

Top Trainers of Today

In general, the very top German riders and trainers are less removed from their counterparts in Austria, France, and Portugal than people would like to make out. As Müseler very wisely observed '. . . The classical art of riding can best be defined as the method that aims at obtaining perfect harmony between rider and horse in a natural way and in full consideration of the psychology of the horse . . . The German and Romanic Schools are both based on this same conception. They are closely related to each other. The difference between them lies simply in the difference of temper and character of the two nations. The German is more thorough and indulges more in theories, the Frenchman is much lighter and has an outspoken sense of elegance.'

One must also add that these differences stem from the temper and character of their horses. Most people now admit that a certain heaviness of style prevailed in Germany between the wars which no doubt came about by an increasing use of heavier blood in the cavalry horse. Roughhanded practices in the showjumping arena has also been reflected in some areas of dressage riding, but thankfully rarely at advanced levels.

Schultheiss and Theoderescu

Nevertheless modern German trainers have been determined to break away from any image of heaviness and under the influence of influential figures like General Stecken, artists on horseback such as former national coach, Willi Schultheiss and competitor and trainer, George

Theoderescu have worked hard to promote a lighter style of riding with their pupils at home and at Warendorf. Both very individual riders, such is their strength of seat and brilliant sense of timing that it is often hard for pupils to folllow them. Horses however respond by never forgetting a lesson derived from these masters, and the Canadian horse, Dynasty was a good example of a horse which had received the magical Schultheiss treatment.

George Theoderescu is not German by birth but comes from that once great Baroque capital of Bucharest in Romania, taking German nationality when defecting from the Communist regime in 1959. Running his own popular training establishment south-west of Hanover, many foreign visitors are trained by him, the talented Dane Rawlins of England being one of many, and he has also worked in both the United States and Canada, coaching their teams. George is enjoying the results of much of his hard work in seeing his daughter placed fourth in the 1989 European championships – a triumph in the tough world of modern Grand Prix.

Boldt

As Germany's national coach, Harry Boldt, Olympic and European medallist, is also based at the DOKR where he passes on a wealth of technical skills to new Olympic hopefuls. A man with a quite unique feeling for the competition scene, he works quietly and tactfully with the steady stream of German and foreign riders who come within his grasp, and in many ways he epitomises the German system. Cool, calm, classical and correct, Boldt's brilliance with horses should not be underestimated, although he may lack the flair or even flashiness of other well known modern trainers. A tall, trim figure, most of Europe's top riders have passed through his hands at some time or another, and amongst the better known horses he has trained is Woyceck with whom he achieved enormous international success. His latest book *Das Dressur Pferd* (*The Dressage Horse*) is yet to be fully translated into English.

Klimke

Reiner Klimke is probably the most professional amateur dressage rider in the world. A successful lawyer, he somehow finds the time to ride up to four or five horses a day, at his yard just outside Munster, and has produced a number of extremely good event and dressage horses over many years. Today, he is generally known for his two great dressage stars, who have shone not only in national and European championships, but each has represented Germany in the Olympics. Mehmed and Ahlerich are two exceptional horses, but the latter, a highly strung bundle of hotblood power could so easily have gone wrong with another rider and it is a testament to Klimke's tact over many years and a pleiad of competitions, that Ahlerich has come to epitomise correct classical dressage success.

Klimke's most rewarding medal was probably the indidivual gold won at the Olympic Games in 1984. He describes the occasion of winning at Los Angeles as 'the most beautiful moment of my life' since for him Ahlerich had given his all. 'I have seldom sensed such an intimate connection between horse and rider as I felt on that day.'

With his tremendously supportive and wise wife, who schools his horses in the early stages, as well as his son, Michael who, with his quiet, centaur-like seat, is now proving his own talent for Grand Prix competition with the Entertainer, the Klimke success story is obviously very much a family affair.

Klimke's style is distinctive. A tall, slim man he personifies straightness, absolute control and total precision in the saddle. An obviously deeply thinking and tactical rider, his is the academic approach and he rides with such steely determination that one cannot even contem-

Jennie Loriston-Clarke working-in prior to competing with Masterlock Recruitment's Dutch Bid. This talented chestnut, home-bred horse, won eight national championships in dressage and jumping events by the age of eight; he was also the first British horse to win at a European Championship when he took the Prix St George at Goodwood, 1987. There is a pleasant, sparkling quality about the overall picture. (*Photo : Chris Skarbon*)

PLATE 13

Ahlerich, ridden by Reiner Klimke at the 1984 Los Angeles Olympics. The horse bounds lightly into the flying change at canter, assisted by the upright but very light seat of his rider. This photograph exemplifies lively but controlled energy and expression and the attitude of horse and rider would not be out of place in either 1910 or even 1710, although in the old days, the flying change was not a specific movement of the classical manège. (*Photo : Kit Houghton*)

Dutch Courage, Jennie Loriston-Clarke's veteran partner of national and international success, obviously enjoys his outings in the New Forest. Jennie has always maintained the value of schooling horses out of the manège as well as in, and remembers how she first taught 'Bill' his one-time flying changes following a line of trees out in the forest. (*Photo : Kit Houghton*)

PLATE 14

Nicole Uphoff during her medal-winning performance at the Seoul Olympics on the Thoroughbred Rembrandt. Light, still, straight and at one with the horse, Nicole is able to obtain precision with the quietest of aids and gentle hands. Suddenly, lightness appears back in fashion – a heartening sign for world dressage. (*Photo : Bob Langrish*)

plate anything ever going wrong during one of his beautifully executed tests. Yet it has done, and there have been bitter moments of disappointment. Through it all however, Klimke is always the first to blame himself and to determine that the next time, there will be crowning success. Usually, this happens.

Of all the great dressage riders of Germany, here is a man who has made it his business to seek an all round experience of horses. From bringing the young foal on from babyhood to the first stages of schooling, from Olympic three day eventing to Grand Prix dressage, Klimke has done it all – a very different breed of competitor to the one who buys a ready-made horse, dons top hat and tails and proceeds to the competition arena after his or her trainer has worked in the horse for an hour or so first.

Klimke is against the current fashion for bringing on the young horse too quickly. 'Nowadays three-year-old horses are offered at auction sales as top potential dressage, jumpers or event horses in the belief that these horses, which have only just been backed, will reach the top in these disciplines. To the experienced horseman this is sheer nonsense. He knows that patience is needed on the long route which brings a horse from basic training to the top of a discipline. But how many lovers of horses have enough knowledge of horsemanship? . . . Often a horse is regarded merely as a piece of sports equipment. Hence, knowledge of training and horsemanship has generally diminished.'

Taking each day at a time, the Klimke way is slow and painstaking. Once the horse's basic education is complete, he may work him hard, but tries never to make the mistake, so prevalent nowadays of pushing him beyond the limit thus losing trust and natural generosity. A new and difficult movement once successfully accomplished, will be left alone whilst he takes the horse back to basics, before that line is pursued again.

In his latest book *Ahlerich – The Making of a Dressage World Champion* Klimke describes with intimate clarity the psychological approach used throughout the training of this sensitive beautiful Westphalian gelding. On the one occasion, after some persistent trouble in the piaffe,

he gave in to force instead of tact, 'punishing him with powerful spurs and angry words . . .' The result was a Pyrrhic victory: 'After his initial resistance, Ahlerich finally resigned and obediently piaffed' but thereafter remained 'reserved and distrustful . . . The price I would pay would be my horse's expression.'

This and many other personal glimpses show us a man who builds on his relationship with his horses to an extent of tremendous understanding and shared intimacy. Discipline is always there, an iron determination to win, and everything is analysed with the thoroughness for which the Germans are famed, but for all the desire for victory,

In true classical tradition, Dr Klimke and Ahlerich move as one through an expressive, well elevated and technically correct passage. (*Photo courtesy Reiner Klimke*)

Klimke displays a psychological understanding of the horse which is compatible with all the old classical principles. A man who obviously admires in others that elegance which is not always apparent in modern riding, and softness in the horse which people rarely connect with the German school, Klimke must rank as a modern master. It is not enough to ride brilliantly, he declares, the horse must be brilliant in himself. Perhaps, if more competition horses were ridden with the ideals and understanding of a man like Klimke, we would see many more brilliant horses. (*See Plate 13*)

Other books by this extraordinarily accomplished man include his original small handbooks *Cavalletti* and *Horse Trials,* written in his eventing days, followed by his first mainly dressage book, *Basic Training of the Young Horse.*

Herbert Reybein, who runs a beautiful establishment near Hamburg is another trainer who has achieved considerable influence in this great equestrian country and among visiting pupils from the United States. A pupil of the legendary Bubi Gunther (died in 1974) he is a very clever teacher, often driving horse and rider to the limit, but always getting the results. The real benefit of his teaching however is in his riding the horse. Horses go athletically for him and with his strong seat but remarkably light touch, he is able to achieve results where many others have failed.

Since the proof of a good trainer must, in most opinions, lie in the number of successful horses which have passed through their manège, then perhaps of all the Germans, Schultenbaumer deserves this accolade. His own son Uwe, a doctor, has enjoyed international fame on two stunning horses, Slibowitzch and Madras. The first to enjoy his father's schooling and training, he was quickly followed by others, and the most recent successes have been the gold medal winning performances worldwide of pupils Margit Otto-Crepin and Nicole Uphoff. Since the great, bold-striding Corlandus, and the slight, sensitive Thoroughbred Rembrandt, could not be more dissimilar in looks, temperament, and way of moving, one from the other, the success of Schultenbaumer's schooling of both horses is all the more remarkable. Corlandus, is more reminscent of the type of horse so favoured by the judges in the seventies when sheer size and strength seemed everything; happily, with Rembrandt, we are seeing a new era in the international arena, when once again lightness and delicacy will be greeted with more enthusiasm by all.

Von Neindorff

Herr Egon von Neindorff, now in his late sixties, differs from his peers in modern Germany in that he is little concerned with competition riding, and abhors any method of rushing the horse and placing too many demands on it. Working in his own Baroque type riding hall, tucked away in the busy industrial town of Karlsruhe, he takes students from all over the world who wish to study riding as an art. Classical music, Iberian horses, the dramatic lighting and the pillars of the classical manège seem more akin to a riding hall in Versailles or Lisbon than Western Germany. The effect is dramatic however and cleverly places the pupil in the right mood for the study of art from a bygone era.

Here the emphasis is on the collection and lightness of the horse. There is to be no domination, no relentless driving forward – rather the cultivation of the horse's suppleness, his beauty and happiness being the ultimate aim. Since von Neindorff believes the demands of competition cause duress to the horse, von Neindorff rejected it long ago.

Training methods are similar to the school of Baucher and Oliveira. Much emphasis is placed on developing the technique of back and weight control from a deep, still seat and supple loins. The legs must be deep, relaxed and still, the aids featherlight. Here there is no place for Müseler's driving back or seat bones, and every reason for La Guérinière's *descente de main et des jambes*, a gift to the horse too often neglected and rejected in today's international arena.

Summing up the German School

Readers will now see that it is impossible to make generalisations. The German seat, the German school, all have come in for criticism, yet Germany, *per capita*, may well boast a larger number of classical riders than any other country in the world. Who can say? Competitors like Reiner Klimke, Monica Theoderescu, Nicole Uphoff and Ann-Kathrin Lisenhoff all display different small characteristics in their riding, but there is a general classic uniformity and straightness about them, which has to be admired.

Rarely at this level, unlike some of the sights observed on the way up, are there signs of punishing legs or a heavy-handed contact. Difficulties in the execution of the High School movements which often lack real engagement are not peculiar to Germany. Reiner Klimke is one of the few Grand Prix medallists whose horses display a real dancing quality. It is a universal problem that engagement and flexion are too often forfeited for the impressive thrust which may emanate from an artificially suspended back and the pendulum action of stiff hind-legs. Not all judges seem aware of this inconsistency however although followers of the Versailles school would blame this on insufficient freedom in the neck and jaw of the horses concerned. This is generally caused by too much schooling into an ungiving fixed contact. As Klimke points out, 'The horse should move with the *softest possible* [my italics] contact in a good self-carriage.'

This difference between the very top German riders and their contemporaries on the way up was remarked upon by Nuno Oliveira in one of his books.[11] 'I possess a film of Schultheiss on a grey horse showing the Grand Prix movements. You can often see the reins slack, almost loose, when the horse flexes his haunches well. In the 1982 World Championships at Lausanne, Reiner Klimke also demonstrated very often in his test, this *descente de main*.'

Setting aside the work of these two masters, most Germans will admit there is a tendency in the German (particularly male) character to dominate and the French writer and dressage judge, Decarpentry complained of too much submission in their horses which he described as '. . . constrained and sometimes dull' with '. . . a strict precision that was more mechanical than animated'. At the same time however, he clearly regretted the 'nonchalant leniency of the French . . .' which is mainly responsible for their lack of success within competition. Even their elegant gold medallist, number one rider, Otto-Crepin is not French, but German born.

Perhaps if the French competition riders made more use of their talent for extracting lightness and gaiety from the horse, in the way of their traditional masters, instead of trying to mimic the Germans who are past masters at application and thoroughness, the world dressage scene would be very much more interesting.

Von Neindorff is certainly the exception to any form of dominant school. It is said that he is more influenced by the Romantic School than his fellow countrymen. Yet Podhajsky refuted such descriptions and wrote of the Olympics at Helsinki, 'the representatives of the so-called Romantic school rode partly with a very strong contact with the bit . . . the representatives of the so-called Germanic school, on the contrary showed their horses on a long, sometimes even slack, rein. Such observations prove once more that 'classical equitation is not the property of one particular nation.'[12]

[11] *Classical Principles of the Art of Training Horses.* [12] From Handler's *The Spanish Riding School of Vienna.*

SEVENTEEN

The Spanish Riding School Today

Creamy white horses with dancing feet and bobbing manes move in soft unison away from the central gallery and file in perfectly matched pairs along the perimeters of the historic school. There is something so splendidly gentle, so rhythmic, about the rise and fall of each horse's rounded, elastic back, matched only by the rise and fall of the rider's chest – everything else is still – that if one half-closes the eyes, you begin to imagine yourself being lifted gently on the white crested waves of a deep ocean, as the sweet strains of a Mozart concerto serenade you far out to a dreamlike sea.

Time stands still for the Spanish Riding School's stately carousel. The white feet move sideways, appearing to converge for a moment in the centre, then clearly separate and move on to the other side, momentarily crossing in front of each other; then horse and rider resumes his dressing (place) in the exercise and two partners meet again as they bend, turn and come purposefully foward down the centre line. Then you see the dark eyes of the horses, fathomless eyes, now concentrating, now proud; fine aristocratic noses, long, gleaming, quivering nostrils turned towards you, pink and open with fervour and desire to excel.

Lipizzaners are noble, years of proper training and progressive discipline have developed a horse generous to serve. The music changes, a more impressive march, some strident chords and the horses take up passage, a stately bouncing gait which flexes the fine joints of their legs, thigh, hock and fetlock, and enhances the roundness of their necks and rumps without losing the rhythmic softness of the gait. So they sweep by. A timeless procession, a step back into splendour, you sense the achievement and wonder at the emotions it draws from within you, as though perhaps you had been there before, and understood it all the time.

This display by four of the most accomplished stallions in the School, which had been preceded by a flowing ride of the young stallions, is followed by the breathtaking Pas de Deux which brings members of the audience to the edge of their seats. Even those who understand nothing of horsemanship cannot fail to appreciate the apparent marriage of four minds – two horses', two riders' – the weaving patterns of four pairs of hooves, perfectly timed, perfectly in unison, the subtle quietness of two pairs of hands which rest at the base of two proud highly crested necks, and the intricacy of the steps and figures which unfold. Today, *Oberbereiter* Artur Kottas and *Bereiter* Johann Riegler are the elegant riders; they epitomize the classical ideals of the still, restrained artist on horseback.

Boccherini's 'Minuet' accompanies the fourth section of the programme, work on the short hand rein, ably led by the First *Oberbereiter* Tschautscher, a big man whose gentle handling of the leading stallion, one of the Neapolitano strain is matched only by his attention to detail. A solo performance follows by a clearly older, but brilliant horse Maestoso Palmira and for this specialised work on the long rein, the highly experienced *Oberbereiter* Eichinger displays those skills and practices which are rarely seen anywhere else in the world.

The airs above the ground! The last entry on the programme before the School Quadrille, brings alive all the old battle manoeuvres of the seventeenth century. Only the School's strongest, most gymnastic, and noblest of horses are suitable for this desperately demanding

Pegasus – the winged horse! The Lippizzaner takes on a light magical quality as he flies through the air in the supreme test of strength and obedience – a beautiful, timeless capriole. (*Photo courtesy of the Spanish Riding School*)

mounted work. No stirrups are worn by the riders, the classical three reins in one hand is employed and whilst the horses of the levade and the courbette retain their long flowing tail, the horse of the capriole has his tail braided up and tucked neatly under his dock. The strains of Strauss pervade the arena and the horses anticipate the extra hush from the galleries. In preparation for these exciting and extravagant leaps high above the head of a man, the stallion begins to bounce on the spot. Gathering himself with sheer physical strength and willpower, he must accomplish an extreme point of collection in order to make the spring. The beauty of the capriole is the visual sight of an apparently winged horse, Pegasus – no longer bound by earthly forces – momentarily flying with great force and impulsion into eternity. Spectators are transfixed, a great sigh goes up, and the weight of privilege at having witnessed such a feat is not easily forgotten.

It is almost with relief that one greets the School Quadrille, the seventh and final section of a programme that has remained the same over many decades. The white ballet of eight dancing stallions lulls the spectator back onto his ocean of contentment. Silver crested necks rise and fall, the bright bobbing fetlocks waltz over the tan, and cause a mesmeric effect of harmony and ease. There is a liquidity about the movements of the Lipizzaners which is rarely seen in other arenas. Nothing jarrs, nothing is forced, even the extended trots show no staccato movement; instead rhythm, cadence and impulsion ebb and flow as softly as a summer breeze. Beauty and art reign supreme.

To spend a Sunday morning at the Hofburg Spanish Riding School is to evoke history. This is no pleasant parody of the past. The performance is the result of the same effort, the same hardships, the same discipline and adherence to unswerving principles, created with the same strong sense of purpose that the masters of the sixteenth, seventeenth, eighteenth and nineteenth centuries found under the inspirational skies of Imperial Austria.

To appreciate all this, it is not sufficient only to see the Lipizzaners and their riders. The true connoisseur must wander the *Plätzes* (squares), the little *Strassen*, the great avenues, and the grandest parade grounds and the meanest alleyways that make up Vienna. They must breathe in the clean mountain air and feast the eyes and the brain on the richness to be found all around. For Vienna is truly the Centre of Europe. Into Vienna from gateways to the east, west, north and south flood the cultures of all Europe and beyond. The influences of the orient permeate this ancient of cities, like a thin gold thread which may appear with sudden boldness and extravagance in a surprise encounter with a Viennese tapestry, cupola or canvas. In Vienna the traveller feels a closeness with those mysteriously romantic countries which once made up this mighty empire, neighbouring Bohemia, Hungary, Transylvania, Romania and mountainous Yugoslavia. The artistic splendour of bordering Italy which opens the sea route to Spain, Portugal and France, together with the order and grandeur of Germany to the northwest have all converged on this most ancient of capitals to give it an identity which is totally unique and can only be described as Central European.

Austria's empire which reached its zenith under the Habsburgs in the mid eighteenth century was one of the greatest of European history. The capital shows its sheer supremacy. Huge buildings, built of hard granite, billow magnificently in the luxury of the Baroque style; powerful statues, fountains and gateways boast of Imperialistic might. Etched sharply against a vivid Viennese sky, they push importantly upwards towards the heavens themselves – a remarkable testimony to a period when nothing seemed impossible and the wealth and strength of the Holy Roman Empire was touched by immortality. The Palace of Belvedere, the Opera House, the Natural History Museum dominated by the memorial to Maria Theresa who sits grandly and weightily on a throne guarded by four frock-coated horsemen, the Schwarzenberg, the vast Summer Palace of Schönbrunn, with its magnificent horse pictures by George Hamilton – all must be visited, lingered over and appreciated. For this forms the backcloth to all that is accomplished in the Spanish Riding School of Vienna, and to pass these glorious monuments by renders the picure incomplete.

And so, the thinking visitor comes to the Hofburg with a sense of continuity, touched by the endeavour of the past. On their homeground in the centre of this heaving capital, he can now appreciate the work of the Lipizzaners to the full. Solemnly

Baroque Vienna! Everywhere one goes in this great, intrinsically Central European city, the visitor is reminded of Austria's glorious history. The much loved equestrian statute in the foreground is to Prince Eugene who defeated the Turks at Belgrade in 1717. (*Photo by the author*)

resolute, the horses emerge in an orderly file from their stables at the Stallburg, their four-storied quarters in this 1556 palace, and as the city traffic grinds to a respectful halt for them, they clip-clop across the age-old cobbles to the Winter Riding School. Humility, one of the keywords in the teaching of equitation at Vienna, is epitomised by the simple apple-wood sticks carried by each rider. From their masters who are entrusted to retain that important human ingredient, the Lipizzaners derive confidence for the task ahead. To remind people of the glory that once was Vienna and the spirit of the people who lived there after the Renaissance and whose dream it was to create a heaven on earth by displaying all that was noble, grand, ordered and beautiful in their music, art, architecture and equitation – that is their inheritance. As Handler once wrote: 'We are links in a long chain of men who pass a treasure into grateful hands from generation to generation. It is our task to preserve a heritage, and to make sure that it is transmitted intact to others yet to come.'

What place does the Spanish Riding School hold in today's modern world? The question is constantly asked. There are many who patronizingly suggest that the School is but a charming anachronism, another splendid money-spinner for the Vienna Tourist Board. Idle spectators with no knowledge of equestrianism could be forgiven for such suppositions, since they are based on ignorance. It is altogether more serious and tragic for the horse world when these sentiments are expressed on the lips of dressage judges and critics, yet this has occurred. Despite the tremendous strides forward which have taken place in recent years which have brought dressage within the reach of thousands of riders all over the world, and focused attention on the intricacies, difficulties and challenges of the craft, earning it real respect and a separate place in the Olympic scheme, there are still those who have made up their minds that what is required and produced in competition should bear little relationship to the reality of Vienna. It is these same people who have turned their own dressage into a sport, removed from the ideals of riding as an art.

This attitude has, over the years, given real concern to the custodians of the Spanish Riding School as well as to the *aficionados* of classical equitation. In a serious interview with Dr Jaromir Oulehla, the present Director of the Spanish Riding School, we discussed the resistance by some FEI dressage judges to the work being undertaken at Vienna and of the merits of the Lipizzaner horse.

'Many modern critics have little idea of the past and indeed of art. They fail to appreciate that our Lipizzaner was bred for representative purposes by the Imperial Court. These horses personify all that is elegant and proud. It is their compact shape and high rounded movements which fill the eye and paint a very beautiful picture. Regrettably, because of the influence of two centuries of sporting riding, many judges have unconsciously replaced the pursuit of beauty with that of size, power and rapidity. Slow, stately, collected movements, the essence of the High School, are less understood than the extended movements of the sporting horse. Yet whilst we practise extension here, it is certainly not everything and does not particularly represent beauty.

'Classical riding is like the ballet, you look for the overall effect. The precise intricate steps, the control and the height are what make it graceful. The big strides across the stage, or in our case, the arena, are impressive but have little to do with the art. Unfortunately, in dressage the judges are not always able to recognise that the shorter, rounder frame is as correct for the horse as the longer extended one. The action of our Lipizzaners is in keeping with their frame. Mechanically, their whole way of moving is sound, and you can see it through the swinging back, the deeply flexed hocks. The proof of this is the horses' continued suppleness

Dr Jaromir Oulehla is the first person to direct both the Spanish Riding School of Vienna and the Austrian Federal Stud at Piber. A sensitive man who shows a great love for the Lippizzaners in his charge, he is shown here with Favory Alea I. (*Photo courtesy of the Spanish Riding School*)

long after other horses are retired from work.'

No one is more capable of looking at dressage from the point of view of the horse than this distinguished veterinarian, who was born and studied in Czechslovakia before settling in Austria. The first Director of both the School and the Austrian Federal Stud, Dr Oulehla's primary concern is the health and mental wellbeing of the horses. This has alienated him from some of the modern methods of dressage training which he observes outside Vienna. He feels these are not only misguided but unwittingly employed to the ultimate detriment of the horse. He is particularly against overfeeding the young horse to achieve early maturity, and the use of body-building additives. Neither can he tolerate intensive training on young horses which even if physically, are certainly not ready mentally to accept such demands. 'I am afraid much of the competition world has now moved a long distance away from the Spanish Riding School,' he observes. 'I will tell you why.

'Classical riding is concerned with the slow, systematic training of the horse over many years to prepare him gymnastically and mentally for dressage training. The programme of schooling is performed always with the enhancement and happiness of the horse in mind. We pay great attention to the role of man and horse as one unit and stress that the psychological harmony between the rider and his horse must be right – this starts from day one. The hallmark of the great classical and cavalry schools has always been to protect the horse by insisting upon standards and proper procedures. We look first therefore to the ultimate development of the horse in body and in mind. The proof of correct training is quite simple. It is a horse which grows in beauty and happiness. By happy I mean a relaxed supple horse, not one who is tense and artificially bright. The majority of horses brought on in this way are long-lived and active over many years.

'Too many people in the competition world are concerned only with equine material. The results of their effort are seen in the auctions; two-year-olds that are big and magnificent through intensive feeding later show flaws, particularly in the joints. Horses break down at a very young age. Despite commanding enormous prices as potential dressage horses, only a small percentage make it to the advanced arenas. Without the protection and the discipline of the cavalry schools, there are few who can protect the horse from hurried, forceful methods. As with everything, too much is governed by finance, so the old principles are lost.

'Not long ago, people were saying the Spanish Riding School was nothing but a museum. Now, they are beginning to come back and take a closer look. They ask why every one of our horses makes it to the top level of training, and how it is that they can continue happily for so many years. I am encouraged nowadays because it is so often the competitors themselves who want to know these answers.'

Dr Oulehla went on to highlight the root cause of the problem which he firmly believes lies in the attitude of judges. 'Unfortunately the majority are not clear in their minds what constitutes good dressage. Too many are concerned with sheer mechanical locomotion as opposed to the overall picture of man and horse moving through a series of movements in the most correct, beautiful and harmonious way. These are still judges who keep their eyes at ground level and only look at legs, legs, legs. This is not the way to judge an overall picture.'

A former Director, General Albrecht, himself an international dressage judge of the highest repute, backed up these sentiments. 'Ideally and in theory, there should be no difference between the Classical School and the Competition School but unfortunately, in practice there is. The goals are different. The Classical School is looking first and foremost to make the horse gymnastic through logical training and psychology. The Competition School is looking for horses to learn movements in order to compete. In the Classical School we believe that competition should only be used as a very last topping to the cake, a finishing touch to show and to prove (for those riders who wish this) that the horse has been successfully trained.

'My concern is that horses are taken out to compete whether they are ready or not. It is painful to see these horses stiff and resistant through incorrect riding and insufficient preparation being taken to show after show. It is a travesty of the aims of equitation and demeans the horse. I am afraid this happens not only in Holland, England, America and Germany, it occurs in Austria too. Horses go week after week to shows. All the riders want is to achieve better marks. If they do not do well one week, they go back the next hoping to do better. To get better, there is only one way. To stay at home and work for months, years, until you and the horse are ready for such activities.'

General Albrecht believes there should be no actual competitions until at least Medium/Advanced level. The rider should judge his horse on the way up not by competition, but by training, clinics and observation. 'Every rider can see whether or not his horse is growing in beauty, suppleness and if he is mentally happy. If the rider finds this too hard, then he needs the help of an expert, but certainly he is not ready to *compare* his horse with others.

'The dressage world must be awakened to the fact that what is happening is far from ideal. Judges and competitors alike must be educated to understand that real dressage means soft, beautiful, happy horses, and that there is only one way. This is through a consistent psychological approach combined with correct, slow training in the ways that have been laid down by the great classical masters.

'The Spanish Riding School is an island. It is the last stronghold of classical equitation in its most correct and purest form. It will not change; its future is secure. Riders who really care look to it for inspiration and for guidelines. The judges may think they know better, but even they will come back in the end for help and guidance. The Lipizzaners of the Spanish Riding School give people pleasure wherever they go. People love to see horses working with such pride and ease; it brings tears to their eyes and like a beautiful piece of music, or a superb painting, it lifts the heart. That is the ultimate of dressage.'

The programme of schooling for each horse at the Spanish Riding School has changed very little in 400 years. Close observation of the early morning training sessions with the young horses does much to explain why the Lipizzaners are confident in their work and are often able to continue far into their twenties. First and foremost the riders seem at peace with themselves. Whatever their own personal problems or worries, they are sufficiently disciplined to leave these far behind them when they enter the school to salute the portrait of the Emperor Charles VI, the founder of the Winter Riding School. They sit still on their horses, quiet,

The levade (shown here in hand) requires tremendous generosity, balance and strength on the part of the stallion. Here Favory Europa displays the depth of engagement necessary in the thigh, hock and fetlock to enable the elevation of the forehand, whilst still maintaining a compact rounded outline. The handler is *Bereiter* Harrer. (*Photo courtesy of the Spanish Riding School*)

upright and elegant; the white-gloved hands handle the reins with absolute precision and care. Months of work on the lunge made long ago, early in the training of each *élève* has paid off. With a deep secure seat, they have learned to feel and absorb every movement made by the horse so that he never senses the discomfort of a hard bumping or the resulting bruised back.

The first concern of each trainer is to look for forward impulsion and straightness. Colonel Podhajsky constantly quoted Steinbrecht, 'forward and straight at all times is our *lietmotif*!' New work is very gradual and riders concentrate on following the horse's movement, rather than influencing it. Purity of gait is all important and this cannot be obtained if the horse is not relaxed. Only when he begins to gives his back to the rider, will any form of collection be attempted.

The young horse is never forced into an outline, but rather ridden forward on a light elastic contact which follows through but does not attempt in the early stages to place him on the bit. Frequent encouragement is given with the voice and hand, and training sessions last no more than half an hour. Before the horse is led away, the rider, now dismounted, spends time at the head of his horse and personally acknowledges his efforts. Not only is there the inevitable lump of sugar kept in a pocket in the tail of the coat, but gentle caressing of the face and looking into the horse's eye establishes a real personal contact.

During the second year of training, concentration is on helping the horse through carefully laid down suppling exercises on the circle, shoulder-in, voltes and so on, to develop and strengthen the muscles behind the saddle. This will later enable the horse to take more and more weight on the hocks and transfer the balance back. Collection therefore is developed slowly and arises naturally as the horse becomes lighter on the forehand from deeper engagement behind, and he learns to respond to the rider's gentle contact by chewing on the bit. The rider's hands remain still, only the fingers and wrist conducting a minute giving and taking of the contact which keeps the horse's mouth fresh and happy. Pulling back on the rein is completely foreign to this school.

Only when collection is firmly established with the horse pleasant in the mouth, and the muscles of neck and back now well developed, will the rider begin to use the useful weight aids of the seat associated with more gymnastic work, without ever deviating from the still, upright body position. By this time the horse will be in the third to fourth year of training and meticulous attention is paid to the execution of the school figures, looking always for cadence, lightness and rhythm through all the gaits and transitions. Once this has been achieved, the horse is ready to work towards the two or one tempo changes in canter; passage and piaffe will also be developed, and as suppleness, balance and strength is attained in the joints of the hindlegs, rudimentary preparation for the airs above the ground is made.

Chief Rider Artur Kottas explains that not every horse which excels for example in one tempo changes will make a capriole horse, and vice versa. 'Tremendous strength and impulsion is required for the airs above the ground, but it is more a question of smoothness and balance for the changes. Certainly, not every horse can produce the same brilliance in both. For most Lipizzaners, the trot gaits are easier than the canter but when the foundations have been correctly laid with straightness a priority from the beginning, the changes should not present too great a problem.'

Oberbereiter Kottas is one of the few riders at the Spanish Riding School who has competed for his country. As national dressage champion, he was actually selected to ride for Austria in the Olympic Games at Montreal in 1976 but was unable to accept this honour due to his

Concentration on the part of the horse and rider highlight the degree of finesse required to produce the correct piaffe. Here Chief Rider Artur Kottas drops his weight a little forward, helping the horse to round his back and gently lower the croup. With the hind legs now well engaged the movement takes on a dancing quality. The reins are not slack, but the contact is light from an unclenched hand and half-open, asking fingers. (*Photo courtesy of the Spanish Riding School*)

commitments at Vienna. For him personally, competition holds the attraction of challenge which he enjoys.

Other *Bereiters* are clearly not in favour of competition, regarding it as a threat to the high standards they have learned to accept and to admire at Vienna. As *Bereiter* Riegler put it, 'Dressage tests nowadays are too often designed to catch horses out rather than to help them accomplish a flowing output of work. This makes perfection almost impossible to achieve. Mechanical perfection means little if obtained under duress.'

A few *Bereiters* have their own teaching yards which keep them actively in touch with all that goes on in the competition world, and is a way of helping to raise standards. Kottas emphasized that he schools and teaches in exactly the same way outside the Spanish Riding School as he does inside. 'I will not take shortcuts,' he says 'and even if it takes a year longer, I insist on teaching all my students the classical way.'

For him the biggest problem worldwide is that of the rider's seat and this even occurs at Olympic level. He regrets that trainers do not take the trouble to establish a good seat in their pupils before they ever start to improve the horse. 'So often the good horses excel in spite of their riders, not because of them,' is a sentiment heard over and over again at Vienna.

Similar to General Albrecht, *Oberbereiter* Kottas feels strongly that a horse should only be entered in competition when he is ready and really good. 'The competition must only be the proof of the horse at his best.'

Commenting on other problems which he encounters outside the School, *Oberbereiter* Kottas realises that collection is a problem for many riders. Again, he blames the lack of a good seat but he is often surprised at the choice of horses. 'Some competitors just choose the wrong horses. The Lipizzaner for example is a natural for collection, so is the Lusitano and Andalusian, but the ex-racehorse naturally finds it very hard. He has been developed for a totally different purpose. It is vital that the horse is strong and supple in his back before he is asked for collection and this cannot be achieved if the horse is weak behind the saddle and if his neck is not muscled along the top line.'

The most refreshing aspect of teaching at the Spanish Riding School is neither the constant quest for perfection, nor the glittering trappings of traditional tack and turn-out, nor even the upholding of a system which has changed little in four hundred years of empirical teaching. What emerges forcefully from Vienna today, is the underlying concern for the well-being of the horse. This is classical riding at is best.

So often, in the outside world ignorance is the root cause of abuse. Riders do not intentionally cause their horses pain, but every day, even in the most lavish of stables, there are all too many examples of equine suffering. Worried horses, horses under stress cannot speak but as *Oberbereiter* Kottas said, you can read the sadness in their eye. Little resistances give them away, quietly gnashing teeth, flailing tails, setting the neck and back against the rider, unhappiness in the stable. Signs like these show that all is not well, yet too often they are ignored.

Fortunately, ignorance has no place at Vienna. Set in that noble hall of learning, against the whitely austere background of Fischer von Erlach's rows of double columns and connected galleries rising up to four stories high, a flourishing work of love and dedication goes on. Human failings are quenched, prejudices and pre-conceived ideas set aside. Once the doors to understanding and enlightenment have been opened, there is no retreat. No rider of calibre and stature can ever again return to shortcut methods or abuse. There is only one way forward, and that is to pursue the order, the discipline and the rules of nature. For that is what classicism is all about. The horse must be as relaxed, as balanced and as beautiful in his work as Nature intended. It has been said that Nature can exist without Art; but Art cannot exist without Nature. Nowhere is this better exemplified than at Vienna.

EIGHTEEN

Nuno Oliveira and the Modern Portuguese School

A CLASSICAL UPBRINGING

The final research on this book and its translation into a chapter form was almost all complete when a telephone call from Portugal broke the news. Mestre Nuno Oliveira had died the night before in Australia at the age of sixty-three. The words from an official source in Lisbon bore out the esteem in which he was held, 'This is a tragedy for the world.'

Dramatic as that phrase may sound, for those who knew him, studied under him, rode his horses, saw him ride, listened to or read his words, there was no overstatement – the Master, with all his faults and there were a few, was a genius with horses. With his dark brooding looks, colourful and powerful personality, unmistakeable riding figure, and gentle hands, he was undoubtedly the most revered classical horseman of our time. He embodied a last living link with those great classical Masters of seventeenth, eighteenth and nineteenth century Europe. It was not for nought that he himself was called Master by people of every nationality.

Not everyone liked his style, indeed some disapproved of his refusal to ride modern dressage, yet there can be very few serious horsemen who saw him at work who could truthfully disagree with the description above. It is interesting therefore to consider why such a trainer *sans pareil* commanded such a position and was held in such respect far into the 1980s. How, as we approach the twenty-first century, when dressage worldwide has gone through such a transformation and classical riding as an art is often more a sentiment than a reality, could just one man exert such influence? For in this ephemeral world of changing values, the Oliveira school will for certain live on.

Portugal's Historic Cultural Backcloth

To provide some of the answers, it is necessary first and foremost to understand Portugal. Without some knowledge of Portuguese traditional equestrian life it is hard to imagine how a figurehead such as Nuno Oliveira could have emerged, let alone remained as a pinnacle of riding aspiration.

The answer is bound to some extent in Portugal's proud past. Behind that once great naval history, the raising of colonies and building of empire, lies a small rugged country, tucked away to the most westerly point of Europe. Here, in the same way as within that other great seafaring nation, Britain (her oldest ally since the 1386 Treaty of Windsor[1]), a strong culture developed. Portugal boasts the oldest working universities and libraries in the world,[2] and because of her geographical isolation from the rest of the Continent, ancient countryside traditions have also thrived uninterrupted over the centuries.

Her very natural inaccessibility except by sea has now of course changed with air travel, but not that sense of national independence. Therefore whilst Portugal's resurgence into the mainstream of integrated European life is achieved through tourism in the south, and commerce

---

[1] After 600 years of friendship, celebrated anew at Windsor in June 1986, between HM The Queen and the Portuguese President.
[2] Coimbra University and the Library of Coimbra and of Braga were built in the tenth century.

on the western seaboard through Lisbon and Oporto, there is yet another Portugal, deep inland, which few tourists or foreign business men know or even comprehend.

Unknown Portugal

This comprises Portugal's hidden interior, the overlooked agricultural lands which lie to the north of the Algarve, sheltered behind range after inhospitable range of thickly wooded, often scrubby, rocky mountains. Here there is little habitation on a grand scale, only small villages with modest cottages sometimes without running water, and good roads are few. Winding inwards amongst mile after mile of sandy track it is not difficult to fancy oneself in an enchanted, endless world of eucalyptus, cork oak and pine forests. Where the wildcat and wild boar roam, there is the lingering thought that if your car broke down, no one would ever find you. Of course this is not so, for around the next corner there is a welcoming *monte* (hamlet) and round the one after that, a great house rears up against a brilliant sky, an oasis of green setting off beautiful stables, shady courtyards, and a Baroque *picadeiro* (manège). Trailing pink geranium, crimson bougainvillea and violet morning glory spill over whitewhashed walls and archways and give a pleasant homeliness to what is evidently an important *Quinta*. We know that here in the plains of the Alentejo, horses have been bred since before the time of the Romans, and it is here as the land levels out to meet the green fertile plains of the Tagus long before it reaches the sea at Lisbon, that probably the oldest form of equitation in the world has developed.

The End of Monarchy

Portugal's ancient monarchy came to an abrupt end in 1910 when King Don Manuel II was exiled to England, after the assassination of his father Don Carlos and the Crown Prince Ferdinand two years before. Thus the Portuguese Republic was born. Recognised, but officially titleless, the Bragança dynasty lives on, as do those (Dukes) of Lafões, of Cadaval and Palmela, whose names remain familiar abroad through the excellence of the wine that comes from their ancient estates.

Generally, it is still the aristocratic families with their deep cork forests, vineyards, and tracts of hilly olive groves that produce horses for gentlemen to ride as well as bulls for gentlemen to fight. Retaining an empire with her important African provinces well into the seventies, Portugal seemed an unlikely place for a revolution when the troops marched against their President on 25 April 1974. The landed classes' peaceful life with horses seemed perilously close to disappearing when the Communists began to commandeer whole estates after a second uprising in March 1975, yet in some miraculous way a counter coup at the end of the same year saved the day for democracy. Although early on a number of Lusitano mares were slaughtered, and many stallions sold or smuggled abroad, thanks probably to the bullfight,[3] many great estates and studs struggled to survive.

The Last Fighting Horses on Earth

In a unique way the traditions of High School riding had become so interwoven with the bullfight, there were but a few hardliners who considered the continuity of Portuguese equestrian life as a threat to a more egalitarian social structure. Thus, whilst depleted of some of its former grandeur, Portuguese High School remains surprisingly intact. Conversely, this phenomena of court riding and fighting horses is still an accepted way of life in a country which lost its king over eighty years ago. This is one of life's paradoxes since other countries which still enjoy a monarchy lost the tradition centuries ago.

[3] In the Portuguese bullfight the bull is not killed.

Portugal apart, only in Vienna, as we have seen, has this concept of riding been upheld from its sixteenth century origins. The difference between Austria and Portugal is that in the former, the classical art of High School riding is supported by and belongs to the state; in the latter, it receives no assistance whatsoever from the state and classical riding remains in the hands of the people. For the Portuguese it is still a practicality.

Into this climate therefore came Oliveira. Fortunate enough to study under the last of the Portuguese Royal Masters of the Horse, he was only one of the many young men brought up to pursue equitation as an art. There are still gentleman riders of the Oliveira vintage alive in Portugal today. Not all made equitation their career, having inherited industry and large properties to run, and few are known outside the Portuguese and Spanish speaking countries, but names like Don Diogo de Bragança (son of Lafões and cousin of the Pretender), the Palha brothers, David Ribeiro Telles, the late Guilherme Gião, the Veigas and the Coimbras, Fernando Sommer d'Andrade and the late João Nuncio, share with Nuno Oliveira the respect of the Iberian world.

The Beginning

What initially separated Oliveira from the majority of his fellow aspirants was perhaps his lack of great wealth. His family was well-travelled and educated (he had an English grandmother), enjoying responsible posts in the diplomatic service and overseas, but unlike the Andrades and the Veigas, there was no country estate to come to this only son. His father was a banker and later head of the Lutheran Church in Portugal, and the young Nuno had to make his own way in the world as soon as he left school. Fresh from his studies under Portugal's last Master of the Horse, his godfather, Mestre Miranda, he set off to earn his living from breaking and schooling horses.

After gaining valuable experience with military horses, he was soon noticed by Portugal's great landed families. An indefatigable rider, his career was launched when the de Barros family took him under their patronage at their delightful Azeitão property just across the Tagus from Lisbon. Here he rode and schooled up to fifteen horses a day, and seemed as fresh and enthusiastic for the last one at eight o'clock in the evening, as he was for the first at dawn. This early rising was a habit which never left him. Even in the last years of his life he was always out with his horses as the sun rose over the eucalyptus-clad hill. This was only one facet of his tremendous sense of personal discipline and dedication.

His next patron was Julio Borba of Loures. The old man virtually took Oliveira into the heart of the family, giving him the break he needed. The young man was provided with his own *picadeiro* and was soon to have carte blanche with the Borba's magnificent stable of Lusitano horses at Povoa de St Adrião, the Borba's home on the outskirts of Lisbon. The riding school which Oliveira set up there was named after the old farmhouse, Quinta do Chafaris. Sr Borba's two young sons Julio and Guilherme spent every free moment watching their new hero, and after university, Guilherme continued to assist and train with Oliveira for over twelve years. Finally, a master in his own right, he branched out on his own to organise and produce horses for the great Spanish sherry family, the Domecqs of Jerez (see Chapter 5).

Portugal's Last Master of the Horse

One thing of which Oliveira was justly proud was his early training. Mestre Joaquin Gonzales de Miranda, who served Portugal's last royal family, was a distant relation of Nuno's father. He took the young boy under his wing at around the age of nine, and in Portuguese fashion,

Monica Theoderescu rides Ganimedes into an impressive extended trot at the 1988 Olympics. The degree of contact shown with the hands emphasizes the strength and power of the big Warmblood horse which, to be channelled correctly, often require the most determined riding. Successful combinations such as this have held the majority of dressage judges enthralled for over three decades, but since Seoul there has been an increasing awareness of other qualities besides sheer size and strength, although these horses arguably show the best defined gaits. (*Photo: Bob Langrish*)

PLATE 15

Yugoslavia, the host country at the European Championships of 1989 provided some interesting combinations for spectators with their nationally bred Lipizzaners. Here, Dusan Mavec on Pluto Canissa IV demonstrates the collected elevation for which the Baroque horses are famed. The time is surely coming closer when a greater variety of breeds will enter international competition but the ability of judges to assess each type according to its build and natural way of moving will become even more vital. (*Photo: Bob Langrish*)

Piaffe into passage is one of the most difficult movements for most competition horses. Here Cynthia Ishoy rides her beautiful mount Dynasty for Canada in the Seoul Olympics showing impressive height and definition, although normally the horse was more engaged behind. (*Photo : Bob Langrish*)

PLATE 16

This pleasant picture of Margit Otto-Crepin with her World Championship horse, Corlandus, preparing to ride for France in the elegant setting of Goodwood House, illustrates the very best of competition dressage, combining a high standard of harmony, vivacity, expression and grace with which to inspire all future competitors. (*Photo : Chris Skarbon*)

he developed his seat on a fully schooled horse of the manège. First it was months of work without stirrups in a Portuguese traditional saddle, later both the English and Portuguese saddles were used. Miranda instructed in the way of all the great court riding masters. Faithful to the principles of La Guérinière and Marialva, he taught first and foremost that equitation was an art. Later, when Nuno was old enough to appreciate such things, he was told that this Art was so full of subtleties and sensitivity that it would refine all the feelings within the rider for literally everything that surrounded him. In other words it would give him new eyes in which to view life itself, eyes which would constantly search for that which was beautiful, straight and true.

But this gift, first discovered by the Greeks, could not be developed without first practising discipline, civility and a total lack of impatience or force. Miranda also taught Nuno that the dignity of man could never be acquired without understanding these three important prerequisites, and intense was his fury if at any time pupils strayed from this path.

There is an amusing story in *Notes and Reminiscences of a Portuguese Rider* which runs '. . . once someone entered the school wearing a hat.[4] Mestre Miranda's fury was unimaginable and the rebuke he gave Mr So and So was so strong that the hat was immediately removed and the man stayed hidden during the whole time he was in the school . . .' Another quote gives us an inkling of the inspiration the young Oliveira drew from his teacher. 'He insisted on absolutely correct movements, so that all his pupils knew how to make every act of High School dressage. Flying changes at the canter were the most brilliant I have ever seen, done in a big stride but having total fluidity at all times, as were the passages which had the greatest suspension I have ever seen, much more than you see nowadays.'

An Elegant Figure on a Horse

Old riding friends who remember Oliveira in those teenage years, recall an earnest young man who hung on every word that was uttered in the manège. His obvious devotion to Mestre Miranda provoked much teasing and he was labelled something of a sycophant.

Another side that amused the crowd of young people as they grew up together was the matter of Oliveira's good looks. It was obvious the young man had no pretensions to modesty on this subject. He realised he cut an elegant figure on a horse and said so. This led to invitations to present his horses in public, and he enjoyed a rapturous response from the public when in the way of Baucher, he gave a number of exhibitions in the early days at the Coliseu dos Recrios, a great orchestra hall in the heart of Lisbon where ballet, displays of circus and travelling acts were given in the summer. Quite seriously, he told a friend that he would never have problems finding pupils because everyone liked a good-looking riding master. No truer word was ever spoken, but it was not only his looks which drew international pupils from novice to Olympic level for the rest of his life .

Nuno Oliveira ran his school at Quinta do Chafaris until the year before the Portuguese revolution. During this period he became recognised not only in Europe, but worldwide. Pupils who made the long journey from America, South America, the Far East and Australia surprised even themselves by returning year after year to study under the Master. No one quite knows when this title began to be used, but it was probably started by one of his many Portuguese students. It was also at this time that he rode in so many exhibitions abroad.

Until then, relatively few people had ever heard of the Portuguese Lusitano horse and at this time Oliveira rode no other. During his foreign trips, he presented several brilliant Lusitanos

---

[4] Considered *infra dig* in those days.

which he had trained to the highest levels. Beau Geste, who was renowned for his beautiful balanced levades, was an Alter Real from the royal line of bays, bred in this case by Fernando d'Andrade. Euclides was a stunning dappled grey, and Corsario, another bay, drew gasps from the crowd in the Philippines when Oliveira drove him in long reins as he first passaged, then completed a circuit in Spanish Trot under the spotlights of the Polo Club to the music of Verdi's 'Nabucco'. To Geneva and Lucerne he took Beau Geste and Euclides; to Paris, Euclides, but by the time he appeared at the 1966 Horse of the Year Show at Wembley, he was presenting two more Alter horses, Ansioso and Curioso who received a standing ovation from the English crowd. Exhibitions in Portugal and Spain were frequent; once he rode with Colonel Podhajsky in the Campo Grande Bullring of Lisbon, on another in Spain, the Prince of the Asturias, now King Don Juan Carlos of Spain hushed the excited crowd before Oliveira rode.

Portuguese Students

In deference to the many distinguished Portuguese riders who passed through his hands, Oliveira made an amusing allusion about an incident which took place at the International Horse Show in Brussels, leaving the reader in no doubt both of his royalist sympathies and an ever present empathetic arrogance. 'One evening Queen Fabiola came to watch and a member of the committee came to instruct me, a citizen of a Republic, in the necessary courtesies due to a member of the Royal Family. I replied curtly that I had members of the oldest Royalty in Europe as students and that I was quite versed in Court manners.' Of those Portuguese riders who dedicated years, rather than months, to the study of classical equitation, many have gone on to earn the name of Master for themselves, although so far none have used it. These include the highly respected and hardworking Dr Guilherme Borba of whom we have already spoken, now *chef d'equipe* of the Portuguese School of Equestrian Art, D. Diogo de Bragança (*see Plate 10*), the Veiga brothers, Luis Valenca, D. José Athayde (recently retired *écuyer* at the old Portuguese Royal Stud of Alter) and Felipe Graciosa, Director of the Portuguese National Stud. Oliveira also left a son, João,[5] whom he called his dearest friend and pupil and who continues to run the school which he opened at Quinta do Brejo, Avessada in 1973.

The Portuguese Government honoured the work of the Master by conferring upon Oliveira in 1984 the Order of the Infante Don Henrique, thus giving him the distinction of being the only Portuguese riding master to be decorated in his own lifetime.

A LASTING CONTRIBUTION

Nuno Oliveira was a tireless worker. Often deeply religious, sometimes superstitious, he lived off a fount of nervous energy, inhaling cigarette after cigarette and constantly complaining that there was not enough time to accomplish all he wished to do in his life. He was committed to helping people to see the Art as Mestre Miranda had described and taught it to him, but felt a helpless sense of frustration when he saw how some riders rode and consequently sometimes dried up during a lesson.

Oliveira the Writer

His one great hope lay in his books. 'If I can open their eyes through my writing, then that is something,' he said, but there was much sadness in his face.

Oliveira lived to see his six books all published. The first, *Brief Notes on a Fascinating Art*

---

[5] Who took his first training clinic in England in November 1989 to much enthusiasm from pupils and the equestrian press.

'Equitation in bedroom slippers' . . . Oliveira constantly quoted from Baucher. Pupils were 'to try to ride all horses without exception, using the reigns and legs with the utmost gentleness and the least effort'. Here, with bowed head, a habit he rued and blamed on encroaching age, the Master works Soante, his Alter Real Lusitano in the traditional High School Airs. (*Photo by Menut, courtesy of João Oliveira*)

was written in Portuguese and privately published in a limited edition; this and the next two were later translated into English. His last three were written in English in Australia where he spent so many of his latter years teaching.

There is no doubt Oliveira's greatest contribution to equitation lies in these small gems of equestrian literature. In the simplest language he passed on what he found best in La Guérinière, Marialva and Baucher, and whilst he would have been the first to argue that his methods were as old as the hills, there is something fresh and easy to assimilate from his writings. Here, there is nothing heavy or portentous, just little secrets and much commonsense to be shared and enjoyed. Oliveira's readers are left in no doubt that every lesson one could ever hope to receive in a lifetime is contained within those pages.

Oliveira once told me that if he had not dedicated his life to horses, he would like to have become an opera-singer. His riding school daily rang with the voices of Pavarotti and Placido Domingo. A quote from his favourite composer Verdi at the beginning of his last book, *Horses and Their Riders*, could not be more appropriate for someone who deliberately shunned the modern trend and went out with pride and deep conviction to show the world the true meaning of equitation as an art, determined to prove that it had a role to play in the twentieth century. 'When you write do not worry about what others do and do not try to imitate them. Write what you feel sincerely and without bias. In art what matters is sincerity and not ill-will.'

High School riding originated with hand to hand combat. Today that tradition of the fighting horse on whom the rider depends for his very life lives on in Portugal. This *cavaleiro*, Antonio Ribeiro Telles, rides in the old classic manner, reins in the left hand, weapon in the right. Note the lateral suppleness of his Lusitano, the horse that first inspired Oliveira. (*Photo from 'Cavalo Lusitano – O filho do vento' by Arsenio Raposo Cordeiro*)

Sound and Simple Tips

Never given to long-winded explanations, much of Oliveira's writing appears in short, easily remembered sentences. These, if considered carefully as the author obvious intended, stand out like golden milestones on a carefully laid path. For example, in the section on lateral work:

'In shoulder-in you must feel that the power comes from the inside hind-leg . . .

'In the shoulder-in, the horse takes his weight on the inside hindleg and not the outside shoulder . . .

'If the hands are too strong you block the movement . . .

'Relax the inside rein. . . .

'Do not block the horse with your hands . . .' etc.

Equally helpful, is the following advice concerning the half-pass.

'Begin the half-pass around the inside leg. . . .

'Control the half-pass with your inside leg and outside rein . . .

'Finish the half-pass with more inside leg than outside, this proves the impulsion . . .'

And to sum up the aids for all lateral work, this invaluable reminder ends the page: '. . . when you work with one leg you stay quiet with the other.'

Oliveira's first major English success was a book translated by his pupil, the late Phyllis Field. Entitled *Reflections on Equestrian Art* it sums up in modern language so many forgotten thoughts from past masters. Below are some random quotes which are well worth mentioning, but this book should not be missed; it remains an inspiration to those dressage students who, above all, really love their horses.

'The relaxing of the aids, the *descente de main* conceived by Baucher has nothing in common with fake lightness. Rather it is the reward of superior impulsion in which the horse maintains his collection without needing the continuous aid of the rider.

'The talented rider who is tactful will reward [upon] the slightest indication of obedience on the part of his horse who will then respond calmly, confidently and pleasurably to any further demand. The true horseman should put into practice these words of Captain Beudant's, 'Ask for much, be content with little and reward often.'

'Generally, riders seem to forget that the basis of the horse's schooling is given by constant transitions and variations between gaits.'

'The memory of a horse is astonishing and if this is ever forgotten by the trainer, there will certainly be great difficulties during dressage training.'

The Legendary Oliveira Lightness

Above all, Oliveira is remembered for his lightness. This was partly achieved by a remarkable use of the seat and lower back which we shall discuss shortly, but first let us examine what he himself has to say on the subject. One quote of which he was very fond was from General l'Hotte: 'It is the lightness of the horse which gives great cachet to advanced dressage, and at the same time expresses the indubitable talent of the rider.'

For himself, he admitted, 'I cannot control my rage when I hear it said that the horse must be permanently pressed against the bit as though this is the only way to vary the speed as wished, and the only way to have a completely straight horse. Obviously, results may be achieved by the method of pushing the horse hard against the bit, given a methodic gymnastic programme. But the same results may be better obtained, by relaxing the aids (*descente de main*) . . .

'The true lightness is the one which assures the instant obedience of the horse at the slightest solicitation on the rider's part.'

True to his ideal of a light, obedient and happy horse, Oliveira's books not only explain what training is necessary to achieve this result, but in his latter volumes, carefully designed exercises are illustrated which will supple and gymnasise the horse so that he will gradually learn to take a contact from his own free will, and not because the rider has imposed force.

A realist when it came to the different types and breeds of horse, Oliveira recognised that many German and Dutch horses could take more hand than the far more sensitive English Thoroughbred, Arab or Lusitano. Probably thinking of his old favourites, the Iberians, he wrote that horses which have shorter and thicker necks cannot be light when in hand if in a fixed contact, but must sometimes be allowed to come slightly in front of the vertical due to their physical shape.

After he moved his school from Quinta do Chefaris to the isolated but charming village of Avessada up in the mountains of Malveira, near Mafra, Oliveira turned more and more to foreign-bred horses. For him it was a challenge to train a highly strung Thoroughbred to the level of High School once reserved for his Lusitanos and Lipizzaner. He once said of Baucher, 'the man was a genius twice over because he entered the world of *haute école* when the Thoroughbred was taking over from the Baroque horse.'

During his last five or six years Oliveira began to import the Russian Akhal Teke horse. This breed attracted him enormously partly because of its elegant beauty and also its ability to achieve brilliant extensions; he was commercial enough also to recognise a market abroad for these horses in the competitive field.

On Competition

Although Oliveira never competed himself, he did not actively discourage others from doing it. What he did say on the subject was this: 'Art is not a competition. Competitive dressage cannot therefore be an art; it is a sport. The German system is *the* system; it is the best in the world, and if you want to win the only way is to join the system – that is if you want to compete. One thing however is true. The very very best in the world are basically all the same in their riding. It is on the way up and the lower levels that we see such huge and disturbing differences.'

Whilst many competitors came to his school, others stayed away. It was interesting to note how the majority of the best-known British competitors had neither the curiosity or the inclination to attend the two last national clinics the Master gave in this country.

Whilst generous in the extreme with his advice, Oliveira could be curiously enigmatic when pressed about his own riding. Those who understood equitation recognised that there was more to his riding than the gentle hand, and the elegantly-booted, long legs which scarcely seemed to touch the horse's side. Those who did not, were mystified at the apparent lack of aids. For hours they would sit in his small gallery, scrutinising him for some outward, visible clue to the results he got from his horses. More often than not they waited in vain.

The Oliveira Seat

It takes a real horseman to understand the importance of the back. Those who understood this realised that Oliveira had a remarkable back. Considering Oliveira's repertoire of up to fifteen horses to school a day, it was scarcely surprising that he had developed enormous strength and suppleness in the lower back or loins.[6] Without the slightest appearance of movement

---

[6] Which he usually referred to as the kidneys.

D. José Athayde, former lead rider of the Portuguese School of Equestrian Art working his Alter Real stallion in hand at Goodwood during the 1986 Treaty of Windsor celebrations between Portugal and Great Britain.

in his proud shoulders and upraised chest, he was able to hollow or straighten his back with the utmost ease. This had the effect of rotating the pelvis forward or back depending on his requirement, and gave him that depth of contact so necessary for advanced dressage. Thus he enjoyed unsurpassed subtlety over the weight-giving aids of the seat to a degree of brilliance which few horsemen ever attain, particularly of course if not started correctly.

Thus, in an apparently effortless, almost magical way. Oliveira enjoyed total mastery of the horse. He could collect and balance a young, fit, unschooled horse within seconds; he had taught horses which had never been trained to changes in their lives, two and even one time flying changes in less than a week; a passable piaffe and passage could be extracted from untalented riding hacks before unbelieving eyes. Often the horses themselves seemed as surprised as their owners. It was almost as though he rode with an angel at his elbow. It was this total control, this wonderful technique which lent this Portuguese master of our time, the quality of greatness.

The respected late Colonel Crossley, dressage correspondent for *Horse and Hound* for so many years, and author of a number of training books, came close to explaining this apparent phenomenon when he wrote an in-depth profile on Oliveira for *Riding* magazine in 1977. Entitled 'At the Feet of the Master', the Editor had added an apt subtitle, 'It's all in the Back'. Crossley was perceptive enough to realise that the famous *lightness* achieved by the Master, was the product of his 'unusually strong and controlled back'. The following passage is noteworthy: 'The Oliveira theme, unmistakably apparent in the horses they [Oliveira and his son, João] train for themselves and for clients is embodied in the three principles of collection, impulsion and lightness, the first and the last being taken to a degree beyond the conception of most riders. But of the three it is lightness that makes the most vivid impression on the average visitor and which is Nuno Oliveira's greatest contribution to twentieth century dressage. Such heights of artistry may be out of reach for the average rider, but the visual awareness that they are a practical reality, and not just something that occurs in books, must raise and enrich the conception of what dressage is all about for any devotee who makes the pilgrimage.'

When asked to explain how he used his back, a question which was brought up again and again at the many overseas clinics given by the great man, Oliveira would reply with his usual enigmatic simplicity. 'Just take the stomach to the hands' was the usual reply; or 'take the horse by your waist'. Over the period of time he was there, Crossley was able to define this simplistic answer into four salient points:

1) 'To relax and supple the whole body of the rider but to keep the stomach forward and the back braced [forward] under a greater or lesser degree of driving tension applied through the seat.
2) 'To use the back before, and probably instead of, the legs.
3) 'To keep the hands very still but alive and talking to the horse, the reins being not too short, but the contact extremely light and generous.
4) 'Never to use force of any kind.'

The Portuguese Saddle

In fact, Oliveira's strong use of the back was not peculiar to himself. All the great High School riders of the Peninsula develop a similar posture, assisted enormously by the design of the Portuguese classical saddle which has changed little since Marialva. The beauty of this saddle is that it places the rider in the correct central position, so necessary for executing the more collected work. There is the important 'hand's breadth between the rider's seat and the cantle', the wide barrel-like twist which opens and relaxes the buttocks and ensures a broad base of support, whilst the protruding sword guard places the thighs a little back and prevents the knee from straying upwards. The result of this gentle positioning not only prevents a chair seat (so often encouraged by some English saddles) but actually encourages the rider to take up the classical posture with the stomach and chest advanced, the lower back supportive and taking up its natural S shape, and the legs remaining long and relaxed.

There is also the argument that this distinctive proud posture suits the physique of the Iberian people. One encounters the same characteristic of arched back, and upraised torso every day in the market place where the people carry themselves with great pride often accompanied by a pronounced swagger. This inward hollowing of the lower back is also noticeable in flamenco dancing, and in the stance of the pedestrian bullfighter as he plays the bull with his cape.

So Many Dedicated Pupils

In addition to his books, Oliveira's other great contribution to the equestrian world must lie in the continuity of his work through all his pupils worldwide. There are many of these, some now freelancing in Australia, New Zealand and the Philipines, others heading their own establishments. In the United States there is Bettina Drummond, in France, M. Michel Henriquet of whom we shall read in the next chapter; in Belgium, there is Helena Arianoff and Oliveira's daughter-in-law, Sue Cromarty-Oliveira who train to High School levels, as well as M. Ivan Kirsch, president of the *Promotion et Studbook du Cheval Lusitanien*. Two English girls, Jane Turley and Lucy Jackson, who worked with the Master for his last few years at Avessada, are also making their debut in international teaching. Both participated in seminars given by Oliveira in the South of England at the invitation of the Association of British Riding Schools in 1987 and 1988. In Australia, there is Ray van der Drift and Joy Howley; another British *aficionado* is Patricia Finlay and there are countless others, too numerous to mention. But perhaps nowhere can the results of this great Master's work be more clearly represented than in the Portuguese School of Equestrian Art in Lisbon and in Spain's famous Andalusian School of Equestrian Art, as already discussed.

The Horses of the Peninsula

Oliveira must also take credit for the revival of interest in the breeds of the Peninsula. For a time, both Portugal and Spain, due to influence from the military began to shun their own purebred in favour of horses from England, Germany and France. Whilst this was understandable for crosscountry purposes, there was a creeping tendency to look down on the Iberians as an anachronism from the past which had no further part to play in modern life.

Today, a much healthier attitude exists. Horse people in Portugal admit there are two schools: one for competition riding where the European Warmbloods obviously excel; and one for Baroque or classical equitation where the Lusitano and Andalusian is without equal.

The Portuguese Cavalry School

Not many people are aware that Portugal is one of the few countries in Europe to continue with a fully-fledged Cavalry School. This is based at Mafra, an ancient walled hillside town just ninety kilometres from Lisbon. Over the years Mafra has produced many talented and extraordinary horsemen[7] particularly from her Officer Instructors' Course. In recent times these included Olympic riders Pereira Almeida and Jorge Mathias. In addition to her own instructors, there has been a healthy interchange of staff and ideas from Saumur.

True to her army traditions, Mafra is not interested in artistic virtuosity, but in preparing suitable horses for outdoor cavalry purposes. Three day event riding and showjumping take priority although the dressage at Mafra is undoubtedly superior to any European civilian academy. All breeds of horse including Irish, Thoroughbred, Anglo-Arab, European Warmbloods are used; the versatile Lusitano crosses, particularly the Anglo-Lusos are very popular in all phases of work. Every officer at Mafra has come into contact at some time or another with the Master who lived just down the road en route for Lisbon, and are immensely proud of his achievements particularly on the international equestrian scene.

When asked about the two schools of thought and how they worked in modern day Portugal, a captain at Mafra summed up the situation easily and succinctly: 'Mestre Oliveira often came here to watch and to teach officers in the manège. He was enormously respected. All of us recognised the huge benefits his style of teaching gave our horses, suppleness, athleticism, straightness and correctness of gait. Unfortunately, for competition riding his ideals of lightness were too high, that is beyond the capability of most competitors, even the best. So one had to compromise and accept that for competition we were looking at a sporting concept with accuracy playing a more important role than just beauty; with Mestre Oliveira and the traditionalists we were looking at the complete empathy of horse and rider, sheer art. Provided one can recognise there are two schools, then people should not become confused.'

For Oliveira of course there was no compromise. One cannot help reflect that if people had been as wise as the young Portuguese captain, he might have died a happier man. Always fighting for a cause which not enough people understood, he was often frustrated and sad. For him it was so simple. I shall never forget the last words he said to me: 'Art is not a competition; art is love. Now I ask you, how many people realise that?'

NOTE

A surprising but fitting tribute came from Colonel Taton, who, in his nineties is the doyen of Saumur. In conversation at the Goodwood National Championships, we got on to the subject of Oliveira's recent death, 'Ah yes,' he said, '*Cet homme* . . . he truly was a Master of our old School of Versailles.'

---

[7] One of these, G. N. Jackson, wrote a useful book, *Effective Horsemanship*, based on his course at Mafra.

NINETEEN

The Quest for Olympic Gold and Other Influences

We have now followed the course of dressage history from its birthplace in Ancient Greece, through the centres of civilisation to those times and events where its very nature was either threatened or transformed by circumstances beyond the direct control and often the comprehension of the most dedicated adherents of the art.

Thanks however mainly to the Swedes and the Germans, competition has given dressage an acceptable face and place in the latter part of the twentieth century. Whilst the traditionalists amongst us regret the passing of that age of elegance and grandeur, we must be thankful for the resurgence of interest and endeavour. Today, competitive dressage thrives in virtually every country of the world which breeds and enjoys horses. Once again there is space for different schools of thought and emphasis to emerge.

Within one book, it is impossible to follow in every detail and continuity the development of dressage in every country involved. Of necessity, there has therefore been a concentration on those Schools and those periods in time which, in the broad, international context, have provided the most formative, influential stages.

There is however the very real importance of the smaller countries such as Switzerland, Holland, Denmark and Sweden which continue to produce leading competitors and horses of international repute.

Then there are those once proud duchies, principalities and kingdoms of Central Europe which either formed or were joined to the proud Austrian Empire. Romania, Yugoslavia, Hungary! – home of the most wonderful classical horsemen . . . even now, as these pages are being printed, we are reminded of their strong national identity as the Iron Curtain crumbles. By focusing on the culmination of much of their shared culture at Vienna, particularly during the age of the Baroque, the reader can appreciate the breadth and depth of their great traditions.

Mother Russia, a vast land of continental proportions, with a history of dashing cavalry, in particular the Cossacks, etched against a backcloth of empty plains and sweeping steppes, came reluctantly and somewhat late to the discipline and confines of the riding hall. Yet the Russians had for centuries boasted a tradition of ring riding, travelling entertainment, the finest circus riding in the world. Today, aided also by the enlightened teachings of Fillis at the Cavalry School of St Petersburg, there remains a strong artistic dressage presence. The Russian riders, Sergei Filatov (Olympic gold, Rome 1960), Elena Petushkova (World Champion, Aachen 1970), Ivan Kizimov (Olympic gold, Mexico 1968) and Victor Ugriumov (Olympic bronze, Moscow 1980) surprised the world with their medal-winning dressage performances at the World Championships and Olympics Games from 1960 to 1980. The late Dorian Williams described their horses as 'the most attractive, light-footed, light on the hand Russians, as different from the heavy Germanic breeds as it is possible to imagine . . .' in his Introduction to a book on the Wilton Riding House collection.

Let us now review, albeit briefly, some places and people which will add the final bright touches of colour and balance.

Denmark

It is little known that Denmark has for almost five centuries enjoyed an illustrious history of classical horsemanship. In Chapter 3 we remarked how the Danish king Frederick II was one of the first of the European monarchs to organise court riding. This he achieved at Rosenberg in 1562, through a number of imported Spanish and Neapolitan horses which provided the heart of his stud and manège. A magnificent collection of equestrian portraits, similar to the Riding School collection at Wilton, in England, hangs today at Rosenberg Castle in the centre of Copenhagen. This depicts the Danish Royal Family mounted on their favourite High School horses executing the various airs of the manège. Two centuries later, an important Danish stallion from this line, named Pluto, was sent to the Austro-Hungarian Empire in 1765 to improve bloodlines within the Lipizzaner breed. One of the foundation stallions of Graf Gynther of the Oldenburg Stud was also from the Danish Royal Stud.

From those early Baroque horses crossed with the sturdy native Danish stock came the Fredericksborg. This breed was then lightened and heightened with Thoroughbred blood, and reached its height of popularity in the early nineteenth century as a carriage breed of great presence and stamina. More recent discerning breeding from a mixture of bloods has provided Denmark with the handsome Danish Warmblood. The progress of these horses, developed over the last century in a similar way to the German Warmbloods has resulted in a brilliant competition mount. Amongst the best known Danish horses in international dressage today are Marzog, Ravel and Aconto, the latter representing Britain.

Danish Riders and Writers

Like the Germans, the Danes ride at clubs, and although only a small minority of the population actually own their own horses, there is an air of dedication and professionalism amongst those who do. Perhaps the best known instructor of modern times to emerge from Denmark is Gunnar Andersen, whose pupils include Liz Hartel, the brave and highly talented Danish rider who entered the Olympics (having defeated polio) when women had just been admitted. With her lovely mare Jubilee, she succeeded in winning the first ladies' Olympic medal in equitation. Today, there is also Tony Jensen who schooled Anne-Grethe Jensen, Børge Rasmusson, Nis Valdemar Mansen, Hasse Hofmund and others. Several British riders have been helped by the Danish approach which is considered less rigorous and demanding of the horse than that of the Germans and very much closer to the classical French School. One of the best books (translated into English) to come from a modern Danish writer is A.K. Frederiksen's *The Finer Points of Riding*. This small but highly informative book should (in the words of Charles de Kunffy) 'be read like a poem' containing as it does 'a lucid condensation of vast knowledge of the classical dressage principles.' The Danes have always been recognised for their quiet seats. The overt bracing of the back as seen in some Continental riders, has no place in this book. Frederiksen describes the rider's seat as being 'on the two pelvic bones (not the seat bones) and the crotch, that is three points of support'. Much emphasis is put on the importance of feeling, co-ordination and timing in the preparation of the horse for dressage.

Denmark's most recent international successes have been achieved by the calm, minutely accurate work of Anne-Grethe Tørnblad (previously Jensen) with Marzog who won the silver medal in the 1984 Olympic Games at Los Angeles and the World Championship.

Denmark, still enjoying a monarchy, has one of the most beautiful royal indoor riding halls in the world at Christiansborg Castle, Copenhagen. According to one Danish scholar,[1] 'The

[1] Bente Branderup

This harmonious combination of Danish rider and Danish horse, Anne Grethe-Jensen on Marzog at the 1984 Olympic Games, not only achieved many medals for this horse-loving nation, but drew tremendous support from the crowds for their elegance and style. (*Photo: Kit Houghton*)

Royal Danish School of Equestrian Art lived at Christiansborg like the School of Vienna. In 1685, King Christian gave a brilliant carousel of High School riding, and a painted manuscript of the period shows brilliant costumes and magnificent horses.' Under the Royal Stud Controller, Baron Anton Wolf Haxthausen, who oversaw the imperial stud at Oldenburg, frequent interchanges of blood was made between the Danish Stud and those of Dresden, Hanover, Berlin and Vienna. Today, under the command of the present Danish Master of the Horse, the royal manège at Christiansborg is still used for festive riding occasions reminding visitors of Denmark's classical past, together with the nearby Royal Stables.

Sweden

Quite apart from the consistently important role Sweden has played in the revival of equitation, as well as collecting more Olympic dressage medals than any other country except Germany, Sweden too is fundamentally rich in equestrian culture and history. In 1658 territory which had belonged to Denmark passed to Sweden under the Peace of Roskilde. Charles X of Sweden established an important Royal Stud at Flyinge in the province of Skane, which was to produce suitable horses for the royal manège and for the cavalry. The breeding of fine horses at Flyinge has continued up until the present day from an initial stock of Danish Fredericksborgs, Spanish, East Prussians, French and English blood.

Sweden's old nobility was fascinated by the high ideals of courtly equitation and in 1621 King Gustav Adolph opened a stud in the grounds of what would become Stromsholm Castle, for the breeding of horses for war and the manège. The covered school became an illustrious centre for equitation which was visited by Engelhardt von Löhneysen (see Chapter 6) in the seventeenth Century.

In 1855 the beautiful White Riding School was built, and when in 1868 the army took over Stromsholm for the training of cavalry, the natural outlet for the horseloving sons of the aristocracy or wealthy merchant classes was here at the *Militar Central Ridskolan*. In its lake, castle, moat, fields and woodland setting, the Swedish Cavalry School became the ideal training centre for all sporting riding. Talented officers further advanced their already widely comprehensive equine education at Hanover, Vienna, and Saumur and when finally in 1968, exactly a century after they came, the cavalry took their leave of Stromsholm, it was the end of an era not only for Sweden, but in so many ways for the whole equestrian world.

Swedish Riders and Writers

Today's civilian riders who are privileged to train at Stromsholm, now run by the *Svenska Ridsportens Central Forbund*, have much to live up to. In the first Olympics of 1912, Sweden through a combination of superb horses, excellent facilities and a balanced viewpoint of training from all over the world, was able to sweep the board in the dressage events. This success was repeated in 1920, the most illustrious names coming to the fore at that time being those of Count von Rosen and Lt Colonel Bertil Sandstrom. Later, just after the war, it was Major St Cyr from Stromsholm, who gained two gold medals for Sweden in the 1952 and 1956 Olympics, not only leading a victorious Swedish team but on both occasions winning the individual dressage medal. St Cyr had studied at Saumur and was a fervent follower of Baucher. International riders of that time recall his helpfulness and sportsmanlike approach. Joan Gold, one of the first ladies to compete abroad for Great Britain marvelled at his brilliance on a succession of 'very moderate horses'.[2]

More recent celebrated names include that of chief instructors Boldenstern and Wikne. Major Boldenstern, Olympic medallist and former student at Saumur, coached many foreign students as well as contributing to a very high standard within his own country; Major Hans Wikne, who studied at the Spanish Riding School was the highly successful national coach in 1968.

In many ways, the two men personify the Swedish approach which is generally lighter than that of the Germans with great emphasis on feel, never overdemanding of the horse, always generous with reward. A nineteenth century saying inscribed on a wall at Stromsholm reflects the Swedish philosophy: 'The true art of riding never grows old. Where art finishes, force begins.' So true.

In Britain we are fortunate enough to enjoy the teaching of another former Commandant from Stromsholm. Baron Hans von Blixen-Finecke whose cavalry father distinguished himself in racing and by winning the Bronze medal at the 1912 Olympic Games, is himself a most distinguished horseman. In the 1952 Olympics, Hans rode for his country at Helsinki and won the individual gold medal in the Three Day Event on his own horse Jubal.

As a coherent and often amusing writer, von Blixen-Finecke's approach to dressage in his book *The Art of Riding* is rich in commonsense and how to make things easier for the horse. The section dealing with work from the ground and making the horse think, with many useful hints from the *Swedish Army Manual* is stimulating; a better basic handbook would be hard to find. Interestingly, but indicative of the Swedish tradition of taking the work of the manège out into the fresh air – this author advocates a seat which will be more familiar to the cross-country rider than the High School rider. Somewhat in contrast to La Guérinière's seat of advancing the waist through the small of the back, pursued by Baucher and Oliveira, von Blixen-Finecke advises the rider to work from a position '*behind* the vertical, and gradually straighten up. This leaning backwards must come from the base of the spine, and not from the waist; the small of the back should always be kept almost straight.' This growing tall (through the spine rather than the chest and abdomen) position, easily adapts to a driving seat and has become very popular with modern competition riders. It is obviously well suited

[2] In conversation at personal interview with the author, 1987.

to the big, athletic Swedish horse which in the heyday of cavalry training was required to 'carry a substantial load (about 20 stone) over long distances without wearing itself out. . .'

Colonel Nyblaeus

A Swede who became a world figure on the international competition circuit until his death in 1988, was Colonel Gustaf Nyblaeus, President of the FEI Dressage Committee, and an Olympic judge. Son of a Strömsholm chief instructor in the latter part of the nineteenth century, his first love was eventing, but as he became involved in the world of dressage, his academic and thoughtful approach was much admired and he worked tirelessly to promote this rapidly growing competitive discipline. He strove never to lose sight of what constitutes the ideal in classical riding, and was refreshingly ever ready to quote the words of La Guerinière written in 1729: 'A horse which is not absolutely supple, loose and flexible cannot conform to the will of man with ease and carriage'.

The Swedish Warmblood

Today's Swedish Warmblood horse is purpose built for all competitive work. Originally, local stock crossed with Friesian, old Iberian and Neapolitan blood, evolved into a sturdy military horse. Later, as more emphasis was placed on extended work, regular infusions of Thoroughbred blood led to a streamlined, tall, spectacular all-rounder. Where the Swedish horse perhaps reigns supreme over all the other Warmbloods is in his excellent character. Kind, quick to learn and willing to please, this has made him sought after by dressage riders all over the world. One of the most famous Swedish horses to win at the 1972 Olympic Games was Piaff, gaining a gold medal for Germany. Krist, the mount of Bar Hammond, a top British international rider is also Swedish.

The Netherlands

During the sixteenth century, modern Holland and Belgium fell under the rule of the Spanish through the Habsburg dynasty (see Chapter 5). During this period of turbulent history, the heavy coldblood horses of the Low Countries were greatly improved by the Spanish hotblood. The Flemish painter Van Dyck, court painter to Charles I, portrayed the superb Baroque horses of the period in his great equestrian portraits of the noble Dutch overlords. Today's Dutch breeds, particularly the Friesian and to some extent the Gelderland still bear some marked resemblance to their earlier Iberian ancestors whereas the Dutch Warmblood, with its Oldenburg bloodlines, has become very much more streamlined and refined through English Thoroughbred blood. Two of the best known dressage competition horses to come out of Holland are the famous Dutch Courage, and The Optimist, now ridden by Anni MacDonald-Hall for Britain.

Although little is recorded, the nobility of the Netherlands enjoyed a brief period of High School riding in the seventeenth century possibly inspired by the Antwerp school school of the exiled Duke of Newcastle. Later, the French influence prevailed in Holland when La Guérinière's book was translated worldwide. According to the French authority, André Monteilhet, 'Equitation in the Netherlands has successively followed the old French school – Gaspard de Saunier taught there from 1720 to 1748. Later in the nineteenth century it was the German School (Steinbrecht), and from 1900 onwards, the contemporary French School (Saumur), as well as from 1920 the *sisteme* of Caprilli over fences and in horse trials.'

Over the centuries, these influences have left Holland with a strong tradition of refined cavalry riding. The last great cavalry school was at Haarlem in 1857. Sadly, it was dissolved just after the last war from its more recent quarters in Amersfoort. Even the last military riding school, the *Rijen Tractieschool* at Eindhoven, which has provided Holland with some knowledgeable instructors over the years, has recently closed down (a museum to horsemanship left in its place), but the dressage tradition is as strong as ever.

One of the most profound modern Dutch books on equitation is that of Ernest Van Loon's *Ruiters en Rechters* (*Horsemen and Judges*), but many classical riders still refer to La Guérinière. The horses of Holland have played an increasingly important part in both Olympic and European dressage events. One consistent Dutch international rider is Ann-Marie Sanders Keyzer, another now coming to the fore is Mrs Tineke Bartels. Dressage is not only making a revival amongst the minority who ride, but major dressage events held at Rotterdam, Amsterdam and s'Hertogenbosch draw large crowds.

Belgium

Belgium too has benefitted in modern times from a fine cavalry tradition. In 1842 Leopold I set up a military equitation school which evolved into the well-known Cavalry School of Ypres. This, together with the School of Brasschaet, promoted a disciplined style of riding with the greatest outside influence coming from Saumur in France. During the early Olympics, the Belgians distinguished themselves in the jumping events, and were the first European nation to instigate organised long-distance riding. Dressage, although forming a valuable part of the old military training, has probably developed with more enthusiasm since the last war, despite the closure of both cavalry schools. The excellent tradition of Belgian military school riding has been maintained through the writings of Captain Henri Lame who was chief instructor at Brasschaet from 1933–1940 and by the civilian population in more recent times. One of many sports centres with riding run by the Government for the Flemish region is in St Ulrickscappele near Brussels, which specialises in dressage and boasts a number of highly schooled Lipizzaners. There is also a revived taste for High School riding through the frequent visits of the late Nuno Oliveira, together with Portugal's energetic chef d'equipe Dr Guilherme Borba who has a strong following in and around Brussels. This movement is non-competitive, but displays and exhibitions are given by the schools of Helena Arianoff, Susan Cromarty-Oliveira and Alain Godeau, just outside Brussels, where the traditional Baroque horses of Portugal are used. The reigning Belgium champion in international competition for several years running was the very talented Anne Ieteven.

Switzerland

Switzerland, unlike Sweden, Denmark and Holland, has only recently caught up with producing her own national Warmblood of which Christine Stückelberger's Gaugin de Lully is a strikingly successful example. Swiss dressage has benefitted from a combination of bloods and ideas, and for many years the Swiss were content to import the best horses from Germany, Sweden, England, Ireland, Holland and Denmark for their competition success.

The once renowned cavalry school at Berne (built in 1890) has given way to the Federal Military Horse Depot which provides horses and basic training in all disciplines for mounted infantry but whereas in the past visiting specialised dressage instructors generally came from nearby Austria, government sources are now encouraging more national training from within. *L'Association Suisse de Professionnels de l'Equitation et Propriétaires de Manège* gives a framework for future young government trained instructors, although it is still the great traditional trainers who dominate the Swiss international scene.

George Wahl

The best known instructor in Switzerland is Austrian by birth and education. George Wahl, who trains the former World Champion Christine Stückelberger is now national coach and based at St Gallen, near Zurich. A former rider of the Spanish Riding School who rose in 1967 to the position of chief rider, he chose to resign from this classical establishment after four years in order to concentrate on training for competition which has never been considered compatible with the ideals of the School, although today as we have seen, there are a few individuals who have done both.

Wahl is considered by many to be the most successful trainer of dressage horses and people in the world. With a sixth sense for competition technique and his own classical skills and understanding, he remains a giant amongst ordinary men. Although always associated with the successes of just one particular worldbeating combination, the lightweight Christine Stückelberger and the hefty magnificent Granat, Wahl has probably had more famous riders and horses through his school than any other trainer. As he approaches old age, he continues to draw pupils of every nationality, and horses still transform themselves under his beguilingly iet but powerful seat.

Stückelberger

People have commented on the fact that whilst Wahl is so classical, the slender Stückelberger rides in an individual style that is at variance with her trainer. To this Wahl smiles and says little for he knows, as he watches over and minutely directs his protégée daily in the manège, that it is no accident of fate which has ensured a permanent place for Christine and the horses they together produce in the world record books.

For a small country, Switzerland has achieved much in dressage. First there was Moser, a Swiss cavalry officer who won the Grand Prix of the 1948 Olympics; he was followed by Fischer and Chammartin who also brought back the coveted Olympic gold and silver. Today there is Otto Hoffer and the newcomer Daniel Ramsier but for the most, it is still the distinctive figure of Stückelberger who dominates the scene. Her world-beater Granat the Holstein will always be remembered for his powerful, flowing half-passes; his extravagant extension drew gasps from spectators all around the world (*see Plate 12*).

Stückelberger's list of successes is formidable. Her first European Championship individiual gold medal was in Kiev, 1975, and two years later she won the same event at St Gallen. World Champion in 1978, she then went on to take the European silver medal in Denmark, 1979, which was followed by another silver in Laxenburg, Austria, two years later. Her Olympic successes are nonetheless impressive. She won the individual gold in Montreal in 1976 as well as the team silver. At the Alternative Olympics held at Goodwood in 1980, it was a repeat result. Runner-up in the World Championship in 1982, she retired the formidable Granat, but was back in the top international echelon, with a team silver in Los Angeles, 1984. Finally with her new horse, Gaugin de Lully, she earned the individual bronze at Seoul in 1988.

CONTEMPORARY PERSONALITIES
AND SCHOOLS OF PRESENT INFLUENCE

Let us now look briefly at some isolated but important contemporary personalities whose influence, either through teaching or writing or both, has gone far beyond their country of birth, and who can be deemed as truly international in every sense of the word.

Some of these have been as concerned with event dressage and the jumping disciplines as with pure dressage. This makes their contribution no less important; in fact, such is their success in the coaching of riders of all disciplines, that had they concentrated only on dressage, the riding world would have been the poorer for it.

Two Hungarians

Two important instructors to fall into this category, and both from post-war Hungary, are (the late) Lieutenant A. L. d'Enrody and Charles de Kunffy. Both have represented their country of birth in Three Day Event riding, yet both have enjoyed an artistic leaning towards dressage which has been much enjoyed and put to successful use by their pupils overseas, particularly in Britain and the United States.

D'Endrody's book, *Give Your Horse a Chance*, although primarily aimed at the jumper contains some very useful information on the mechanics of the horse, which is extremely useful to the dressage rider. De Kunffy's book, *Creative Horsemanship*, is lighter and more elegant in style, and forms an important contribution to our understanding of the gymnastic development of the horse to help achieve elasticity, suppleness and ease of understanding in the various stages of dressage training.

Henriquet

A Frenchman, for whom the three day event holds no temptation since his interest lies in an epoch long before the days of competitive riding, is Michel Henriquet. Based at Bailly, just outside Paris, Henriquet is a devoted follower of the late Nuno Oliveira and prolific writer on the subject of *haute école*. A successful businessman, historian, bibliophile and architect, Henriquet now devotes most of his time to the schooling of horses and the many international pupils who come to his private manège at Bailly. Despite his refusal to enter the competition arena, Henriquet is frequently requested to demonstrate his beautiful horses at international shows and exhibitions. Together with his elegant pupil, Dr Catherine Durant who has worked with him since childhood, Henriquet appears in a class of his own. A master of lightness and precision, he strives to provide a last living link with the School of Versailles in his own country.

In his book *L'équitation, un art, une passion*, Henriquet explains that whilst the national school of Saumur was initially moulded on the traditions of Versailles with mostly civilian instructors, this changed drastically after 1855 when it became strictly military. Thenceforth, Saumur moved in a new direction, producing horses for campaign riding and the dressage of the Olympic arena.

Far from alienating himself with these views, the present-day administration of Saumur accept such pronouncements as the logical truth, a necessary fact of modern life. M. Henriquet is therefore welcomed and respected by the two chief *écuyers*, and the School's Director, Colonel Durand illustrates the admiration and respect that is felt for Henriquet by informal consultations on matters of *haute école*. In addition, he teaches a number of young officers from the *Cadre Noir* at Saumur, whilst others attend his clinics at Bailly where mainly Lusitano schoolmasters are used. Schools above the ground are taught between the pillars as well as under saddle; the latter are only used when the horse is already well established in each movement in order to improve lightness and precision.

Highly read and articulate, Henriquet has produced a number of books over the years which illustrate his deep understanding and appreciation of French equitation from the age of enlightenment. In addition to the above mentioned, these include *A la Récherche de l'Equitation,* and a number of useful training books. Much importance is placed on maintaining a good seat which he sums up in one sentence. 'Sit in the saddle with a wide and open seat – pull the waist forward and downwards on a triangle formed by the seatbones and the crotch, in an imaginary attempt to have the waist meet the hands, keep the hands low, the thighs back, use loose, relaxed legs and the horse is yours!'

Two Austrian School Directors

Since Podhajsky, a number of world class trainers have emerged from the background of the Spanish Riding School into the international field of training and judging. These include such venerable and distinguished riders as Franz Rochowansky (Chief *Oberbereiter* between 1950 and 1957) and now based in England, Ernst Bachinger, and Franz Mairinger (died in 1978) of whom more later.

In the tradition of Spanish Riding School Directors, both Hans Handler and Kurt Albrecht, who consecutively followed Podhajsky, have left their own important contribution to modern equestrian literature.

Hans Handler had the unenviable task of taking over command of the Spanish Riding School from Podhajsky in 1965. An able cavalry officer who had successfully competed internationally for Austria before the war, later fought at the front and been taken a prisoner of war, and finally served at the School for more than a decade, Hans Handler tackled his task with sensitivity and a true feeling for what had gone before. At all times he was concerned with preserving 'the art of the High School' in order that the Spanish Riding School might 'remain the mecca of dressage riding.' Sadly, his health was not good, but before his death in October 1974 he was able to complete a work of dedication and love, the massive *oeuvre*, published in English in 1972 under the title *The Spanish Riding School of Vienna and the Training of the Lipizzaner.* This beautifully bound masterpiece of historical fact, technical explanation and the most evocative photographs and reproductions, not only recounts the full stirring story of that great academy, it also explains much of its ethos, the training methods and the disciplines in easily understood language. It is therefore rated as a great contribution to our understanding of the classical art.

After Handler, came Brigadier General Kurt Albrecht, an artillery officer with a distinguished war record, who directed the Spanish Riding School from 1974–85. With a similar idealistic vision for the school as Handler, he guided the School through a period of great change in the world outside. With a constant eye and ear open for diverging developments within the competition world, he strived to maintain standards at Vienna whilst always keeping morale high. Since his retirement, he has had more time for lecturing and judging, and in his role as an international dressage judge is able to influence to some extent the understanding of his contemporaries in the world of judging.

Uncompromising in his concern for the horse, Albrecht the *horseman* is the author of four important books all written in German. The first, now translated into French, *Dogmes de l'Art Equestre* (1986) deals convincingly with the technical aspect of school riding. Like Handler, he has strong views of the necessity for a perfect seat if the vital weight aids are to be correctly utilised. He stresses the need for an allround contact in the centre of the saddle with sufficient flexion in the rider's loins,

The second book, now available in English as *A Dressage Judge's Handbook,* is written by Albrecht the international *dressage judge*. This too is an invaluable addition to modern horse literature but regretfully we can only here include a few of the important and perceptive statements made throughout the book. The judge has a responsibility not only to the rider but to the horse. One of these is '. . . to ensure that the sport does not deteriorate into a comparison of equine material in which size and power play the predominant role. Dressage must always remain an inspiration for all riders: purely the art of training a horse to move gracefully in self-carriage, and to respond instantly to the barely visible indications of its rider.'

Riders should be rewarded for riding well. 'Effectiveness combined with discreetness in the use of the aids naturally deserves to be marked generously. Regrettably it has to be said that many riders have an ineffective seat and counteract its ineffectiveness by inordinate activity of legs and hands.' In relation to novice events, his remarks would have found an echo in the views of Wynmalen, McTaggart and Hance. 'There are judges who believe that some stiffness of the poll must be tolerated in novice tests and even maintain that a relatively poked nose is part and parcel of the relaxed body carriage . . . They are mistaken, but the reason for their mistake lies in the controversial subject of *flexions of the poll and jaws.*'

From individual writers and trainers and their influence worldwide, we must now remove to those English-speaking countries whose progress within the international field of competitive dressage in the last two decades can virtually be attributed to a handful of powerful personalities.

Great Britain

After the closure of the cavalry school at Weedon in 1939, an all-round form of military training continued at Melton Mowbray, Larkhill and within the barracks of the Household Cavalry at Knightsbridge, and the Royal Horse Artillery in North London.

By the end of the fifties, riding was no longer male dominated. The watershed occurred when in 1952 Olympic contenders were no longer required to be commissioned officers. Quite suddenly, the field was open to every rider of whatever rank or sex.

British women took up competition riding with enthusiasm. The first woman rider in the world to be placed in an international three day event was Vivien Machin-Goodall at Badminton in 1949. In pure dressage, Olympic or European leading ladies included Brenda Williams, Lorna Johnstone, Jook Hall, Joan Gold and Dominie Morgan, all of whom enjoyed classical training abroad. Apart from the exceptionally talented however, dressage training was generally achieved under the discipline of former British army instructors or a few well respected professionals such as Richard Stilwell who came later. As discussed in Chapter 4, dressage at this stage appealed to most only as a necessary part of the three day event. Then British dressage went through a remarkable transition.

It was particularly due to the efforts of one dedicated lady, Dame Mary Colvin, a former pupil of Jack Hance, that dressage was brought to the attention of the ordinary rider. In 1966 she became Chairman of British Dressage under Horse Trials and continued in this role when the Dressage Group was formed in 1973. During this formative time the the teaching of two highly influential and somewhat revolutionary trainers, Lars Sederholm and Robert Hall made a great impact. Sederholm, Swedish by birth, a three day event and showjumping enthusiast taught dressage in a manner which was based on the most natural way of moving for the cross-country horse. His training centre at Waterstock in Oxfordshire, was always full of big, rangy horses suitable for clients to purchase, and ex-eventers were generally used in the manège as schoolmasters. With a well organised system of working pupils enrolling at Waterstock, studying within the framework of the British Horse Society examinations, and later passing out as assistant or full instructors, Sederholm's natural methods were carried far and wide within the country.

Hall

Robert Hall, founder of another enormous establishment, this time at Fulmer in Buckingham-shire, was also responsible for educating literally hundreds of young British people who wished to teach riding. Less oriented to jumping (although able to provide all the facilities required), his first love was dressage. Anticipating a decline in the number of teachers available for this discipline as the hunting and military influence sharply receded, he was the right man arriving at the right time to carve out a new method for British riders. Fresh from his training at the Spanish Riding School of Vienna, Hall with his enthusiasm and energetic personality, was eagerly embraced by the British riding establishment. His own style was elegant and light, and that of his ex-wife, Jook, bore testimony to her training at Vienna, as she represented Great Britain in the Rome, Tokyo and Mexico Olympic Games with her Lipizzaner stallion, Conversano Caprice. Other distinguished pupils also bore the mark of more traditional train-ing; these included the trainer Pat Manning and the familiar figures of Diana Mason[3] and Elizabeth Joicey who have gone on to considerable international success in Grand Prix competi-tion, although more recently both have received help from classical Continental instructors Ferdi Eilberg and Artur Kottas.

Gradually, however, Hall's methods, which came to be known as the Fulmer System, began to move away from the classical principles of the Spanish Riding School. Because he believed the Thoroughbred was unable to sustain any depth of seat from the rider, Hall eventually discouraged pupils from seat and back aids altogether. Contrary to centuries of classical think-ing, knees were encouraged away from the horse's sides, arms away from the rider's. Not unnaturally, these ideas caused heated debate at home, as well as apprehension and bewilderment at Vienna which is still remembered.

British Riding Schools

The Fulmer philosophy appeared in many ways very similar to that of Caprilli, i.e., one of deliberate non-interference or *laissez-faire*. Similar to Caprilli, the new method became enor-mously popular amongst the British riding school system since it was regarded as a safer, less demanding way of teaching the growing number of dressage enthusiasts without the risk of a 'razor in the hands of a monkey' (i.e. collection in the hands of the unskilled, see Chamberlin). By the end of the seventies, remarkably few British instructors would teach the use of the rider's seat and back. The average riding school horse was seen to work on precepts of relaxa-tion, encouraged to find its own balance generally through a variety of exercises in working trot. Even with mature horses, there was little emphasis if any on collection '. . . Let the horse find his own balance when he wants and how he wants!'[4] became a familiar maxim on the lips of many young instructors.

With new centres opening up in Scotland and Yorkshire, Hall's methods were highly influen-tial in the preparation of students for the new Assistant Instructor examination run by the British Horse Society. There was no doubt that the Fulmer System had great merit in the initial schooling of the novice. Whether or not it improved the level of dressage generally in Britain is open to debate. Not every rider had the brilliant feel and sensitivity of Robert Hall, and unfortunately many of his ideas were misinterpreted and taken out of context by less knowledgeable people.

---

[3] Diana Mason represented Great Britain at the Seoul Olympics in 1989 with her British-bred horse Prince Consort.
[4] Compare this theory with that of Austrian *Bereiter* Riegler: 'The horse left to his own devices give way to unwanted weight making his back and raising his head.' (*Dressage & C.T.*, USA, December 1981.)

Lorna Johnstone, the grand old lady of British dressage, riding El Farruco. French competitors and instructors from Saumur used to admire her riding because she gave her horse that freedom which often allowed the head a little in front of the vertical in all movements except the piaffe.

Other British civilian schools such as Porlock Vale in Somerset, Crabbet Park in Sussex, Moat House in Kent, and the still successful Talland School of Equitation in Gloucestershire run by the Sivewright family, were organised on more conventional lines. Molly Sivewright's books *Thinking Riding* and a follow-up by the same name has helped many young dressage enthusiasts with their elementary training. The Sivewrights combine the best of English crosscountry traditions with the more refined work of the Swedes and other Continental schools, and have specialised in bringing to England a number of foreign instructors. This has maintained a happy balance between three day event dressage and dressage for its own sake.

Britain's First Medallist

It was Jennie Loriston-Clarke who through her sound training abroad[5] on disciplined classical lines seemed destined to bring new hope to British dressage. The earlier pioneers had made the way possible, now there was a need for a figurehead. What caught the imagination of the riding nation was the successful partnership which Jennie established with the attractive Dutch Courage (*see Plate 14*). Her World Championship bronze medal, achieved at Goodwood in 1978, a real proof of modern dressage success, was desperately important to such a competitive nation as Britain. For two brilliant decades, the British had basked in the limelight of success after success in the fields of three day eventing and showjumping. At last, the unthinkable and unattainable had happened, a breakthrough into dressage itself.

From then on, it was the riding women of the country who flocked to this not widely known discipline. The demand for foreign trainers with a more classical approach grew swiftly. In the early days there had been Harry Assleberg from Belgium; then came von Blixen Finecke from Sweden, Eddie Goldman from Hungary, and Franz Rochowansky from Vienna, all of whom became well established in England. Younger men followed such as the German Ferdi Eilberg, and the Israeli, Daniel Pevsner. British born trainers such as John Lassetter went to study at Vienna, the late Anthony Crossley in Germany and probably the only trainer who survived with his own very English methods, was David Hunt who teaches with the wisdom of enormous competition experience.

Today, the instigator of recent enthusiasm, who has now represented her country in five

[5] Jennie Loriston-Clarke has trained under the following international trainers: Gunnar Andersen, Franz Rochowansky, Willie Schultheiss.

Olympic Games, works from the family stud at Black Knoll House, on the edge of the New Forest. Stallions at stud not only include her old partner, Dutch Courage, but the best of his progeny out of English Thoroughbred mares. One such, Dutch Gold has been Jennie's partner at a variety of highly competitive musical Kürs as well as in straight dressage, including the Seoul Olympics. Together they achieved not only the highest place on the accumulated points system of the Western European League for the 1988/89 Nashua World Cup, but the highest points on record. All three Grand Prix qualifiers were won at Zuidlaren, Brussels and s'Herto-genbosch by this talented combination.

This line of homebred Dutch x Thoroughbred stock is proving highly successful in all spheres of competition, and successful moves to sponsor performance tests and championships for the homebred competition horse in England have been made possible through the enthusiasm and dedication of Jane Kidd, and the generosity and business acumen of Canadian born Desi Dil-lingham as well as the support of the British Horse Society.

Goodwood House in West Sussex, home of the Duke and Duchess of Richmond and Gordon and for so long synonymous with English flat racing is now for some, more associated with dressage. The classical lines of Goodwood House has provided the perfect backdrop for interna-tional and national dressage championships in the last two decades. The support from Good-wood, together with that of the Earl and Countess of Inchcape who brought in much needed sponsorship and publicity as Britain began her real challenge abroad in the seventies, has done much to enhance the sport for Britain.

With improved dressage, British three day event riding has also benefitted. Princess Anne, Mark Philips, Richard Meade and Lucinda Green set new world standards in the seventies with their magnificent jumping but the public generally underrated the importance of the first day. Today it is generally agreed that because performance has improved all round in the crosscountry and jumping phase, a very high mark in the dressage phase is critical in obtain-ing a head start in the points system on the second day. Virginia Leng and Ian Stark owe their Olympic and European successes as much to their sense of discipline and sympathy in the dressage arena, as they do their strategic boldness across country.

Then there are the event riders, people like Richard Davidson and Christopher and Jane Bartle, whose dressage has been so talented that they have successfully combined both forms of competitive riding in their busy lives. In complete contrast, another international rider who is consistently successful is Tanya Robinson (formerly Larrigan) who comes from a background of circus and High School. Thanks to these and many others, as well as to experienced and dedicated trainers such as Sarah Whitmore who works with young people, Britain is moving informedly ahead. There will always be room for improvement, particularly in ideas of artistry and lightness, but the last decade has brought Great Britain closer into line with the other competitive European countries than most ever thought posssible just fifteen years ago.

Canada and the United States

Due to the huge problem of distance, training in the United States and Can ada is more loosely organised than in small countries such as Britain or Sweden. Although scattered, Americans and Canadians have over the years benefitted enormously from the great exodus of highly skilled trainers from countries like Hungary, Romania, Poland and Yugoslavia who arrived either just before or not long after the last world war. Those who had strong cavalry associa-tions, taught in all three disciplines, but generally their dressage on strict classical lines, far surpassed the average home-based instructor or instructress. Too numerous to list by name, this extraordinary breed of courageous horsemen, who often arrived in the New World penniless and friendlesss, have influenced riding to such an extent that those from the West are now beating the Europeans at their own game.

In 1961, Littauer, in comparing American riders to the Germans, spoke of their 'particularly homogenous and pleasant style'. In the absence of a centralised school, the rules and conditions for competitive riding in the United States are organised through the AHSA (American Horse Show Association) whilst the USET (United States Equestrian Team) provides specialised training for international competition at Gladstone, New Jersey.

William Steinkraus, former president of the USET, has made a deep and lasting contribution towards the objects of the USET, as have joint team trainers Bertalan de Nemethy and Jack le Goff who have worked unstintingly to raise standards all round. Hungarian born de Nemethy, now approaching his eighties, served as a riding instructor within the distinguished Hungarian Cavalry just prior to the war. Later, he competed for Hungary in international showjumping before emigrating to the United States in 1952. French born le Goff, who trained at Saumur, rode for France in the three day event at the Rome Olympics, and having trained the United States team for many years, is now coaching the Canadians.

In this tradition of all-round riding, Sandy Pfleuger and Bruce Davidson are US dressage and event riders, whose work is particularly pleasant to watch, whilst in dressage only, America's Kay Meredith, Robert Dover and Carol Lavell have all benefitted from training in Europe and from visiting coaches, such as George Theodorescu, Hinnermann and Klimke.

For a number of years now, Canada has shone in international dressage. Whether this is sheer natural talent, or the fact that many competitors spend months rather than weeks training with Schulheiss in Germany is open to argument. Cindy Ishoy and her beautiful horse Dynasty excelled themselves for Canada in recent times coming fourth individually at Seoul, and with team mates, Ashley Nicoll, Ana Maria Pracht, and Gina Smith, took the bronze medal for the team dressage. The tragedy of Dynasty's death from colic shortly before publication of this book shocked the competitive world.

South African Lipizzaners

South Africa is banned by a form of international agreement from competing abroad, yet within the country a healthy state of dressage riding exists. One centre of which South Africans are justly proud but which stands independent of the government or cavalry, aligning itself to the Spanish Riding School of Vienna, is the Lipizzaner Centre at Kyalami, to the north but close to Johannesburg.

The foundations for this establishment, now funded by private enterprise but continually threatened by market forces, were laid in 1948. In this year Count Elmer Jankovich-Besan, a refugee from Hungary, arrived with the first Lipizzaner in South Africa. With Podhajsky initiative, he had transported a number of stallions from his native Hungary across Europe and by sea to Natal. Here, he settled and concentrated on training his team for driving. Later, meeting up with another Lipizzaner enthusiast and political emigré, this time from Poland, in the form of the highly skilled cavalry rider Major Iwanowski, the idea of a school was launched. To confirm their beliefs, Iwanowski schooled one of his horses, Maestoso Erdem to High School level and the result was that this combination went on to win the South African National Dressage Championships for five years in a row.

Today, the Lipizzaner Centre at Kyalami has its own training system. The riders are all women, mostly South African, but there are always visiting pupils from abroad. The centre is ably run by Maureen Dalgleish with consultant, Gillian Meyer who led the team for twenty years. Protégées of former *Oberbereiter* Lauscha of the Spanish Riding School in Vienna, these dedicated women strive to retain the old classical values at Kyalami, whilst providing an interesting cultural and touristic attraction to bring in the funds necessary to keep the school alive. The programme of work is moulded on that of Vienna. A magnificent indoor school, complete with pillars, is the setting for work on the long rein and short rein, airs above the ground, the pas de deux and the ever popular school quadrille. There are 30 stallions in work, ranging in age from five to 25, and visiting instructors from Vienna, including Ernst Bachinger, over the past 15 years have given much support and active help to the work of the school.

Altogether, there are about 100 Lipizzaners in South Africa. With around 30 horses at Kyalami and another 30 at stud for the school in the hilly areas of Natal, the existence of this little known equestrian oasis is precarious. Without some form of government assistance, and in the context of economic sanctions, it is doubtful if such an establishment can continue for very long. Kyalami serves as an important reminder that there is a place for such artistic virtuosity today which can be regularly supported by an enthusiastic public.

South Africa is one of the few places in the world where the Lipizzaner is accepted by dressage judges on an equal footing with European Warmbloods and Thoroughbreds. This adds greater interest for the general spectator. There are increasing occasions in Europe when the Hungarians and Yugoslavians have sent competitors mounted on this old classic breed. Formerly so appreciated, they have been much overshadowed in the seventies and eighties by the massive German breeds. With a belated return to the idea of lightness, it is now hoped that judges will soon be able to take a broader viewpoint and encourage all the classic breeds back into the international arena.

Australia

Australia also had her centre of High School and exhibition riding in the days of Ray Williams in the late 1970s and early '80s who imported and bred purebred Spanish horses in Perth. At its height, a very high standard of classical equitation was achieved under various Spanish instructors, including Manolo Mendez from the Domecq School in Andalusia, but with the Williams departure for America, taking his best horses with him, the work of El Caballo Blanco faded.

Generally, Australians are the first to admit that the country is still very young in dressage, but they are proud of their horses, which are good, sound, staying types from mostly Thoroughbred and TB cross stock. Showjumping and the three day event has probably suited these horses more than advanced dressage until now, but it is hoped that Australian riders will persevere with their superb horses and not all bow to the fashion for imported Warmbloods. The success of New Zealand event rider Mark Todd has inspired many New Zealanders and Australians into a strong competitive spirit, and Australia has been proudly represented in Olympic dressage by Judy Mackay in 1980,[6] Margaret McIver in 1984 and Erica Taylor in 1988. As sympathies and fashions change, there is a continual stream of clinics from European dressage instructors. At present the national coach is Clemens Dierks from Germany; in contrast to his very competitive style, was the influence of Nuno Oliveira who gave regular bi-annual clinics for the last decade of his life and left a dedicated coterie of pupils.

[6] Alternative Olympics at Goodwood.

Mairinger

The figure who made by far the greatest impact on Australian dressage however at a very formative time was Franz Mairinger, a former *Bereiter* of the Spanish Riding School. His riding career started at the famous Hanover Cavalry School where he was particularly involved in eventing and jumping; after a further twelve years of dedicated study at Vienna, he arrived in Australia in 1951. A man of quite unique sensibility and love of the horse, he made a tremendous impact on Australian riders and as national coach, succeeded in helping the Australian Olympic team to win a credible fourth place in the Stockholm Olympics of 1956, followed by a gold in the team three day event at Rome in 1960.

Mairinger's book *Horses are Made to be Horses* (see Chapter l) deals with all aspects of riding, from jumping to advanced dressage. The style is philosphical rather than purely instructional, which gives great insight into the delicate techniques of a real master. His description, for example of teaching a horse the piaffe is illuminatingly simple: 'It works like this – the rider pushes him with weight and legs and he [the horse] says, 'That's too much work,' and so he tries to step out his near hind to get rid of that gymnastic exercise. The rider pushes him with his left leg and then he tries to go out again, and if the rider doesn't let him out near hind, then he goes out off hind. Then he could go wide . . . crooked . . . lose impulsion . . . crawl along. This is the degree of the gymnastic exercise that has to go into the horse – you must have him on a long rein to start with and then you must push him a little more and he still keeps going, still accept. Then you push him a bit more and then you have him! And there is piaffe . . .'

At the end of the book, a chapter on judging is full of fair comment and constructive ideas. Mairinger stressed the importance of looking at each horse as though seeing him for the first time, never 'I have seen that horse go a lot better'. He exhorts judges to view the test as a whole and not to '. . . get carried away with too many little technicalities . . . Don't concentrate only on the hindlegs or the front legs; try to see the whole horse or the whole picture.'

Australia's history of horses is essentially a practical one. There was no classical background, since initally Australia was a British settlement. Gradually, as bush hunting, stock riding and campdrafts developed, the Australian 'bushies' developed a not dissimilar seat to the cowboys of Mexico and Western America. The Australian stock saddle, apart from its horn, is not so dissimilar to a deep-seated dressage saddle. With his weight spread in a very centralised way, causing less fatigue to the horse, the Australian bushman is a proud sight as he canters out of the dust. As the helicopters move the cattle on in all too many states, let us hope he is not a dying breed.

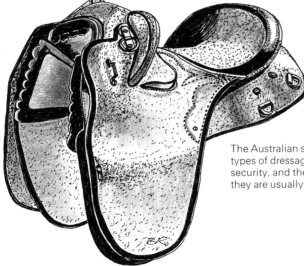

The Australian stock saddle, apart from its supportive wings, it is not unlike certain types of dressage saddle. Whilst the design of the seat encourages depth and security, and the weight of the rider is generally well spread over the horse's back, they are usually rather hard and are often used with a sheepskin over the seat.

TWENTY

Reflections on the State of the Art

ESSENTIALS

Enveloped by the bright hustle and bustle of the modern scene with its excellent communications and efficient transport enabling horses to be jetted round the world, it must be clear we have come a long way since the beginning of equitation or ring riding amongst the warriors of Western and Eastern Europe. Or have we?

The horse is still the horse, gentle, sensitive, easily alarmed, a quintessential creature of flight, of sinewy power, of iron-hard feet and lightening speed – amongst, if not the most beautiful member of God's creation. Man is still man, a natural aggressor, capable in civilised circumstances of great creativity, but nevertheless a compulsive exploiter of his surroundings, often displaying the same greed, obsession for power and success in a more private, covert manner than the long dead citizens of an ancient despotic empire.

In many ways, little has changed. We no longer fight battles on horseback, but the world is as steeped in revolution, oppression and famine as ever it was in the days of the Romans or even Xenophon. In many ways we are artistically and spiritually the poorer than many of our counterparts from history.

Where is the yearning for purity and beauty so beloved by the ancient Greeks? Where is the burning idealism of the Classicists, the supreme effort and the cultivation of an art which ennobles the soul and 'obliges man to live soberly and orderly'? What would the children of the Renaissance have thought of the seamy streets of our cities, the soft porn shops, the books we read and the violent films that intrude nightly into our homes?

What would the masters of equitation have made of our steeplechase, event and showjumping courses and particularly our dressage arenas where the athletic demands of competition riding often impose great stress on our sensitive four-legged friends who have no choice but to comply. A French *écuyer* from Saumur, Commandant Saint-Fort Paillard, wrote with shocking clarity: 'Let us try to imagine for a moment what the atmosphere in the riding hall or around a show ring would be if the horses yelped whenever they were hurt as dogs do. Wouldn't certain jumping competitions be punctuated by howls of pain? And wouldn't certain dressage classses by punctuated by plaintive whimpers. What a nightmare!'[1]

A Bird's Eye View
It is important closely now to examine the broad spectrum of school riding over the centuries to see where we have made headway, and where we have regressed. Only by being totally honest as we follow this fascinating craft from its early source, through its great academic period, through the change from courtly to military emphasis, to the modern age of riding for the masses, can we hope to discover some form of continuity, some form of order and illumination which will clarify the way ahead.

Of course there are always those for whom the present is so all-pervading that they are

[1] From *Understanding Equitation*.

unwilling to detach themselves. Full diaries, ambitious fixtures, new goals crowd their lives. Of what relevance is the past when everything is here and now and the latest training video from the local tackshop is waiting to be played? Let the tomes of past masters gather dust in the libraries. There is no time, no room for ideas from antiquity. Here is where it's at!

The Importance of the Past

Yet to ignore the past, to disregard history, is to deny the substance of equestrian art itself. From every era, from every country, from every school of riding of which we have spoken in these pages there is something of relevance for today. From some it may comprise a mere fragment, from others a bounteous wealth, yet throughout the passage of time, a strong classical culture has emerged and our friend, the horse has a right to enjoy the fruits of this inheritance.

To pass over the writings of men who spent not hours but every waking moment in the saddle and who dedicated their lives to understanding the psychology and physical ability of horses better than most of us will ever dream of, not only results in unacceptable ignorance, it endangers the very subject we love the most.

Complacency is the enemy of excellence. Yet there are well-known figures in the public dressage field today who who are proud to say dismissively, 'I never read those books.' It is, alas, sometimes these people who preside on committees, judge dressage tests, rewrite rules and instruct the young. Happy to deny the source of knowledge itself, they are the first to pass on the limitations of their own experience to others.

A Real Philosophy

The old adage practice makes perfect is laudable, but only as or after knowledge is acquired, and who amongst us is so brilliant he or she can afford ever to stop? La Guerinière provided the clue when he wrote in 1729: 'Every science and every art has its principles and its rules that lead to new discoveries and to perfection. Why should horsemanship be the only art for which practice alone is needed?'

There cannot be one natural horseman who has produced a horse to the highest level of *haute école* who can honestly claim not to have read a book on the subject. Like it or not, riding is bound by scientific rules and precepts; so often a few words of logical explanation from an authority can solve a problem with which a rider and his horse have been grappling for months, even years.

Feel is a wonderful gift to a horseman, probably the most important, but to produce a finished dressage horse, feel is not enough. De Souza, writing from America in 1927, explained: 'Just as one may like music without knowing anything of its theory, yet enjoyment of it is infinitely greater when one understands the theory, so of horsemanship and practically every game, art or science. It is almost axiomatic that the more we know of the theory and technique of an art the more pleasure and profit it affords us.'

Where credo and philosophy are not denied, there is usually humility. It is these precious commodities which carry equitation into a higher realm. Without a philosophy is is very difficult indeed to teach others, especially if their feel is less developed. Without humility you are unlikely to gain the respect of your pupil and certainly not the love of your horse.

Opening the Mind

The downside of a disregard for the academic is a closed mind. Experience of life arms us with our likes and dislikes, our pride and prejudices, but it is reading and study and travel

Jane Bartle-Wilson, a consistent winner in the freestyle Dressage to Music competitions. Her performances on the popular Pinnocchio sparkled with gaiety and lively impulsion, but rarely at the expense of lightness. Second in the World Championships at Toronto (1986) and two European Championships at Aachen (1983) and Copenhagen (1985), this combination seemed entirely at one with each other. (Photo: Kit Houghton)

which opens the mind to other customs, other viewpoints, other ways. The wonderful thing about the Renaissance was that it spread like wildfire across Europe. The rediscovery of civilised ideas, the thirst for knowledge, the travelling and exchanging of information, the humanist element, the writing, absorbing, stimulation, yearning for improvement, made this an inspiring, valuable time for mankind and particularly for equitation.

What partly distinguishes this period from nowadays was the openness. These people were willing to learn from the past and with the fruits of their discovery they explored, improved and embellished. Yet through the modifications and the adornments, the purist logic of the Greeks burned through. Xenophon's philosophy, based on Nature's laws, stood the test of time because it was clearcut, logical and good.

National Academies

One of the tragedies for many of the English-speaking nations is the lack of a national academy of classical equitation. Surprisingly, too many in international dressage competition fail to see the need, yet constantly rue the difficulties encountered in producing dressage judges of knowledge and calibre. It is little wonder conflicting ideas abound in this area when there is no Mecca to which to turn. In Britain, in particular, writers have regretted the lack of a national school for generations.

In 1801, Philip Astley wrote with bitter resignation, 'There is not a scientific riding school in this kingdom, nor any regular professor of Equestrian Education!...' Not long after, another writer, J. G. Peters commented, 'In surveying the pages of history, we find scarcely an instance of any nation of importance that has not had proper institutions for their young nobility, gentry and military, for the express purpose of initiating them in all manner of riding from the plain hack on the road to the fine manège horse ... but, strange to say, in England, whose immense importance is acknowledged all over the habitable world, we look around us in vain for such an establishment, and ask, *where is it to be found*?'

Such sentiments have been echoed in the United States, Canada, New Zealand, South Africa and Australia, but strangely it has only been in the latter two countries that attempts have been made to establish a classical school based on idealistic vision rather than commercial and competitive enterprise. Equitation, as any other art, benefits from a seat of cultural inspiration. It is no accident of fate that those countries which still maintain a national academy of classical riding, on however modest a scale, enjoy a higher allround standard of equitation in general.

Let us look therefore to the Schools of Austria, France, Romania, Portugal, Spain and Germany (still basking in the shadow of the great School of Hanover) and try to understand their influence. The old classical ways may differ somewhat from the neo-classical school of most Olympic riders, but by upholding traditions of slow, systematic training, the establishment of the rider's seat, the psychological and muscular development of the horse, and his ultimate happiness and beauty, inspiration is derived by all.

It is now recognised by the medical, and to a large extent, teaching profession, that the learning process which take place in our brain is subdivided into that which is acquired consciously, and that which enters the memory cells subconsciously. In fact two sides of the brain are used, the left for the storing of facts and for logical reasoning, the right for visual images, recognition of beauty and form, in short that part which constitutes 'the mind's eye'. It is the subsequent drawing from the latter which results in intuition, creativity and artistry.

Nowhere is this double use of the brain more pronounced that in the study of equitation. Whilst learning techniques through books, lectures and articles is invaluable to all thinking riders through the left side of the brain, the right side processes an equally great store of information through watching. In dressage, visual memory plays a remarkably vital role; the picture of a great master on his horse, if seen enough times, can literally burn itself into the brain and create spectacular physical and mental results. For the dressage rider, these will manifest themselves in an automatically improved position, and finer use of the aids, often accomplished quite unconsciously at the time. For the dressage judge, too little exposed to sights of near perfection, such valuable visual feasts tune the eye to what is truly good, classical and correct, and what is not, leaving him more discerning and clearer in his judgements.

Raising the National Standard

If some form of national academy was established in those countries which seriously participate in dressage, it is clear the national standard of riding generally would also be raised. This would lead to greatly improved safety in roadriding and hacking out. In terms of actual dressage, the benefits both to horse and rider would be magnified. The forgotten values of quietness, gentleness and real empathy between horse and rider, would rapidly become vividly apparent if and when they exist for all to see.

Concepts so often overlooked and forgotten in the busy humdrum of the commercial yard, take on new meaning once people realise that there is a better way, a more classical approach. Even non-dressage riders will recognise quality of work. People who have never received a formal riding lesson in their lives are often the first to say 'he and his horse moved as one', after seeing a good rider. How much more so then would competitors, instructors and judges benefit from such an example. With a real living source of inspiration to which each country will relate, thousands more would understand and rate the words of L'Hotte who wrote 'the use of the rider's hands and legs were so secret that the eye could not catch them'.[2]

Different Seats

Throughout this book, we have discussed how different influences affected different schools in different countries over the years, more often than not caused by the type of horse in fashion at the time. The reader will have taken note of the different seats and saddles and it would be foolish not to admit certain national differences usually determined by the type of horse being ridden and what he was required to do. These were broadly summed up by Jane Kidd in her book *Horsemanship in Europe* when she wrote: 'In every dressage school a good seat is considered the prerequisite of successful riding but this position differs between countries. The German likes to be straight upright and appears to be in much the same position as if he were standing up. The Swede tends towards a rounded stance, but the French push their loins forward and scoop their tail bone forwards and upwards.'

[2] From *Questions Equestres.*

This book has dealt generally with the seats of many different authors throughout these chapters and the conclusion must be that where the emphasis has been on mainly very collected work in the pursuit of the High School, the three point, hollow-loined seat[3] first outlined by Newcastle and La Guérinière, has continued and developed into that of Baucher, Oliveira, Frederiksen, de Kunffy and Albrecht. In those instances, where a dressage writer has developed his theories from a strong background of crosscountry riding or hunting, the preference has leaned toward the two point seat, (see the works of Wätjen, Seunig, von Blixen Finecke, Crossley and van Schaik). Both are classical in their own way provided that one uses the word advisedly, i.e., in reference to what is required of the horse at that particular time.

Classical Movements

What united every school of classical foundation, despite the obvious nationalistic traits and characteristics, was striving always for that which was natural in the horse. This precept of Xenophon's was re-emphasized again and again by La Guerinière and his contemporaries and is still the basis for all classical teaching today.

Nevertheless, considerable hypocrisy exists about the different movements used in dressage and whether or not they are truly classical (i.e. natural) or unclassical (unnatural).

It is readily accepted that all the airs practised at Vienna are classical (natural) as are every one of those exercises demanded in the various competitive dressage tests organised within the framework of the FEI. Anything else, particularly movements once favoured in the circus, are deeply frowned upon. Whilst I personally abhor laboured movements such as the canter on three legs for which poor Fillis was condemned for life by the establishment of the time, it does seems odd that the free-moving Spanish Walk and Trot which are recognised by many authorities to have a schooling value for the suppleness of the shoulder, should have been condemned as unnatural. They are certainly no less natural than the rein-back.

To condemn movements out of hand is in many ways a dangerous stance and indicative of the prejudices of the modern age. Not long ago there was a move afoot within the FEI to remove the piaffe and passage from the Grand Prix dressage tests since these were deemed too difficult.[4] How long would it have been, one wonders, before they too would be described by future less informed generations as unclassical and unnatural, and how tragic for equestrian art to be denied movements of such beauty when well executed?

All this is very academic. Yet perhaps one owes it to the High School trainers of the circus, where we still see some brilliant horsemanship and happy horses trained on reward, to enlarge on this controversial point. Has anyone, one wonders, ever seen a horse in his natural state cantering a complete circle in counter canter? Most horses will put in a few strides of counter canter when they are excited and have forgotten to change legs, but there would have to be something physically wrong with the horse to make him voluntarily continue in this imbalance for a whole circuit. Similarly, can it truly be said that half-pass is a natural movement, and what about one time flying changes?

This last demand certainly concerned the authorities at the Spanish Riding School when it was introduced into the Grand Prix, and it put such immense strain on the horse that many highly talented animals are today precluded from entering the highest levels because of this one movement alone. It requires a certain type of balance in the horse to make one time changes,

---

[3] See *The Classical Seat.*

[4] It was General Margot of Saumur who was so sickened by poor attempts at these movements in the competitive arena that he felt the only alternative was to abandon them completely.

and there is no doubt it is much easier for the more horizontally built horses.

Are the efforts of others who have achieved an almost magical understanding with their horses and who are able to extract happily certain movements from a particularly supple partner to be condemned? In England, one immediately thinks of patient trainers such as Mary Chipperfield, or the quietly brilliant Sylvia Stanier, author of *The Art of Longreining*, an expert on work in hand and sidesaddle. The Knie family from Switzerland, and the Portuguese and Spanish are masters of canter on the spot, which still has a practical value for the latter in their work with the bulls. Even at the military base of Saumur some very extravagant airs and leaps have their place. Many horses enjoy this flamboyant work but like all else it must be achieved through great patience and proper preparation.

Different Schools of Thought

A cliché which appears in the writing of almost every major authority discussed so far is that many roads lead to Rome. Nevertheless, all agree that results of excellence cannot be achieved unless the training of the horse has been based more on reward than on punishment. It seems however, that this one desperately important factor is often overlooked in formal lessons today.

Fortunately for the horse, at top level dressage, riders learn from experience that more and more emphasis on reward is vital if the horse is to work harmoniously and without tension. (In this respect as pointed out before, we are not talking about sugar lumps, but on the gentleness of the aids and the quietness of the rider's seat.) On the way up however, divergences occur. Whatever the country, or national school, riding ceases to be classical when punishment becomes apparent in the form of a relentless, harsh contact, rough driving seat and legs with an apparently constant use of the spur. Punishment may also comprise simple ignorance – insufficient relaxation periods for the horse between exercises is commonplace, a total absence of praise even more so.

Abuse exists. Littauer wrote '. . . it is easy to abuse your horse mentally without noticing the little inconsiderate things which one may do without meaning harm . . . Omitting rewards while exaggerating punishments is an abuse.' Asking too much of the horse in one stressful session occurs in every country, competitive and non-competitive alike. Under the rules of competition however, there is an excellent chance to eradicate it, but one of the problems is to ensure that more people are first able to recognise it, and second prepared to admit it. We will return to this at the end of the chapter.

The late Nuno Oliveira had some very interesting thoughts on the subject of the different schools in his book *Classical Principles of the Art of Training Horses*:

'. . . in riding circles there is a tendency to speak of different schools, the French School, the German School, the Swedish School and so on. It is the purpose of this small paper to seek the essential unities that are fundamental. We must be aware of those differences in riding techniques or philosophy that have substantive differences – as against those that merely show the difference in the breeding, conformation and temperament of the horse being used.

'The Germans, through their character, their sense of organization and discipline, do have strong horses with good backs, and very correct and large movements, and especially, with an appropriate temperament for dressge competitions. These horses are more stable and less excitable than the Thoroughbreds and the Anglo-Arabs which were the fashion in France in the nineteen-thirties, forties, fifties and sixties.

'We do not speak of a superiority of any Method (e.g. the German method) but it must be recognized that dressage is very popular in Germany and there are many junior riders capable of competing in Prix de St Georges. Of course German riders are not all top class riders, having a tendency to ride and work their horse with a rigidity and harshness which induces a very strong contact with the reins.

'But if you observe the top riders such as Schultheiss, Klimke, etc., you will notice that this is not what happens. They are not ignorant of the *descente de main* which is the result and reward of real collection . . .

'If a horse is not truly light, exercises such as the pirouette, the passage, the piaffe and especially the transition from passage to the piaffe are not really accurate and brilliant.'

Suddenly talk of lightness is back in fashion. The technique described above for achieving such lightness must once more be respected, and if the French expression seems too obscure to some, let us examine Klimke's own words on the subject. 'The horse should learn to work alone as much as possible, with minimum aids. The hands must emply a "nursing" effect, immediately lightening as the horse steps forward, then just a touch of the reins again in order to "catch the step". As the horse becomes more and more established in each movement, so the pressure (of legs and feel on the rein) is decreased.'

The School of Force

Despite these encouraging signs from enlightened individuals, in many international competitive yards, the school of force is still the dominant one. Even the British, renowned for their love of the horse have too often fallen under the spell of the iron glove and the iron boot. Through a lack of traditional philosophy which constantly seeks a state of perfection, the majority of riders and judges continue to be more concerned with mechanical obedience and submission (even if obtained through force) than lightness. Paillard's criticisms of the modern methods of achieving impulsion illustrate the harshness of some current ideas.

'Impulsion! Impulsion! How many errors have been committed in thy name!

'One of the most common and also most serious is to drive young horses forward in rapid gaits by energetic leg actions on the pretext of giving them impulsion . . . Another one is to *drive into the hands* on the pretext of establishing a *tension* that would amount to the famous impulsion, a horse that as yet understands well neither the leg actions nor the hand actions . . . Such behaviour, notwithstanding the clever words often used in an attempt to present it in another light, amounts to no more than "pushing and pulling at the same time".

'Legs! Legs! Drive! Push onto the bit! All this can certainly *force* a horse to move forward . . . but it will never give the horse impulsion, that supplementary quality of obedience composed of generosity and almost- spontaneity. . .'

Dr Van Schaik, a Dutch born writer from America, who has written a thoughtful book *Misconceptions and Simple Truths in Dressage* blames the composition of the FEI dressage tests for the lack of harmony and ease in present day dressage. 'Would it not be possible' he asks 'to have competitions with the emphasis on beauty and not on acrobatics?'

PRIORITIES

'An emphasis on beauty' . . . this must be the fervent desire of every rider who is inspired by classical principles. The situation today could so easily be improved with a lesson from the past.

The camera catches the piaffe just after the highest point of suspension, but nevertheless the picture is pleasing. In adherence to classical tradition, the horse works in comparative freedom, the back is unconstricted and the croup is slightly lower than the forehand. Note the engagement of the near fetlock. Here *Bereiter* Riegler rides his Duch horse, Vindicator, in a manner which is not yet seen enough in the competition arena.

In the early days of dressage competition, only Kürs and freestyles existed. Riders were required, as in the Musical Kürs today, to show certain movements in certain gaits, but the order and sequence of these movements was at the discretion of the rider. This enabled them to demonstrate more naturally the level of obedience, suppleness and pleasantness under saddle their respective horses had reached. Thus the movements were not so much an end in themselves, but a test of the level achieved. Marking these tests was presumably no more difficult than in today's freestyles and no doubt very much more interesting.

The beauty of the freestyle is that it can be tailormade for each horse. Since all the movements must be shown, there is no shirking of the task, but different horses respond to different programmes. An objection to riding to markers is that very often the flowing quality of the horse's movements is hampered by sudden and inconsistent changes and transitions when the horse is least prepared for them. Riders complain that set tests are designed to catch the horse out rather than to help the horse achieve smoothness and ease. That was one of the main complaints Colonel Podhajsky made about modern competition and it resurrects the whole question of non-riders judging and even devising such tests.

Today, there are more and more signs that frustration is felt by both judges and competitors alike for a a system of scoring which favours the concept of *where* you ride a movement rather than *how* you ride it. Too often, particularly at lower levels we witness the ironic situation of a sympathetic combination producing an aesthetically pleasing, flowing and classically correct test to finish several places below a combination where the aids are more abrupt, the horse is less relaxed but marker-accuracy is achieved. Yet the judges cannot be blamed when the system demands tests are judged in this way. On the other hand is it fair to penalise horses which anticipate? Everyone knows that exact riding to markers creates tension and anticipation, but since markers are obviously here to stay, we could offer more choice for the novice horse and rider.

Musical Kürs

Fortunately, an element of freedom has returned to the competitive arena through the musical Kürs. These, not surprisingly, have caused tremendous public interest and can be breathtakingly beautiful. There is however the increasing danger here again that flow and smoothness will inevitably be lost if judges favour riders whose horses are being trained virtually to dance to the music.

The British writer and dressage judge, Pegotty Henriques, wrote a provocative but timely article for *Horse and Hound* entitled 'Freestyle Monster Could Destroy the Classical Art.'[5] Her important point was that if non-equestrian judges are introduced to these events, the results could be disastrous. 'Even if he [such a judge] was very knowledgeable, it would be easy for him to get carried away by a creatively dramatic performance that overwhelmed his judgement.' Another point in the same article concerned the preponderance for over ambitious programmes where a non-equestrian judge could be blinded to obvious faults. 'Triple pirouettes are no pleasure to watch if the horse is seen to be struggling. Extended trot, piaffe, extended trot is only awesome if it is well done.' It is hoped these words will be taken into account.

There is also the concern that the horse's natural rhythm is destroyed through the rider's preoccupation with finding a matching tempo in the music. Sometimes, it would be more honest to describe such tests as theatrical performances rather than straightforward demonstrations of classical dressage. For the future, priorities must prevail and there will be guidelines to dilute the present trend for changing the music with every change of gait which can detract from the quality of the work being enacted.

Once again a lesson should be learned from the Spanish Riding School. At Vienna, the music is important in that it provides a wonderful backcloth for the work of the horses; never however does the music itself become the altar at which we worship. There is no sudden change of tune or of beat to *complement* the movements. Instead the almost spiritual quality of the work is derived from the horses themselves. They dance because they are light and full of lively but submitted impulsion, not because the rider has shortened or lengthened the gait to match the beat! They are high-stepping because their backs are soft and supple, not because they syncopate their steps in time with the tune! They flow because they are unconstrained, not because the music dictates this! This is the true object of dressage to music, which must never become music to dressage.

Recalling Xenophon

As we started with Xenophon, so we must, if we love our horses, end with the powerful humanitarian philosophy of this practical horseman. The time has come for the horse to make his statement. His happiness and comfort should be considered at every level. This cannot happen overnight. Yet the remedies are clear.

Education of the Rider: The way ahead lies first in the way we present dressage to the young. Precepts of kindness and reward must be instilled at the start. Youngsters nowadays are filled with competitive fervour, but little time is devoted to the psychology of the horse. Most people are quite unaware that horses flourish on praise as much as the latest brand of mix or horse cube. The true aim of riding a test is also neglected. This is not to win rosettes by riding a series of movements but to produce a wholesome, finished picture of the horse at a particular level. The following terms would be understandable to most people, however novice. *In dressage, you are to display the level of work you have achieved with your partner the horse. Through the correctness and quietness of your aids, he should be able to carry out your various requests proudly and of his own volition.* (The word *submission* would be better left out since it is open to misinterpretation by far too many.)

If a national academy cannot be provided, at least we can convey this message in all riding schools, riding clubs and at Pony Club level worldwide, as well as in official FEI literature.

Prevention of Abuse: At every competition in every level of the land, organisers must be

[5] 19 January 1989.

made aware they have a special duty to interfere in cases of abuse. Ring stewards at working-in areas must watch for over-use of heel or spur, overtight drop and flash nosebands which prevent easy breathing, and punitive hands. Tack should be examined; excessive booting should bring a reprimand. Sharply jabbing a horse in the mouth with the bit should cause immediate elimination from the class.

Layout of Tests: There should be more Kürs with and without music. In the lower tests, it should be clear from the rules that riders may ask their horse up to three strides before or after the marker for the next movement. This would allow a more flowing quality based on the rider's ability to judge the right moment for his horse rather than being forced to make it at a particular point whether the horse is ready or not.

Scoring: Dressage tests should place more importance on how the horse is ridden. In addition to the specific points for the execution of each movement, the ideal, although probably impracticable, would be a corresponding set of marks *throughout the test* for the aesthetic qualities of lightness, roundness, harmony between horse and rider, quietness and the overall picture. The present system, although destined to include these qualities, almost encourages the judge to concentrate on the mechanical only. As for the collective mark at the bottom of the sheet often, this is added as an afterthought long after the competitor has left the ring, when it is too late to take a second look. As a friend who trained with the Swedish Cavalry, once expressed it, what dressage judging really needs is one set of marks for the prosecution and one for the defence. If scoring could be implemented on this basis, it would inevitably banish for ever the negative or adverserial image of dressage judging.

A reappraisal of the marking of dressage tests is long overdue. No one feels the present system is ideal and no judge enjoys the outbursts of critics when there is a disparity. The implementation of a broader-based system would inevitably raise standards all round. At the highest level, most of our top riders would remain in pole position; at lower levels however, there would be some interesting and fruitful changes worldwide, and judges would enjoy more freedom. For too long, there has been the temptation to stick at the safe sixes when in doubt.

Educating Judges: It is unacceptable that some judges appear to have vastly differing ideas about the correct classical interpretation of certain movements. The FEI rules are abundantly clear, yet confusion reigns. Even at Grand Prix levels, movements such as the pirouette or passage are awarded 6s and 7s when simply not performed according to the rules, yet at lower levels judges will happily award 3s and 4s if a movement shows a lack of impulsion which is too often confused with speed.

Not all judges seem aware that they have a duty to competitors to be classically educated. As General Albrecht points out in his *A Dressage Judge's Handbook*, practical experience alone can never suffice. 'Although routine practice is needed to develop skill, it does not give the *insight* essential for judging.'

One discrepancy observed in modern attitudes to dressage concerns an apparent glossing over the importance of real collection. At lower levels, it has become fashionable to criticise a horse for being tense or 'high in front' when in fact he is well-engaged and proud (if there was no tension, there would be no energy produced by the muscles). At the highest level, horses are insufficiently penalised when those airs which are deemed the proof of collection, e.g., piaffe and passage, are executed, contrary to the rules, with the horse on the forehand.

Work at Grand Prix level is designed for horses working in balanced self-carriage in all gaits. Where judges are quick to penalise lack of extension and forward thrust, they seem reluctant to penalise lack of *contained* impulsion, i.e., collection and suspension. A question

Olympic gold medallist, Nicole Uphoff and Rembrandt make a sympathetic combination of lightness and airness as they take up the steps of passage at Seoul, 1988. Some horses of Thoroughbred blood require especially sensitive riding since they find it more difficult to round the back and lower the quarters in collection, but generally they are aesthetically very beautiful to watch. (*Photo: Bob Langrish*)

mark also hangs over the acceptance by some judges of the sight of a horse ridden on permanently taut reins and which seems in danger of leaving the arena. It is this inequality of emphasis which has led to many observers questioning the direction of modern dressage and suggesting that there now exists two schools of thought. One, the true classical, where the horse must be well back on his hocks and light in hand; the other, the neo-classical, where the horse's frame is horizontal and there is permanent weight into the hand.

Podhajsky however, had no illusions about the dangers of schooling the horse in a continually horizontal outline so that movements like the piaffe had to be forced with the spur. He rued the typical shuffle of the Grand Prix test where 'the majority of the horses more or less doggedly move about on the spot . . .', very rarely offering 'regular and elevated steps'.

Judges must therefore concern themselves with the theory of classical riding, and be helped to attune their eye to the execution of correct collected work which takes considerable more insight to judge than the more obvious extensions.

Whilst visits to Vienna would be wonderfully beneficial, educating judges need not be expensive. Course books from the classical masters should become compulsory for every judge after Elementary level, as well as course videos. Worldwide, the former should include at least the work of Xenophon, translations from La Guérinière, Decarpentry, Podhajsky and Oliveira. For the English, additional help from Wynmalen and Fillis would be beneficial. (Other countries will have their own favourites.) As for videos, they should be of top quality. Mediocrity abounds and dulls the eye. The eye of a dressage judge must be trained to accept as perfect only the perfect. It is logical therefore that only from those truly classical academies who have been steeped in the gentle art of riding for generations should inspiration be drawn. Recently, there has been much in the equestrian press to emphasize a disparity between the Classical School and the Competitive Dressage School. Yet the groundrules for both are the same. A particularly strong letter on this subject appeared in *Dressage*[6] last year from a reader, B. A, Steibelt, who wrote: 'Surely it is time to drop the pretence and call dressage 'Dressage' and not claim that it is Classical Equitation. From this point we can then go forward and attempt to improve dressage by emulating those aspects of Classical Equitation which we most admire. For me, these are lightness, agility and a dancing quality, as opposed to the relentless, lumbering power which is so in vogue today.'

[6] *Dressage*, September/October 1989.

Personally, I do not believe the situation in dressage today is so violently in opposition to what went before, except at the lower levels which should be called schooling tests rather than dressage tests, and in certain areas of the Grand Prix which have been discussed. The majority of riders, particularly those who school their own horses, want to be educated in the classical ways and want to achieve a classical result. If some positive changes could be made within these suggested guidelines, the two schools of thought would blend to the satisfaction of all. As long, however, as we remain complacent about the present system of training, judging, and the presentation and scoring of tests, there must inevitably follow a polarization of the two systems.

In 1989, the Spanish Riding School came once again to London. With ten riders and twenty-four horses, they gave perhaps their best ever Wembley performance (for they have varied in the past) in terms of accuracy, suppleness, range of work, harmony between horse and rider and sheer pride and enjoyment in the faces of the horses. It seems their reappearance has caused people to stop and to reconsider. A shrewd and heartening article in the Christmas issue of *Horse and Hound* magazine, by Pegotty Henriques, struck an optimistic note for the year ahead.[7]

'The other night I looked at a video of the Olympic Games dressage. I began to wonder whether the path international dressage is travelling along is the right one.

'Out of the top ten, there were too many horses with irregularities and impure paces. Too many riders who failed to comply with the requirement that "all the movements should be obtained without apparent effort" (FEI quote).

'Is the system of judging at fault? The system of competing, or the system of training? Are trainers too aware that their pupils have to be successful and therefore tending to orientate themselves towards competition riding?

'If you take time to lean over the stable door on Christmas Eve and listen to that wonderful sound of contented munching, take a moment or two to ponder what you are really trying to achieve and whether the direction the whole sport is taking is the right one.'

When an international judge of the calibre and experience of Mrs Henriques questions the direction of competition dressage, many competitors and non-competitors alike who truly love their horses will find reassurance. Comments such as this certainly re-emphasize the importance of those establishments outlined at length in this book which have kept traditional equitation alive over the centuries. Surely the time has come now to bring those age-old values back into the open and re-examine the current trends? Are today's methods compatible with the best of the past or is it now imperative to the happiness of the horse that we retrace our steps?

To help the reader make up his own mind, I ask every thinking rider to ponder awhile the words of an English High School rider, Philip Astley, who truly possessed that important quality of which we spoke earlier, namely insight. In his rich and lengthy dedication[8] written at the end of the eighteenth century to all horses, I have chosen those passages which seem particularly apt for the world of riding today:

The Horse

In . . . Equestrian Exercises, his fire and courage are irresistible. Amid his boldest exertions, he is equally

[7] *Horse & Hound*, 21 December 1989.
[8] Published in Astley's *System of Equestrian Education*, London 1801, as a preface to the book dedicated to TRH George, Prince of Wales and Frederick, Duke of York.

collected and tractable; not obeying his own impetuosity, all his efforts and his actions guided solely by his rider. Indeed, such is the greatness of his obedience, that he appears to consult nothing but how he shall best please, and if possible anticipate what his master wishes and requires.

. . . Nothing can be more wonderful that the precision with which he performs everything that is required of him; resigned without any reserve to our service, he refuses nothing however dangerous or difficult to execute. He serves with all his strength, and in his strenous efforts to please, oft-times out-does himself, and even dies in order the better to obey!

. . . All he demands from us, therefore, for a life of incessant fatigue, is support and a tender return . . . which creates in him his chief pleasure, which is the sense of our being pleased and satisfied with his unwearied endeavours to serve us.

'A tender return . . .', it is little to ask. Somehow it seems that the men of the Renaissance were right when they wrote that the art of equitation ennobled the soul. The pursuit of beauty and balance in riding makes he or she who practises it, because they love it, look deep into the heart of their horse and see him for what he is. The noble horse – yes! But to be noble, to be himself, every horse requires a modicum of nobility from us.

If there is a little mist in the eyes but more importantly, a stout resolution in the soul to achieve that end, as we come to this final page, then your reading and my writing will have all been worthwhile.

The Modern Dressage Arena. The 20 × 60 metre international dressage arena with letters as used today was universally accepted in 1932. The Olympic size arena allows many horses to work together without crowding. Horses are shown here in half-pass right and left, the shoulder-in and on the volte. For individual competition, the large arena undoubtedly suits the bigger breeds of horse with bigger gaits, a factor which has helped to promote today's most popular dressage breeds.

Glossary of Specialised Equestrian Terms

Appui A French term to indicate the feeling of contact experienced by the rider through the medium of the rein as the horse accepts the bit or mouthpiece on the bars of his mouth. This acceptance or bearing may vary from the very light to the heavy. A light but constant *appui* has always been favoured by horsemen of all times and nationalities. Only in recent years have certain schools of thought suggested that contact or *appui* be determined or measured in terms of weight. The term *appui* whilst still in everyday usage in France is now little used in English, although it was frequently used (sometimes *appuy*) in historic English works, e.g. by the Duke of Newcastle (seventeenth century) and Henry Herbert, Earl of Pembroke (eighteenth century).

Bridling was a term regularly used in England by all horsemen from the early eighteenth century into the twentieth century to denote flexion and control through a mere touch of the reins. Mysteriously, today it is rarely used. The following definition is one of many written before the last World War. 'Bridling is the rendering of the head and neck light and flexible by teaching the horse to bend his neck at the poll and to relax his lower jaw. The lightness of the head and neck reacts on the shoulders and through them on the entire forehand. If our horse is not flexed, the rider feels as if he were dealing with a log of wood with all its deadness and heaviness . . . a flexed or bridled horse on the other hand resembles a fishing rod in which flexibility becomes greater as you go forward.' (From *Sympathetic Training of Horse and Man.*)

Career A battle term, much used in the days of tournament riding and tilting, originally from the French *carriere*, to denote the demarkation of line that a rider must take when making a charge or a tilt at his opponent. Later it was used in the manège to indicate the line to take; in modern terms 'the track'.

Curvet A term much used by English masters of equitation in the sixteenth and seventeenth centuries (e.g. Blundeville, Markham, Newcastle) derived from the French *courbette*. Essentially a skirmish movement of attack, the *courbette* developed into one of the many airs above the ground (aires relevés) which played such an important part in academic equitation. More similar to today's levade with the horse's body poised at an angle of no more than 30 degrees, a high degree of flexion and bending in the haunches was required. From marking time with the forelegs, the horse was to take a series of small leaps either forward or to right or left. It bore no resemblance to today's *courbette* as practised at Saumur and in the Spanish Riding School, where the horse also takes a series of leaps forward, but the body is held at a much higher angle.

Descente de main et des jambes The yielding of the hand and the legs, while the horse remains in the same flexion, cadence and rhythm of the movement being executed. This is described in detail in Chapter 7 and should not be confused with the modern 'stroking the horse's neck'.

Ecuyer A French term used over much of Europe in the seventeenth and eighteenth centuries to denote a recognised, often noble born, Master of equitation who served at court. Henriquet states that 'within the organisation of the *Grandes Ecuries* of Versailles there was: *Le*

Grand Ecuyer of France – at the head of the court. Under him, served: *L'Ecuyer Commandant*; *Monsieur le Premier Ecuyer* who was served by 13 *Ecuyers*. Below this came: 12 *Ecuyers Cavalcadeurs*; 5 *Ecuyer de Ceremonies*; 135 Honorary *Ecuyers* who served when they could. (In addition to the *écuyers* were 1 king of arms, 25 heralds of arms, 80 pages, and 50 musicians all of whom made up the personnel of the *Grand Ecurie*.' Today, the term *écuyer* is still used at Saumur, but for obvious reasons, no longer has royal connections.

Manège Originally French in derivation, this word has now been incorporated into the English language to denote an arena, ring or area (of any shape or size) where horses are schooled or dressed. The main difference between the manèges of the Baroque and Classical eras and today's modern dressage arenas is the size. The former (e.g., that of the Duke of Newcastle, Chapter 8) were often only half the width of a modern arena since the emphasis at all times was on the collected flexibility of the horse, rather than on his extended ground-covering power.

Nagsman An expression used in the nineteenth and twentieth century in England to denote a man who made his living by breaking and schooling horses fit for a gentleman to ride. Some of these individuals were former grooms, often they were dealers. Generally, although often unrefined in approach, having little knowledge of the academic niceties of equitation, they produced relatively well-mannered horses which were adequately schooled for road riding, hacking out in company and which would not disgrace their owner on the hunting field.

Romanic The Concise Dictionary states 1. Descended from Latin . . . 2. Descended from, inheriting civilization etc., of the Romans, Romance-speaking (f. L *Romanicus* (Romanic)). In horsemanship, therefore, the Romanic style denotes one inherited from Roman times or from the Latin-speaking peoples (see Chapter 3). This, over many centuries, came to imply a lightness and dexterity of riding style as employed by warriers mounted on the hotblood combat horses of Southern Europe and Northern Africa.

Terra à Terra (or Terra Terra) An air which was considered the basis for the airs above the ground, but which is no longer recognised in dressage today. The action of the horse is a very cadenced, elevated canter in two-time often practised against the wall or between pillars, either forward or more often to the right or to the left. Newcastle used it to supple the croup and describes it thus: '. . . the horse always leads with the two legs within the volte; his two forelegs are in the airs, as in the gallop, and his two hindlegs follow when he begins to put down those before, in such a manner that the horse has all his legs in the air at the same time, making a leap forwards.' With the hindquarters deeply engaged, so that the leaps were very close to the ground, the effect was a very cadenced rocking movement of small, controlled advancing prances.

Bibliography

Books, Papers and Articles referred to in part or in whole, the date indicated being that edition used by the author, but not necessarily the first edition of the work concerned

Abbate, Francesco, *Roman Art*, Peerage Books, London, 1970

Adams, John, *An Analysis of Horsemanship*, Albion Press, London, 1805

Albrecht, Brigadier General Kurt, *Dressurrichter*, Orac Pietsch, Vienna, 1981
   A Dressage Judge's Handbook, J. A. Allen & Co., London, 1988
   Dogmes de l'Art Equestre, Crepin-Leblon, Paris, 1986

Anderson, J.K., *Ancient Greek Horsemanship*, University of California Press, 1961

Andrade, Manuel Carlos, *Luz da Liberal e Nobre Arte da Cavallaria*, Lisbon, 1790

Andrade, Fernando de, *A Short History of the Spanish Horse and of the Iberian Gineta Horsemanship for which this Horse is Adapted*, Lisbon, 1973

Andrade, Ruy de, *Alrededor del Caballo Espanol*, Lisbon, 1954
   O Cavalo do Sorraia, Lisbon, 1945
   O Cavalo Andaluz de Perfil Convexo, Lisbon, 1941

Astley, Philip, *Astley's System of Equestrian Education*, London, 1801

Aublet, Lt Col, *L'École de Cavalerie de Saumur*, Saumur, 1986

Aure, Compte d', *Traite d'Équitation*, Paris, 1847

Bacharach, René, article 'Synoptique des Écuyers Français du XVI au XX Siecle', *Les Amis du Cadre Noir, Bulletin, no.21*, Saumur, May 1986

Baucher, Francois, *The Principles of Horsemanship*, Vinton & Co., London, 1919
   Dictionnaire d'Équitation, Émile Hazan, Paris, 1966

Beamish, Huldine, *Cavaliers of Portugal*, Geoffrey Bles, London, 1966

Berenger, *A New System of Horsemanship from the French of Monsieur Bourgelat*, printed by Henry Woodfall, London, 1754
   The History and Art of Horsemanship, printed for Davies and Cadell of London, 1771

Beudant, Étienne, *Exterieure et Haute École*, Amat, Paris, 1923

Bezugloff, Ivan, Article 'Equestrian Olympic Games in Retrospect' in *Dressage and CT*, March 1984

Blixen-Finecke, Hans von, *The Art of Riding*, J.A. Allen, London, 1977

Blundeville, Thomas, *The Four Chiefest Offices belonging to Horsemanship*, William Seres, London, 1570

Bowlby, Glencairn, article 'The Two Colonels', *Dressage and CT*, December 1986

Bragança, Diogo de, *l'Équitation de la Tradition Française*, Le Livre de Paris, 1975

British Horse Society, *Dressage Rules Handbook*, 1987

Broue, Salomon de la, *Le Cavalerice François*, Paris, 1646

Burger, Udo, *The Easy Way to Perfect Horsemanship*, J. A. Allen, London, 1986

Calthrop, Everard R., *The Horse, as Comrade and Friend*, Hutchinson, London, 1921

Cavendish, William, Duke of Newcastle, *Methode et Invention Nouvelle de Dresser les Chevaux*, Antwerp, 1658
   A General System of Horsemanship in All its Branches, modern facsimile from the 1743 English edition.

Chamberlin, Col H. D. *Riding and Schooling Horses*, Derrydale Press, New York, 1937
   Training Hunters, Jumpers and Hacks, Derrydale Press, New York, 1937

Clifford, Christopher, *The School of Horsemanship*, London, 1585

Coelho, Alfredo Baptista, hipplogist and

historian, letters to author and translated excerpts from Manuel Carlos Andrade, Lisbon, 1985–90

Corte, Claudio, *The Art of Riding*, London, 1584

Cordeiro, Arsenio Reposo, *O Cavalo Lusitano, o filho do vento*, Ediçoes Inapa, Lisbon, 1989, shortly to be published as *Lusitano Horse, The Son of the Wind*

Crossley, Col Anthony, *Training the Young Horse*, Stanley Paul, London, 1978
article, 'At the Feet of the Master', *Riding*, May 1977

De Grey, Thomas, *The Compleat Horseman and Expert Farrier*, London, 1639

Decarpentry, General Albert, *Academic Equitation*, J. A. Allen, London, 1971
Piaffer and Passage, J. A. Allen, London, 1964

Dent, Anthony, *The Horse Through Fifty Centuries of Civilisation*, Phaidon, London 1974
Cleveland Bay Horses, J. A. Allen, London, 1978

Dent and Machin Goodall, Daphne, *Foals of Epona*, Galley Press, London, 1962

Dionysius, excerpts from writing, *Halicarnassus*, around 25 BC

DOE official handbook, *Bolsover Castle*, HMSO 1972

Dodge, Colonel Theodore Ayrault, *Riders of Many Lands*, Harper & Brothers, New York, 1894

Dossenbach, Monique and Hans D., and Kohler, Hans Joachim, *Great Stud-Farms of the World*, Thames and Hudson, London, 1978

Dwyer, Francis, *On Seats and Saddles, Bits and Bitting*, William Blackwood & Sons, Edinburgh and London, 1869

Chenevix-Trench, Charles, *A History of Horsemanship*, Longman, London, 1970

Eisenberg, Baron de, *Description du Manège Moderne*, London, 1747

Equine Research Inc, *Equine Genetics & Selection Procedures*, Tyler, Texas, USA, 1978

Enrody, Lt Col A. L. de, *Give Your Horse a Chance*, J. A. Allen, London, 1976

Falkus, Christopher, *The Life and Times of Charles II*, Weidenfeld & Nicholson, London, 1972

Felton, W. Sidney, *Masters of Equitation*, J. A. Allen & Co., London, 1962

Fillis, James, *Breaking and Riding*, Hurst & Blackett, 1911 and J. A. Allen, London, 1977

Fleitmann, Lida L., *Comments on Hacks and Hunters*, Scribner's Sons, New York, 1921

Fox, Anthony J., excerpts translated from *École de Cavalerie* received by the author in 1989

Frazer, Capt. William, *A Treatise upon Horsemanship translated from the original French of M. de la Guérinière*, Hircarrah Press, Calcutta, 1801

Frederiksen, A. K., *The Finer Points of Riding*, J. A. Allen, London, 1969

Garsault, François Alexandre Pierre de, *Le Guide du Cavalier*, Paris, 1770

Gibson, Geoffrey, excerpts translated from *École de Cavalerie*, received by the author in 1988

Goubaux, Armand and Barrier, Gustave, *The Exterior of the Horse*, J. B. Lippincott & Co., Philadelphia and London, 1892

Grisone, *Gli Ordini di Cavalcare*, 1550

German National Equestrian Federation, *Advanced Techniques of Riding*, Threshold, London, 1986

Gianoli, Luigi, *Horses and Horsemanship Through the Ages*, Iris Books, New York, 1969

Girard, Jacques, *Versailles Gardens*, Sotheby's Publications, London, 1985

Guérinière, Sieur François Robichon de la, *École de Cavalerie*, Paris, 1733

Hance, Capt. J. E., *School for Horse and Rider*, Country Life, London, 1932

Handler, Col Hans, *The Spanish Riding School in Vienna*, Thames & Hudson, London, 1972.

Hinde, R., *The Discipline of the Light Horse*, London, 1778

Hartley Edwards, Elwyn, *Saddlery*, J. A. Allen, London, 1963
The Country Life Book of Saddlery and Equipment, Quarto Publishing Ltd., London, 1987

Henriques, Pegotty, 'Dressage Viewpoint', articles in *Horse and Hound*, London, 19 January and 21 December 1989

Henriquet, Michel, *À la Récherche de l'Équitation*, Crepin Leblond, Paris, 1968
article, 'L'assiette', *Cheval*, February 1985

Henriquet and Provost, Alain, *L'Équitation, un art, une passion*, Editions du Seuil, Paris, 1972

Herbemann, Erik F., *The Dressage Formula*, J. A. Allen, London, 1980

Hery, H. J., *Reflections on the Art of Horsemanship*, J. A. Allen, London, 1968

Holmelund, Captain Paul, *The Art of Horsemanship*, A. S. Barnes & Co., New York, 1962

Hope, Sir William, *The Complete Horseman*, London, 1717

l'Hotte, General Alexis, *Officier de Cavalerie*, Hazan, Paris, 1958
Questions Équestres, Paris, 1960

Hünersdorf, Ludwig, *Anleitung, Olms Presse*, Hildesheim, 1973

Huyghe, René, *Larousse Encyclopaedia of Renaissance and Baroque Art*, Paul Hamlyn, London, 1964

Jackson, G. N., *Effective Horsemanship*, Compton Russell Ltd., Wiltshire, 1967

Jones, Gilbert H., privately published paper sent to the author in 1986 'The Earliest Ancestors of the Mustangs', Finley, Oklahoma

Jousseaume, Col André, *Progressive Dressage*, J. A. Allen, London, 1978

Jurenak, Kalman de, article on the state of British dressage, *Horse and Hound*, 25 May 1989.

Kane, Henry, *A Concise History of Spain*, Thames & Hudson, London, 1973

Kellock, E. M., *The Story of Riding*, David & Charles, Devon, London, Vancouver, 1974

Kerbrech, General Faverot de, *Dressage methodique de cheval de selle d'apres les derniers enseignements de F. Baucher*, 1891

Kidd, Jane, *Horsemanship in Europe*, J. A. Allen, London, 1977

Kirsch, Ivan, article, 'Equitation Artistique et Competition de Dressage', *Galop*, Brussels, 1976

Klimke, Dr Reiner, *Ahlerich The Making of a Dressage World Champion*, Merehurst Press, London, 1987
Basic Training of the Young Horse, J. A. Allen, London, 1985

Koehler, Lt. Col. G. F., *Remarks on Cavalry*, London 1798

Kunffy, Charles de, *Creative Horsemanship*, A. S. Barnes & Co., New Jersey, USA, 1975

Lewis, Benjamin, *Riding, the Balanced Seat*, W. H. Allen, London, 1947

Littauer, Vladimir, *Commonsense Horsemanship*, Arco, New York, 1976
The Development of Modern Riding, J. A. Allen, London,

Schooling Your Hourse, Arco, New York, 1982

Licart, Commandant Jean, *Basic Equitation*, J. A. Allen, 1968

Livingstone-Learmouth, David, *The Horse in Art*, Studio Publications, London and New York, 1958

Livy, Titus Livius, Books XXV–XXVII, 59 BC–AD 17

Loch, Sylvia, *The Royal Horse of Europe, the Story of the Andalusian and the Lusitano*, J. A. Allen, London, 1986
'The Classical Seat'. *Horse and Rider Magazine*, London, 1987
Series of articles 'The Dressage Dilemma', *Horse and Rider*, July, August, September, 1986; 'Are you in Tune with your Horse?', *Horse and Rider* February, March, April, May 1989; also *The Horse*, Pakenham, Victoria, Australia, February, March, April, May, 1990.

Löhneysen, George Engelhard von, *Hof-Kriegs-und Reit-Schul*, Nurenberg, 1929

Loon, Ernest van, *Ruiters en Rechters*, Zuidgroep, The Hague, Holland, 1978

Machin Goodall, Daphne, *A History of Horse Breeding*, Robert Hale, London, 1977
The Flight of the East Prussian Horses, David & Charles, Devon, 1973

Machuca, Vargas, *Teoria y exercicios de la gineta*, Madrid, 1600

McTaggart, Lt Col M. F., *Mount and Man*, Country Life Ltd., London, 1925 and 1935

Mairinger, Franz, *Horses are made to be Horses*, Rigby, Sydney, 1983

Markham, Gervase, *Cavalarice*, London, 1607
Markham's Maisterpiece, Revised, London, 1688
The Compleat Horseman, Robson Books, London, 1976

Melling, Jeanne, *The Complete Morgan Horse*, Stephen Greene Press, Massachusetts, 1986

Montigny, Conte de, *Équitation des Dames*

Monteilhet, André, *Les Maitres de l'oeuvre équestre*, Odège, Paris, 1979
'A History of Academic Equitation' in *The Horseman's International Book of Reference* edited by Jean and Lily Powell Froissard, Stanley Paul, London, 1980

Müseler, Wilhelm, *Riding Logic*, Eyre Methuen, London, 1965

Muybridge, Eadweard, *Animals in Motion*, Chapman & Hall, London, 1925

Nagel, *Encyclopaedia of Austria*, Nagel Publishers, Geneva, Paris, Munich, 1970

Nimrod, *Remarks on the Condition of Hunters*, M. A. Pittman, London, 1837 articles in *Horse and Hound*, 1893

Oliveira, Nuno, *Alta Escola, Haute Ecole*, J. A. Allen, London, 1965

    Reflections on Equestrian Art, J. A. Allen, London, 1976

    Memorias e Trabalhos de Meio Seculo dum Cavaleiro Portugues, Lisbon, 1981

    Notes and Reminiscences of a Portuguese Rider, Howley & Russell, Caramut, Australia, 1982

    Classical Principles of the Art of Training Horses, Howley & Russell, Caramut, Australia, 1983

    From an Old Master Trainer to Young Trainers, Howley & Russell, Caramut, Australia, 1986

    Horses and Their Riders, Howley & Russell, Australia, 1988

Oman, Charles, *War in the Middle Ages*, 1885

Oettingen, Baron von, *Horse Breeding in Theory and Practice*, Sampson Low Marston, London, 1909

Paillard, Colonel Jean Saint-Fort, *Understanding Equitation*, Doubleday & Co., United States of America, 1974

Patterson, Major T. S., *Sympathetic Training of Horse and Man*, H. F. & G. Whitherby, London, 1925

Pembroke, Henry Earl of, *Military Equitation, or, a Method of Breaking Horses and Teaching Soldiers to Ride designed for the Use of the Army*, London, 1778

Peters, Colonel J. G., *A Treatise on Equitation*, Whittaker & Co., London, 1835

Pevsner, Daniel, article 'Dressage', from *Equestrian News*, 1988

Picard, Captain L., *Origines de l'École de Cavalerie*, Saumur, 1890

Pliny, Gaius, Plinius Secundus, *Natural History*, Bohn, London, 1848

    excerpts *Encyclopaedia Britannica*, 1949

Pluvinel, Antoine de, *l'Instruction du Roy*, Griff, Paris, 1976

The Manège Royal, translated by Hilda Nelson, J. A. Allen, London, 1989

Podeschi, John B., *Books on the Horse and Horsemanship 1400–1941*, The Paul Mellon Collection, Tate Gallery Publications, London 1981

Podhajsky, Colonel Alois, *My Dancing White Horses*, George G. Harrap, London, 1964

    The Complete Training of Horse and Rider, Harrap, London, 1967

    My Horses, My Teachers, Harrap, London, 1969

    The Art of Dressage: Basic Principles of Riding and Judging, Harrap, London, 1979

    The White Stallions of Vienna, The Sportsman's Press, London, 1985

Polybius, Greek cavalry commander and historian, excerpts Book XXXV, 201–120 BC

Powell, Lily, article, 'The Age of Splendour' from *Equi*, London, January/February 1984

Prior, C. M., *The Royal Studs of the Sixteenth and Seventeenth Centuries*, Horse and Hound Publications, London, 1935

Racinet, Jean-Claude, article 'The Shoulder-in Yesterday and Today', from *Dressage and CT*, Philadelphia, USA, October, 1986

Read, Jan, *The Moors in Spain and Portugal*, Faber and Faber, London, 1974

Rebocho, Nuno de, article on Mirobriga, *O Seculo*, 27 August, 1986

Reese, M. M., *Master of the Horse*, Threshold Books, London, 1976

Ridgeway, W., *The Origin and Influence of the Thoroughbred Horse*, Cambridge University Press, 1905.

Riegler, Johann, article 'The Purpose and Meaning of Collection' from *Dressage and CT*, USA, December, 1986

Santini, Captain Piero, *Riding Reflections*, Country Life Ltd., London 1933

    The Forward Impulse, Country Life, London, 1936

Saracin, E. A., 'History of the FEI' in the *Horseman's International Book of Reference*, op. cit.

Saurel, Étienne, *Le Cheval, equitation et sport hippiques*, Librairie Larousse, Paris, 1966

    Histoire de l'Équitation, Stock, Paris, 1971

Seunig, Waldemar, *Horsemanship*, Doubleday, London, 1974

    Meister der Reitkunst, Hoffmann, Heidenheim, 1960

Am Pulsslag der Reitkunst, Hoffmann, Heidenheim, 1961

Sidney, S., *The Book of the Horse*, London, 1874

Shakespeare, William, *Richard III*, 1597/8

Sind, Baron J. B. de, *L'Art du Manège*, Cologne, 1762

Sivewright, Molly, *Thinking Riding Book 1*, J. A. Allen, London, 1979

Thinking Riding Book 2, J. A. Allen, London, 1984

Snape, Andrew, *The Anatomy of a Horse*, Flesher Printers, London, 1683

Solleysel, Jacques de, *The Compleat Horseman*, translated by Sir William Hope, 1717

Souza, Count Baretto de, *Elementary Equitation*, E. P. Dutton & Co., New York, 1922

Advanced Equitation, John Murray, London, 1927

Stecken, Fritz, *Training the Horse and Rider*, Arco, New York, 1977

Steinbrecht, Gustav, *Le Gymnase du Cheval*, Epiac, Paris, 1963

Timmis, Col Reginald S., *Modern Horse Management*, Cassell & Co., London, Toronto, 1915

Uze, Marcel, *The Horse in Nature, History and Art*, Hyperion Press, Milan, 1954

Van Schaik, Dr. H. L. M., *Misconceptions and Simple Truths in Dressage*, J. A. Allen, London, 1986

Vezzoli, Gary C., *Superior Horsemanship*, A. S. Barnes & Co., New Jersey, 1978

Virgil, *Aeneid* and *Georgico*

Wätjen, Richard L., *Dressage Riding*, J. A. Allen & Co., London, 1979

Whyte Melville, J. G., *Riding Recollections*, London, 1878

Wilkinson, Clennel, *Prince Rupert, the Cavalier*, George G. Harrap, London, 1934

Willett, Peter, *The Thoroughbred*, Weidenfeld & Nicholson, London, 1970

Williams, Dorian, *The Classical Riding Master, The Wilton House Collection*, Eyre Methuen, London, 1979

Wynmalen, Henry, *Equitation*, Country Life Publications, London, 1946

Dressage, A Study of the Finer Points of Riding, Museum Press, London, 1953

The Horse in Action, Harold Starke Ltd., London, 1964

Wynmalen, Julia, letters and notes sent to the author 1989–90

Xenophon, General, *The Art of Horsemanship*, translated by M. H. Morgan, J. A. Allen, London, 1962

excerpts from the *Anabasis*; the *Hipparchicus*; the *Hellenica* written at Corinth, Book II, 369 BC, Pelopponnesian War

Also: *Encyclopaedia Britannica*, all 24 volumes for historical research purposes, 1949 edition; Muir's *New School Atlas of Universal History*, seventeenth edition, George Philip, Liverpool, 1947; *The Shorter Oxford English Dictionary of Historical Principles*, Vols. 1 & 2, Caledonian Press, 1978

Index

[**Bold type** indicates principle areas of subject discussion]